SAVOR THE FLAVOR

of
The Edina Country Club

ISBN 0-9654991-0-3

Inquiries and orders should be addressed to:
The Edina Country Club
5100 Wooddale Avenue
Edina, Minnesota 55424
(612) 927-7151

Dear Members and Friends,

It is with the utmost pleasure that the Edina Country Club presents its very own cookbook, "SAVOR THE FLAVOR." The inspiration for this all-occasion collection? The gratifying, ever-increasing number of requests we receive for recipes served in our distinctively different dining areas — the elegant Tartan and Thornhill Rooms, the extremely popular Pub and the Veranda, with its sweeping warm-weather view of the golf course and swimming pool. We continually revise our various menus to reflect Minnesota's changing seasons, the creativity of our award-winning culinary team, and the dining preferences of our sophisticated clientele.

When the idea of publishing a cookbook was first suggested, the enthusiastic response of the staff was immediate and unanimous. "A great idea! Let's do it!" We then decided to include more than Club specialties — to invite members and friends to share their favorite recipes as well. Again, the response was overwhelmingly positive. All types of recipes were submitted to suit every caliber of cook, varying lifestyles and timetables, all occasions, from casual to elegant, and in some cases, nutritional concerns. Generous volunteers — men, women and teens, offered to test in their home kitchens so recipes would be dependable as well as delicious. Along the way, the project grew from just a Club effort to a community effort.

We all appreciate great meals and satisfying snacks. It is our sincere hope that this recipe collection will add to the quality and versatility of your personal eating enjoyment for years to come.

Dale C. Miller, CCM
General Manager
EDINA COUNTRY CLUB

Acknowledgements

Project Coordinator...Patricia Pracht Meyers

Development Advisor ....Dale C. Miller
Edina Country Club General Manager

Editor/Copywriter...Heather Randall King

Edina Country Club Food &
Beverage Director...........................Kenneth R. Galloway, CEC

Edina Country Club Executive Chef.........................Jerry Cegla, CFBE

Consulting Home Economist.......................................Ann Burckhardt

Computer Specialist...Glenna M. Hammond

Proofreading..Mary Morton
Marie Lacy
Romona Tokheim

Photography:
Cover Photo ....Vinton W. Knechtges, D.D.S.

Interior and Exterior Club Views.................................Bob Firth
Sirny Architects
Dale Miller
Gallop Studios
St. Paul Companies

Aerial Views..Steve Smith

Printing and Graphic Design...Patrick Walsh
for LCS Graphics, Minneapolis

Victoria Daley
for Meyers Printing Company, Minneapolis

THIS BOOK IS DEDICATED TO ...

all who have served on the
Edina Country Club culinary staff since
the year of our founding

AND

to faithful members and friends who
enjoy our hospitality and inspire our
perpetual goals of high quality and
excellent service.

Table of Contents

Appetizers

ECC Members and guests eagerly anticipate summer evenings when they can relax on the beautiful Club veranda with a cool sipper accompanied by these savory snacks. For your own patio entertaining, make ahead and keep on hand in tightly-covered containers.

ECC Veranda Seasoned Crackers

2 pounds oyster crackers
¾ cup oil
3.2-ounce package ranch salad dressing seasoning mix
1½ tablespoons dill weed
1 tablespoon garlic powder
1 teaspoon lemon pepper

Preheat oven to 350°. In large bowl, gently combine crackers with oil so they are moistened. Mix in seasonings until crackers are completely and evenly coated. Spread seasoned crackers in a jelly roll pan. Bake approximately 10 to 15 minutes or until golden brown. Watch carefully, especially when they begin to brown.

Serves 12 or more

Uncork the wine, pass these colorful appetizers and be prepared for plaudits. Vine-ripened tomatoes, an aromatic pesto and a duo of cheeses — a winning combination!

ECC Bruschetta

1 loaf French bread
   24 inches long
1 cup basil pesto
2 red tomatoes, diced

2 yellow tomatoes, diced
1 cup grated Parmesan cheese
1½ cups shredded Mozzarella
   cheese

Preheat oven to broil. Split loaf lengthwise. Place on cookie sheet. Broil until lightly toasted, watching carefully so as not to burn. Remove from oven and spread cut sides generously with pesto. Top evenly with diced tomatoes and cheeses. Return to oven and broil until cheese is melted and lightly browned. Cut into serving pieces and serve immediately.

Serves 6 to 8

From Judy Tucker, super snacks with a make-ahead-and-freeze option for harried hosts. Testers Marie Lacy and Karen McKay tried them out on several groups and everyone gave thumbs up! Marie suggests options of using fresh minced garlic instead of garlic powder and lowering calories with low-fat cheese and sausage. Prep time? A mere 30 minutes!

Hanky Panky Party Snack

1 pound lean ground beef	1 teaspoon garlic powder
1 pound hot sausage (in roll)	1 teaspoon oregano
1 pound processed cheese food	Cocktail rye bread

Brown beef and sausage; drain well. Melt cheese over low heat. Stir in meat and seasonings. Spread 1 tablespoon mixture on each slice of cocktail rye. At this point, you can place on cookie sheets and freeze. When frozen, remove from freezer and place in freezer bags. Seal well and return to freezer.

To serve, bake at 350° on cookie sheet for 20 minutes. Serve as is or cut diagonally for smaller bites.

Serves a crowd

Gene Gaasedelen would rather be golfing so she relishes reliable recipes like this gleaned from an Edina neighbor. It's assembled in minutes and bakes while you're getting ready for guests. Serve with crackers and frosty Margaritas.

San Antonio Quiche

One 4½-ounce can chopped green chilies
12 ounces shredded Cheddar cheese
3 eggs
3 tablespoons milk

Preheat oven to 325°. Beat eggs and milk. Fold in chopped chilies and shredded cheese. Pour into 9-inch quiche pan. Bake uncovered for 45 minutes. Serve with crackers.

Serves 6 to 8

This hot (and haute) combo is assembled in minutes and will be devoured just as quickly. Kay and Bill McReavy find this a no-fail crowd-pleaser for entertaining in their Minneapolis or Sanibel home. Tester Sheran McNulty praised the "excellent taste" and suggested adding flaked crabmeat for variety. Short on time? Substitute sturdy crackers, melba toast or sourdough bread slices for toasted pita pieces.

Bubbly Artichoke-Cheese Bake

Two 14-ounce cans non-marinated artichoke hearts, drained
1 cup mayonnaise
1 cup freshly-grated Parmigiano-Reggiano cheese
3 to 4 cloves garlic, minced
2 tablespoons sherry
Dash cayenne
Dash paprika

Preheat oven to 300°. Cut up artichoke hearts. Combine all ingredients except paprika. Place in shallow baking dish. Sprinkle paprika over top. Bake for 15 to 25 minutes, or until bubbly. Great with toasted pita bread pieces.

Serves 8 to 10

Have this hearty party nibbler ready and waiting in a chafing dish. Judy Tillson, ECC Board member, appreciates the easy oven browning of the meatballs and the special sweet-sour sauce made from just two prepared ingredients. Be sure to keep meatballs no bigger than bite-sized for easy eating.

Chafing Dish Party Meatballs

12-ounce bottle chili sauce	1 medium onion, chopped
16-ounce can	1 teaspoon garlic salt
whole berry cranberry sauce	1 cup bread crumbs
2 pounds lean ground beef	Dash of pepper
2 eggs	

Preheat oven to 400°. Combine chili sauce and cranberry sauce in large saucepan.

Mix ground beef with remaining ingredients. Roll into bite-sized meatballs. Place on ungreased jelly roll pan. Bake 15 minutes or until done, shaking pan occasionally to turn meatballs. Then add meatballs to sauce mixture, spooning sauce over. Heat briefly over low heat. Transfer to readied chafing dish; serve hot.

Yield: About 48 cocktail-sized meatballs

The surprise sauce ingredient is ginger ale! Contributor Kathy Schmid of Edina says her guests like the "not-too-sweet flavor," and she likes the pronto preparation. For a thicker sauce, reduce with further cooking after meatballs have been removed to chafing dish.

Easy-Does-It Meatballs

1 pound lean ground beef	Garlic powder (optional)
1 medium onion, chopped	½ teaspoon dill weed
⅓ cup dried bread crumbs	1 teaspoon Worcestershire sauce
¼ cup milk	2 cups ketchup
1 egg	2 cups ginger ale
Salt and pepper to taste	Chopped parsley, if desired

Combine ground beef, onion, crumbs, milk, egg, salt, pepper, garlic powder, dill weed and Worcestershire sauce. Shape into 30 one-inch balls. Combine and heat ketchup and ginger ale in large saucepan. Add meatballs and simmer 15 to 20 minutes. Serve in chafing dish with wooden or plastic picks. Sprinkle with chopped parsley, if desired.

Yield: 30 meatballs (8 to 10 cocktail servings)

An East Indian accent gives Jack Bucklin's recipe pizazz. Now an Edina retiree, Jack "loves to cook, especially appetizers, soups and salad dressings." So, watch for more of his recipes. Tester Jan Nelson found this "very tasty" with only ¾ teaspoon curry. So taste test and add as desired.

Chutney-Cheese Spread

8 ounces cream cheese, softened
½ cup mango chutney, finely chopped
¼ cup toasted almonds, chopped
1 teaspoon curry powder, or to taste
½ teaspoon dry mustard
¼ to ½ cup chopped green onions, including tops
Parsley for garnish
Crackers/fruit wedges

Thoroughly combine all spread ingredients several hours before serving for flavors to blend. Serve with crackers and/or wedges of apple and pear. Garnish with parsley.

Serves 6 to 8

An elegant, mildly-flavored hors d'oeuvre spread from Mitzi Hlavac, Stevens Point, WI. If desired, substitute chopped thawed shrimp for canned, particularly if you like more texture. Tester Heather King baked it in a decorative oven-to-table soufflé dish, five inches across, two inches deep.

Hot Shrimp Spread

8 ounces cream cheese, softened
¼ cup mayonnaise
2 tablespoons finely-chopped onion
2 hard-cooked eggs, finely chopped
One or two 4½-ounce cans small or broken shrimp,
   drained and rinsed
Paprika
Crackers or Melba toast

Preheat oven to 325°. Blend cream cheese, mayonnaise and onion until well mixed. Put half of mixture into small baking dish. Top with shrimp and half the egg. Place other half of cheese mixture over top and sprinkle with remaining chopped egg. Dust with paprika. Bake 45 minutes or until heated through and lightly browned on top. Serve with crackers of choice.

NOTE: Another option? Combine all ingredients instead of layering. Sprinkle with paprika and bake as directed.

Serves 6 to 8

Liz Krezowski of Minneapolis pops this in the oven for a piping hot appetizer to serve a group. "Easy and tasty" comments tester Jaye Vaaler. Festive for a holiday menu with flecks of red and green from the beef and green pepper. Make ahead and freeze, if desired.

Hot Beef Dip

8-ounce package cream cheese, softened

2 tablespoons milk, optional

3-ounce package dried or chipped beef, cut into small pieces

Garlic salt or powder to taste

White pepper to taste (optional)

½ cup sour cream

½ cup chopped green pepper

½ cup chopped pecans or walnuts

2 tablespoons butter (optional)

Crackers or melba toast rounds

Preheat oven to 350°. Soften cream cheese with 2 tablespoons milk or microwave to soften. Combine with remaining dip ingredients. Place in 1-quart casserole. Bake uncovered for 20 minutes. Serve hot with crackers.

Serves 8 to 10

A tasty trio of ingredients combine for this Tex-Mex medley. "People love it," says contributor Gretchen Pracht. Tester Bonnie Damkroger concurs, rating it five-star for ease of preparation and taste. "Heating the chips is a great idea, too," she adds.

Fiesta Dip

Two 8-ounce packages cream cheese, softened

Two 15-ounce cans no-bean chili

2 cups sharp Cheddar cheese, shredded

Warmed corn chips or crackers of choice

Preheat oven to 350°. Spread cream cheese over bottom of 9 x 13-inch pan. Pour chili evenly over cream cheese. Sprinkle Cheddar cheese over mixture. Bake about 20 minutes or until bubbly. Serve with warmed corn chips or other crackers.

Serves 10

Two testers, Anita Anderson and Vicki Kattke, gave high fives to this favorite appetizer spread from Marde Olson. "Excellent on all counts," remarked Anita. "Simple to make and would be wonderful with slices of French bread," commented Vicki. It's definitely make-ahead because topping ingredients should be combined at least two hours before completing layering process. Use low-fat cream cheese, if desired.

Layered Black Bean Dip

<u>TOPPING INGREDIENTS:</u>
15-ounce can black beans, rinsed and drained
4 ½-ounce can chopped black olives, drained
1 small onion, finely chopped
1 clove garlic, finely chopped
2 tablespoons oil
2 tablespoons lime juice
¼ teaspoon salt
¼ teaspoon cayenne
¼ teaspoon ground cumin
¼ teaspoon pepper

<u>TO COMPLETE RECIPE:</u>
8 ounces cream cheese, softened
1 hard cooked egg, finely chopped
1 to 2 green onions, chopped

Mix all topping ingredients; refrigerate 2 hours. Spread cream cheese on rimmed serving plate. Cover evenly with topping mixture. Garnish with chopped egg and green onion.

Serves 8 to 10

Energetic Edina entrepreneur, Liana Peterson, still finds time to entertain and appreciates the make-ahead feature of this boldly-seasoned dip. Proprietor of Edina Hairdresser, she counts many ECC Members as clients and friends. "There's plenty of recipe swapping at the shop. We all enjoy good food!" she confides.

Zippy Veggie Dip

1 cup mayonnaise	⅛ teaspoon cayenne
½ cup sour cream	2½ tablespoons salad oil
½ teaspoon leaf thyme	3 teaspoons vinegar
¼ teaspoon curry powder	Assorted vegetables for dipping
⅛ teaspoon garlic powder	

Combine all dip ingredients. Cover and refrigerate overnight.

Yield: About 2 cups dip

Gerry Mooers gave Judy Tucker's recipe the ultimate test — she tried it out at a potluck with many tasters present. "Everyone liked it very much," she reports. Gerry used low-fat mayonnaise and cream cheese and both worked well. Two tips from Judy — drain artichokes thoroughly, then blot them dry with paper toweling. And, use the thickest portions of the salsa for a drip-free consistency.

Baked Artichoke-Shrimp Dip

8 ounces cream cheese, softened
1 cup real mayonnaise
1 cup thick salsa
14-ounce can artichoke hearts,
    chopped and drained (not marinated)
Two 7-ounce cans small shrimp, drained and rinsed
½ cup freshly grated Parmesan cheese

Preheat oven to 350°. Combine all ingredients. Spoon into baking dish. Bake uncovered for 20 minutes or until piping hot. Serve with corn or tortilla chips.

Serves 8 to 10

For a spur-of-the-moment sensation, serve drop-in guests this dandy dip from Marde Olson, who keeps ingredients "on hand." Vicki Kattke, who tested it with some sampling help from "bridge friends," suggests serving with slices of French bread for a heartier repast.

Acapulco Artichoke Dip

14-ounce can artichoke hearts, drained and chopped
6-ounce jar marinated artichoke hearts, drained and chopped
4½-ounce can chopped green chilies, drained
6 tablespoons mayonnaise (regular or low-fat)
1 cup grated Cheddar cheese
Tortilla chips

Preheat oven to 350°. Grease glass 9-inch round baking dish. Combine artichokes; place in dish. Top with green chilies. Spread mayonnaise over top. Sprinkle with Cheddar cheese. Bake at for 20 minutes or until bubbly and cheese has melted. Serve with tortilla chips.

Serves 8

Marde Olson selects the mild Spanish onion for this simple dip which should be made several hours ahead of serving for full flavor. When shopping for onions of any type, select those which are firm, dry and free of soft spots.

Spanish Onion Dip

⅓ to ½ cup chopped Spanish onion (about ¼ of a large one)
1 cup sour cream
½ teaspoon salt
½ teaspoon Worcestershire sauce

Combine all ingredients. Refrigerate several hours to combine flavors. Serve with chips.

Serves 4

Ray Bentdahl, CEO of Edina's Americana Bank, and his wife Shirley are particularly fond of foods that "float." By that we mean totable treats which they can serve aboard their Lake Minnetonka cruiser. Here's one example of an exotic blend that is make-ahead and travels quite nicely in a cooler. (Just as tasty served at home, too.)

Deluxe New Delhi Dip

1 pound cream cheese, softened 1 cup hot mango chutney
2 cups shredded
  Cheddar cheese
2 teaspoons curry powder
2 tablespoons plus 2 teaspoons
  dry sherry
1 pound bacon,
  cooked crisp and crumbled
6 scallions, chopped
Crackers

Blend cheeses with curry powder and sherry until creamy. Spread in an even layer on the bottom of a 9-inch spring form pan which has been lined with plastic wrap. Refrigerate for 4 hours or overnight. When ready to serve, transfer mixture from spring form pan to serving plate. Top with chutney, bacon and scallions. Serve at room temperature with sturdy crackers.

Serves 12

Jack Bucklin is back with another innovative recipe! It's great as a dip for raw veggies, can be used as a spread for ham and turkey sandwiches or is sensational spooned over hot vegetables like baked potatoes. Because the curry is such an important ingredient, we suggest purchasing a fine-quality product for a mellow, rather than sharp flavor.

Curried Mayonnaise Dip

1 cup real mayonnaise
¼ cup consommé
(or 1 bouillon cube dissolved in ¼ cup hot water)
1 clove garlic, minced
Several dashes of hot sauce
1 teaspoon curry powder
1 teaspoon dry mustard

Beat ingredients with a wire whisk until well combined. Cover and refrigerate until serving.

Yield: 1¼ cups

Jean Giroulx of Bloomington describes her lower-calorie spread as "fast, delicious and economical." Tester Kathy Schmid commented on the "fresh taste" of the colorful combo and suggests it as a congenial candidate for a cocktail buffet. Marie Lacy halved the recipe to serve 10. "The next night I put the leftover portion into the blender and made a creamy dip. That was tasty, too," adds Marie.

Mock Crab Spread

1 small onion
2 cloves garlic
Two 3-ounce packages low-fat cream cheese, softened
2 tablespoons skim milk
1 cup chopped fresh parsley, divided
1 medium tomato, seeded and chopped
1 small green pepper, seeded and chopped
2 teaspoons lemon juice
¼ teaspoon salt
6 ounces imitation crab meat, finely diced
Crackers

Finely chop onion and garlic. Mix onions and garlic with cream cheese and milk until well blended. Spread in shallow oven-to-table 9-inch quiche or pie plate. Mix together 2 tablespoons of the parsley, tomato, green pepper, lemon juice and salt. Spoon over cheese mixture. Flake crab meat; mix with remaining parsley. Sprinkle over cheese/vegetable mixture. Chill; serve with crackers.

Serves 20

Preparation for this bourbon-laced loaf begins the day before serving so ingredients can set and flavors meld. An elegant Act I for your fanciest dinner party from Gretchen Pracht, attorney and hostess extraordinaire.

Bourbon Liver Paté

½ pound braunschweiger/liver sausage
1 tablespoon grated onion
2 tablespoons mayonnaise
3 ounces cream cheese, softened
¼ teaspoon garlic salt
1 tablespoon bourbon
½ cup sour cream
1 tablespoon mayonnaise
¼ teaspoon salt
⅛ teaspoon white pepper
1 teaspoon dill weed
3-ounce jar small stuffed green olives, drained

The day before serving, blend the first six ingredients. Shape into loaf and chill overnight. Several hours before serving, blend the next four ingredients. Use this mixture to frost the loaf. Sprinkle with dill weed. At serving time, arrange olives around loaf for garnish.

NOTE: Paté mixture may be doubled; not necessary to double the frosting.

Serves 4 to 6

Party-perfect presentation with this attractive spread from Rebecca Walser. Tester Pat Meyers shared it at a friend's cocktail buffet and took home an empty plate! Do make a day ahead for convenience and peak flavor.

Frosted Paté

¼ pound fresh mushrooms, chopped
1 medium onion, minced
5 tablespoons butter, divided
1 pound braunschweiger/liver sausage
½ cup sliced black olives
8-ounce package cream cheese, softened
½ cup sour cream
1 teaspoon chicken bouillon granules
Parsley, additional green/black olives and pimiento slices as desired for garnish
Sturdy toast or crackers

Sauté mushrooms and onions in 2 tablespoons butter. Blend remaining 3 tablespoons butter with liver sausage; stir in mushrooms and onion. Using half of the mixture, form bottom half of loaf. Stud with olive slices. Form top half of loaf from remaining mixture. Combine cream cheese, sour cream and bouillon granules; mix well. Frost loaf with cheese mixture. May be garnished with parsley, green or black olives and pimiento slices. Serve with melba toast, party rye or pumpernickel.

Yield: About 2 cups

When there's a party in the offing, Shirley Bentdahl of Edina relies on this crowd-sized spread to satisfy hungry guests. Definitely for braunschweiger lovers with interesting texture enhancers — pistachio nuts and water chestnuts. Halve ingredients for fewer servings.

Party Pistachio Paté

1 pound braunschweiger/liver sausage
¾ cup chopped onion
¾ cup chopped pistachio nuts
¾ cup chopped kosher dill pickle
3 teaspoons celery seed
1 teaspoon garlic powder
3 teaspoons monosodium glutamate
8-ounce can sliced water chestnuts, drained and chopped
½ cup mayonnaise or salad dressing
Parsley sprigs for garnish
Crackers

Combine paté ingredients thoroughly, adding just enough mayonnaise for proper spreading consistency. Garnish with parsley; serve with crackers.

Serves 20 to 30

A take-to-the-lake treat from Jan Nelson of Edina. "It has a trendy salsa-like consistency, stores well in the frig, and is definitely make-ahead," says Jan. Tester Marie Lacy found her guests appreciated the healthy, unique combination. "It was a big hit!"

Texas Caviar

Two 14-ounce cans black-eyed peas, drained
15½-ounce can white hominy, drained
2 medium tomatoes, chopped
2 to 3 green onions, chopped
2 cloves garlic, minced
1 medium green, red or yellow pepper, chopped
1 jalapeño pepper, chopped
½ cup chopped red onion
½ cup chopped fresh cilantro
8-ounce bottle of Italian dressing
¼ cup balsamic vinegar
Tortilla chips

Combine all "caviar" ingredients except dressing and vinegar in large glass or plastic bowl. Mix well. Add dressing and vinegar; stir and cover. Marinate at least 2 hours in refrigerator. Drain or scoop out with a slotted spoon into serving dish (keep marinade for leftover caviar). Serve with tortilla chips.

Serves a crowd

Edina ophthalmologist, Dr. Leslie W. Jacobson, unwinds from a busy practice plus teaching at the University with hunting trips whenever his schedule allows. Not only does he bring home supper, he often prepares it as well. This is one of his unique ideas for sharing your bounty with guests.

Grilled Game Appetizers

Several goose or duck breasts
Prepared teriyaki sauce

Prepare grill so coals are piping hot. While coals are heating, cut game breasts lengthwise into ⅓-inch strips. Marinate in teriyaki sauce (using a glass or plastic container) for no longer than 25 minutes. Grill for 1 to 1½ minutes on each side, or until desired doneness. Serve piping hot. (Vary amounts of game and sauce to suit number of persons being served.)

Ole! to this long-on-flavor, short-on-preparation time dip. Shirley Bard of Eden Prairie was persuasive enough to obtain the recipe from Sue Mills, former catering manager of the Decathlon Club in Bloomington. "It's always on my appetizer table," says Shirley. Hearty enough to keep armchair quarterbacks fueled until the final touchdown. Tester Mary Morton comments, "This is supreme, indeed!"

Mexican Melt Supreme

8-ounce package cream cheese, softened
15-ounce can chili without beans
4-ounce can chopped green chilies, drained
2 cups shredded sharp Cheddar cheese
Taco or corn chips

Preheat oven to 350°. Layer cream cheese, chili and green chilies in a 10-inch round ungreased baking dish. Top evenly with Cheddar cheese. Bake uncovered ½ hour. Serve with taco or corn chips.

Serves 4-6

As a favor to ECC member Terry Swanson, Beth Quinn, proprietor of Beth's Custom Cuisine, Inc., in Wayzata, contributed this unusual appetizer biscotti. Absolutely wonderful with a selection of cheeses or cheese spreads and a robust wine. It also can be served with a dessert platter of fruits and cheeses accompanied by port or sherry. Beth's specialty business "provides heart-healthy meals to busy families." She is a registered dietitian.

Biscotti di Vino

4½ cups all-purpose flour, divided
¾ cup sugar
2 teaspoons salt
1 tablespoon baking powder
1 teaspoon freshly-ground black pepper
⅓ cup finely-chopped walnuts
1 cup vegetable oil
1 cup full-bodied red wine

Preheat oven to 350°. In a large bowl, mix 4 cups of the flour with sugar, salt, baking powder, pepper and walnuts. Add the oil and wine and mix thoroughly. Knead in the extra ½ cup flour to prevent sticking. Cut dough into four sections. Then cut into 10 sections for a total of 40 pieces. Roll each piece into a 5-inch stick and place on a greased baking sheet. Bake for 20 minutes. Then reduce heat to 300° and continue to bake for an additional 15 to 20 minutes, or until golden. Cool and store in airtight containers. Makes 40.

Serves 8-12

Virginia Bodine, a 30-year Edina resident, created this do-ahead recipe at home after "tasting something similar at a party. I cut a wedge each time I entertain and generally, one ball lasts through the holidays." For 17 years, Virginia was Director of the Edina Chamber of Commerce, and she also has served as President of both the Edina League of Women Voters and the Edina Garden Club. She remains active in both, along with The Edina Foundation and she is Treasurer of the Edina Historical Society.

Holiday Cheese Ball

Mix ingredients in food processor in order given.

1ST LAYER:
1 tablespoon minced onion
1 ounce dry sherry
8 ounces cream cheese, softened
8 ounces Swiss cheese, grated
½ teaspoon garlic salt

2ND LAYER:
2 tablespoons milk or cream
16 ounces cream cheese, softened
½ teaspoon sweet basil and/or leaf thyme
1 tablespoon chopped sun-dried tomato
1 large clove garlic, minced or pressed
2 tablespoons minced Italian parsley

3RD LAYER:
1 tablespoon minced onion
1 ounce brandy
8 ounces cream cheese, softened
8 ounces sharp Cheddar, grated
½ teaspoon garlic salt

GARNISH:
Chopped parsley/chopped pecans

Coat a 2-quart bowl with vegetable spray. Line bowl with enough plastic wrap to overlap edges of bowl. Mix the first layer and press firmly in bowl. Combine and add second layer, then third. Bring edges of wrap over top. If they don't cover completely, cover top with either aluminum or plastic wrap. Refrigerate overnight. Unmold and garnish with chopped parsley or chopped pecans. Cut into wedges and serve with crackers.

Serves a crowd

Tester Annette Nelson welcomed the refreshing taste of June Randall's creative curtain raiser. Two tips: Press pineapple in strainer to thoroughly extract juices and combine ingredients the day before serving for peak flavor. Recipe is easily halved for fewer servings. "Takes only minutes to prepare, and it's a nice change from the usual cheese balls," says Annette, an Edina resident and a dental hygienist. Try with crisp cucumber rounds on a warm evening.

Pineapple Cheese Ball

Two 8-ounce packages cream cheese, softened
8½ ounce can crushed pineapple, drained
¼ cup chopped green pepper
2 tablespoons chopped onion
½ teaspoon salt, or to taste
2 cups chopped pecans, divided
Crackers

Combine all ingredients except for 1 cup of pecans. Shape into balls; roll in remaining pecans. Wrap and refrigerate overnight.

Serves 12 to 16

Sparked with bits of red and green, Annette Nelson's recipe is a handsome hand-me-down from her mother's repertoire. Tester Vicki Kattke suggests it as a bagel spread, too. It takes only minutes to toast the walnuts, so watch carefully!

Bleu Cheese Ball

⅓ cup chopped walnuts
4 ounces bleu cheese, crumbled
8-ounce package cream cheese, softened
1 tablespoon chopped fresh green pepper
1 tablespoon chopped pimiento
⅛ teaspoon garlic salt
Crackers

Toast walnuts under broiler until golden brown. Blend cheeses, green pepper, pimiento and garlic salt. Shape into a ball. Roll ball in the nuts to coat. Chill until serving time. Serve with crackers.

Yield: 1 Cheese Ball

When the Auxiliary of the Home of the Good Shepherd sponsored a culinary contest, Marjorie Kugler of St. Paul was thrilled to have her entry judged "Best-in-the-Midwest Cheesecake." Since preparation and baking are done the day before serving, you simply add the garnishing touches at the last minute.

Bleu Cheese Appetizer Pie

1 cup cheese crackers
2 tablespoons butter or margarine, melted
16 ounces cream cheese, softened
8 ounces bleu cheese
1 cup sour cream
3 eggs
¼ cup flour
¼ teaspoon salt
¼ cup picante sauce
½ cup chopped green onions
½ cup chopped walnuts
Tomato rose and green onion stems
Crackers

Preheat oven to 325°. Butter 8-inch spring-form pan. Crush cheese crackers in blender; combine with margarine. Pat into bottom of pan. Blend cheeses, sour cream, eggs, flour, salt and picante sauce. Fold in onions. Pour into pan; sprinkle evenly with walnuts. Bake 1 hour or until toothpick inserted in center comes out clean. Cool, remove outer edge of springform pan. Store overnight in refrigerator. Garnish with tomato rose and additional green onion stems. Serve at room temperature with crackers.

This can be served as whole pie for 20 or divided into wedges and frozen for future parties.

Serves 20

Mary Laukka of Edina describes her favorite appetizer as "a terrific recipe" which she serves with salsa. The make-ahead and freeze option is very convenient and makes cutting the muffin halves into triangles much easier. And, if you don't need all 72 canapes for one party, you have the remaining on hand for another occasion.

Cape Cod Canapes

½ cup butter, softened
6-ounce can crab meat
5-ounce jar Old English cheese spread
½ teaspoon seasoned salt
1½ teaspoons garlic salt
12 English muffins, halved

Combine topping ingredients; spread on halved English muffins. Freeze. When ready to use, preheat broiler. Cut each muffin half into 6 triangles. Place on cookie sheet; broil until triangles begin to bubble.

Yield: 72 canapes

"My mom first made these when I was in high school and they quickly became a favorite," says Rebecca Walser of Edina. "The flavor of the capers is quite subtle, making the canapes universally appealing." The flavor of capers, unopened buds of the caper bush, develops only after the pickling process. Unused capers should be stored immersed in the pickling liquid.

Caper Canapes

6 green onions, thinly sliced
1½ cups grated Cheddar cheese
2 tablespoons capers
1½ cups real mayonnaise
12 English muffin halves

At least 2 hours before serving, combine onion, cheese, capers and mayonnaise. Spread on cut side of English muffins. Preheat broiler. Broil muffins 5 minutes. Cut each muffin half into four pie-shaped pieces.

48 Appetizers

Feta cheese, distinctively salty, pure white and crumbly in texture, is teamed with shrimp and spices for a mouth-watering pita-based pleaser. Shared by Cynthia Quinn, of Edina and Vero Beach, Florida, it can be prepared ahead and frozen, if desired.

Feta Shrimp Triangles

Four 5 to 6-inch pita bread rounds
¼ pound unsalted butter, softened
8 ounces feta cheese, crumbled
8 ounces baby shrimp, chopped
2 large cloves garlic, minced
⅓ cup mayonnaise
½ teaspoon chili powder
½ teaspoon ground cumin
Sesame seed
Paprika

Preheat oven to 300°. Slice pitas in half horizontally. Spread each half with butter; cut into 8 triangles. Place on cookie sheet and bake for 15 to 20 minutes or until lightly browned. Re-set oven to broil. Combine next 6 ingredients; mix until blended. Spread generously on toasted triangles. Sprinkle with sesame seed and paprika. Place on cookie sheet. Broil 4 to 6 inches from heat until bubbly, watching carefully.

(Can be frozen and heated on cookie sheet in 450° oven 5 to 10 minutes.)

Yield: 32 Triangles

"These are the first appetizers to disappear from a cocktail buffet table," confides Rebecca Walser. "With three pre-schoolers, I favor speedy preparation without sacrificing flavor." We suggest trying these for a brunch when a meatless egg dish is the entrée. Slow baking at a low temperature is the secret to success.

Glazed Bacon

1 pound bacon
Brown sugar

Preheat oven to 200°. Cut slices of bacon into thirds. Sprinkle with brown sugar until bacon is completely coated. Bake on cookie sheet for approximately 1 hour or until crisp and brown. Dab carefully with paper toweling to absorb grease. Allow pieces to cool on hard surface without touching each other.

Serves 8 to 10

Soups

Combine ingredients for this elegant number the night before serving and have it ready and waiting to refresh after a brisk game on the courts. And remember this ECC favorite for showers, bridal dinners and other summer celebrations. Serve in chilled bowls brightly garnished with fresh mint and strawberries.

Ginger Peachy Yogurt Soup

13-ounce can sliced peaches, finely chopped
24 ounces plain yogurt
¼ cup honey
1 pinch ground ginger

⅟₁₆ teaspoon ground cinnamon
½ teaspoon lemon juice
Mint leaves
Strawberries

Press chopped peaches into yogurt. Add remaining ingredients. Chill overnight. Garnish each serving with a mint leaf and a fresh strawberry.

Approximately 6 Servings

With an eye to economy, Julian G. Plante, Ph.D., comments, "I've been preparing this soup since 1982 and my cost has ranged from 60¢ to 90¢ per serving." Kielbasa, which can be stored for weeks unopened in the refrigerator, adds seasoning and texture to this plucky potage. Now a consultant to libraries, archives and museums in areas of resource and fund development, Julian served as founding director of the Hill Monastic Manuscript Library at St. John's University for over a quarter of a century. He was also a research professor of classics before his retirement.

Potage Strasbourg

Two 10¾-ounce cans condensed cream of potato soup
1½ soup cans of water (2 cups)
1 pound smoked Kielbasa or Polish sausage, sliced
1 cup peeled and diced tart apple
   (Granny Smith works well)
8-ounce can lima beans, drained
8-ounce can sauerkraut, rinsed and drained
1 teaspoon caraway seed

Combine all ingredients in a large saucepan.. Cover pan and bring mixture to a boil. Reduce heat and simmer for 20 minutes, stirring occasionally. Serve piping hot.

Serves 6 to 8

The popularity of this salad in a bowl has made its way from Spain to the U.S. with little change in the traditional ingredients. For tip-top flavor, use garden-fresh vegetables and serve thoroughly chilled. Other garnishes may be used — crunchy croutons, avocado slices, chopped cucumber and/or diced green pepper.

ECC's Gazpacho Soup

13-ounce can diced tomato with juice
12-ounce can tomato juice
8-ounce can tomato sauce
3 shakes of Worcestershire sauce
3 shakes of hot pepper sauce, such as Tabasco
2 tablespoons lemon juice
2 tablespoons white champagne grape vinegar
4 tablespoons olive oil
1 tablespoon sugar
½ average-sized green pepper
¼ cup celery
¼ cup white onion
2 cloves garlic
6 spring onions and green tops
Small amount of fresh parsley
⅛ teaspoon dried tarragon leaves
2 medium to large cucumbers, seeded
Salt and pepper to taste
Sour cream for garnish

Combine diced tomato, tomato juice, tomato sauce, Worcestershire sauce, hot pepper sauce, lemon juice, vinegar, olive oil and sugar. Using food processor or grinder, grind green pepper, celery, onion, garlic, spring onions and tops, parsley, tarragon leaves and cucumbers. Blend with tomato mixture; add salt and pepper to taste. Chill thoroughly. Top each serving with a dollop of sour cream.

Serves 6 to 8

Tester Nancy Bros liked this recipe from Pat Meyers so much that next time she vows to "double ingredients to ensure leftovers for another meal." A welcome warmer after a chilly autumn round of golf.

Tangy Tomato Soup

14½-ounce can
  stewed tomatoes, undrained
1 cup half-and-half, divided
1½ tablespoons flour
2 tablespoons low-fat
  sour cream

1 tablespoon mild
  Bloody Mary Mix
Seasoned salt to taste
Sour cream
Minced parsley for garnish

Place tomatoes with juice in saucepan. Break up the tomatoes into bite-size pieces. Add ¾ cup of half-and-half, 2 tablespoons sour cream and the Bloody Mary mix. Combine ¼ cup half-and-half with flour and stir gradually into the tomato mixture, stirring over medium heat until soup is slightly thickened and hot. Garnish each portion with a teaspoon of sour cream and a sprinkling of minced parsley.

Yield: 2 generous servings

Don Stork of the ECC culinary staff streamlined this old-fashioned favorite for today's life-style. "Only 30 minutes from kitchen to table," comments enthusiastic tester Jaye Vaaler. "We loved the homemade flavor, and it's great with garlic toast or onion crackers. Recipe can be halved very successfully," she adds.

Cream of Tomato Soup

½ pound butter
1 cup diced onion
½ cup diced green pepper
1 cup all-purpose flour
2 quarts chicken stock
1 quart tomato sauce
½ cup fresh tomatoes, diced
½ teaspoon hot pepper sauce

14½-ounce can diced tomatoes
  with juice
½ cup heavy cream
Salt to taste
White pepper to taste
½ tablespoon Worcestershire
  sauce

Melt butter in 3-gallon soup pot. Add diced onion and green pepper. Cook until vegetables are tender; add flour to make a roux; cook for 5 minutes. Add chicken stock, tomato sauce, and both fresh and canned diced tomatoes. Cook until thickened. Add heavy cream, salt, white pepper, Worcestershire and hot pepper sauce. Cook until hot.

Yield: 16 one-cup servings

If you have been to Hawaii, you have heard of Chef Roy Yamaguchi, restauranteur and cookbook author. Julian Plante of Shoreview has adapted one of Roy's specialties. He serves it with a garnish of low-fat sour cream topped with a sprinkling of sliced scallions. As guests vie to see who can determine flavor origins, this recipe is bound to be a conversation piece at your next dinner party.

Roasted Eggplant Soup

1 eggplant (about 1 pound)
¼ cup olive oil
3 cloves garlic, minced
½ cup chopped onions
½ cup chopped carrots
½ cup chopped celery
1 tablespoon ginger root, minced
2 tomatoes, chopped
1 red bell pepper, chopped
1 quart water
2 tablespoons basil, julienned
Salt and pepper to taste
Sour cream and sliced scallions for garnish

Preheat oven to 350°. Roast whole eggplant in oven for 25 to 30 minutes, or until soft. Remove from the oven. Let cool, peel and chop into bite sized pieces.

In large soup pot, heat olive oil over medium heat. Saute garlic, onions, carrots, celery, ginger root, tomatoes and bell pepper in pot for 2 minutes. Add water, eggplant and basil. Simmer for 15 minutes. Puree vegetables and liquid in food mill or food processor. Adjust seasoning with salt and pepper. Reheat, if necessary, before serving.

Serves 6

A special wine-tasting dinner at ECC inspired Chef Scott Rochat to develop this beautiful bisque. "It was definitely a hit!" he exclaims. Soup goes together quickly once garlic and peppers are roasted.

Roasted Red Pepper and Garlic Bisque

10 garlic cloves, roasted
4 red peppers, roasted and coarsely chopped
½ cup shallots, chopped
⅓ cup flour
2 tomatoes, peeled and seeded
1 cup cream
2 cups dry white wine
2 quarts chicken stock
⅓ cup butter
¼ cup tomato paste
½ tablespoon dried thyme
1 tablespoon kosher salt
1 teaspoon white pepper
Garlic croutons

To roast garlic, coat with oil and bake at 350° for about 30 minutes or until soft.

To roast peppers, cook on open flame until they blister, then peel under cold water.

In medium saucepan, sauté shallots in butter until tender. Add flour to make roux. Cook over low heat, stirring often, for 2 minutes. Add remaining ingredients. Simmer for 20 minutes. In food processor or blender, pureé ingredients. Garnish with garlic croutons.

Yield: 2 quarts

This recipe from Linda Johnson, who recently moved from Edina to Woodbury, was pronounced "a keeper" by tester Mary L. Miller. "It goes to the top of our soup list — we wouldn't change a thing," she says. "And, one could add chopped cooked ham or poultry for variety." Mary reports that it took only 30 minutes to prepare, and freezes well.

Tortellini and Vegetable Soup

8 cups homemade or
  canned chicken broth
9-ounce package
  fresh cheese tortellini
1 cup frozen peas
1 cup julienne-cut carrots
  (strips about 2")

8 ounces fresh mushrooms,
  sliced
3 green onions, sliced
  (include green tops)
½ cup freshly-grated
  Parmesan cheese

Bring chicken broth to a boil in medium stock pot. Add the tortellini and cook 5 minutes. Add peas, carrots, mushrooms and onions. Cook until the vegetables are tender-crisp. Ladle into heated soup bowls. Sprinkle with grated cheese. Can add 1 to 2 cups of diced cooked chicken or ham.

Yield: 11 cups, about 10 servings

Traditionally, Italians are avid gardeners so this soup is aptly named. "It's our family's favorite in the winter," says Sheila Lind of Edina. "And it's tasty and colorful enough to serve to company." Be aware that fresh sausage keeps only a day or two in the refrigerator, so purchase close to preparation time.

Italian Garden Soup

½ pound bacon
1 pound mild Italian
  sausage links
1 large onion, chopped
1 large clove of garlic, crushed
2 tablespoons butter
2 quarts chicken stock (broth)

Two 14½-ounce cans
  diced tomatoes in juice
2 small zucchini, sliced
2 cups carrots, thinly sliced
2 teaspoons Italian seasoning
Seasoned croutons
Parmesan cheese, freshly grated

Cook, drain and crumble bacon; set aside. Cook sausage, drain and slice thinly; set aside. Sauté onion and garlic in 2 tablespoons butter about 5 minutes. Add chicken broth, vegetables and seasonings. Cover and simmer 15 minutes. Add bacon and sausage to soup. Simmer until hot. To serve, top portions with croutons and/or cheese.

Serves 6 to 8

Pat Meyers chose a -50° windchill night to test this slow cooker creation from Annette Nelson of Edina. She served it with toasted cheese sandwiches and pineapple coleslaw for a satisfying supper. Hearty, nutritious, low-calorie and a dinner that's ready when you get home!

Slow Cooker Vegetable Beef Soup

1 pound beef stew meat
3 cups water
3 cubes beef bouillon
2 stalks celery, sliced
2 large carrots, sliced
2 large potatoes, peeled and cubed
15-ounce can green beans, drained
14½-ounce can whole tomatoes, cut up (do not drain)
⅓ cup frozen corn
¼ teaspoon leaf oregano
¼ teaspoon black pepper

Brown meat in a non-stick pan; drain fat. Boil 3 cups water; stir in beef bouillon cubes until dissolved. Place meat and bouillon in electric slow cooker. Add remaining ingredients. Add additional water, if necessary, for a soup consistency.

Cook on low heat at least 8 hours, stirring occasionally.

Serves 4 to 6

Eastern Europeans think of this as "a stout soup for lean times." But anyone sampling Julian Plante's version will appreciate the full-bodied flavor any time. Slav immigrants to Minnesota prided themselves on wasting nothing when it came to stretching the food budget, and sauerkraut and potato-based dishes were staples.

Czechoslovakian Cabbage Soup

2 pounds beef soup bones (sliced marrow bones work well)
1 cup chopped onion
3 carrots, pared and coarsely chopped
3 cloves garlic, chopped
1 bay leaf
2 pounds lean beef short ribs
1 teaspoon dried leaf thyme
½ teaspoon fine quality paprika (more if desired)
8 cups water
8 cups coarsely chopped green cabbage (1 head)
Two 16-ounce cans tomatoes
2 teaspoons salt
½ teaspoon hot pepper sauce (more, if desired)
½ cup chopped parsley
3 tablespoons freshly squeezed lemon juice
3 tablespoons sugar
16-ounce can sauerkraut

Preheat oven to 450°. Place beef bones, onion, carrots, garlic and bay leaf in roasting pan. Place short ribs over the top. Sprinkle with thyme and paprika. Roast, uncovered for 20 to 30 minutes or until meat is brown.

Transfer meat and vegetables to large kettle. Using a small amount of water, scrape browned meat bits from roasting pan into kettle. Add water, cabbage, tomatoes, salt and hot pepper sauce. Bring to boil. Cover and simmer for 1½ hours. Skim off fat. Add parsley, lemon juice, sugar and sauerkraut. Cook, uncovered, for 1 hour.

Remove bones and ribs from kettle. Cool slightly and remove meat from bones. Cut meat into cubes; return to kettle. Cook 5 minutes longer.

Serves 12

Minnesota wild rice plays a starring role in this aromatic meal-in-a-bowl. Remember, it takes longer to cook than white rice, so allow ample time. Wild rice harvesting methods are much the same today as in earlier years, and require hours of labor and several trips through each "ricing bed" to glean grains as they ripen. All the more reason to savor this vegetable-sparked version.

Wild Rice-Vegetable Soup

⅔ cup uncooked wild rice, rinsed
1 medium onion, chopped
1 stalk celery, diced
3 carrots, thinly sliced
1½ tablespoons butter or margarine
Three 10½-ounce cans condensed chicken broth (fat skimmed off)
1½ tablespoons cornstarch
1½ cups fat-free (or regular) half-and-half
Salt and pepper
1 tablespoon Worcestershire sauce
Dash hot pepper sauce
Bacon bits, optional

In a large pot or Dutch oven, saute rice, onion, celery and carrots in butter until carrots are crisp-tender — about 3 minutes. Stir in the broth and 2 soup cans (2½ cups) of water. Heat to boiling, stirring regularly. Reduce heat and simmer, covered, stirring occasionally, about 40 minutes, until rice is popped and tender.

In a small cup, combine cornstarch with a little water until a smooth paste forms. Then stir it into the soup. Cook several minutes, stirring constantly, until soup has thickened. Remove from heat. Stir in the half-and-half and season with salt, pepper, Worcestershire sauce and hot pepper sauce. Ladle into bowls and garnish with bacon bits if desired.

Serves 8

Thanks to The Minneapolis Club for sharing a recipe for this popular Minnesota winter warmer. Founded more than a century ago, the Club stands in the heart of downtown and is renowned for fine food, an elegant atmosphere and a membership dedicated to civic endeavors.

Minneapolis Club Wild Rice Soup

4 to 6 ounces margarine
½ cup diced carrots
½ cup diced celery
½ cup diced onion
¾ pound sliced mushrooms
3 quarts chicken stock
1 cup cooked wild rice
2 tablespoons chicken bouillon granules
1 teaspoon chopped fresh herbs of choice*
½ cup cornstarch mixed with water
Salt, pepper and sugar to taste
1 cup light cream
1 cup dry sherry
Diced sliced almonds, if desired
*Suggestions: Marjoram, thyme and/or sage

In soup pot, heat margarine. Add diced vegetables and mushrooms. Saute for a few minutes. Add chicken stock, wild rice and herbs. Simmer gently for 30 minutes. Thicken to taste with the cornstarch diluted in water. Add seasonings as desired. Finally, add cream and sherry. Heat just until serving temperature; do not boil. Top each serving with almonds, if desired, or mix them in with soup during final heating step.

Serves 8 to 10

The enticing variety of mushrooms available today make them the darlings of home and professional chefs. Choose your favorites to add texture and flavor to this delicate first course dandy from the ECC kitchen. The mushrooms suggested here should be cooked gently to avoid toughening.

Wild Mushroom Soup

½ pound chanterelle, lobster or shiitake mushrooms
½ pound white mushrooms
Juice of one lemon
2 medium shallots, minced
1 small sprig of thyme (leaves only)
½ bay leaf
Salt and pepper to taste
2 cups heavy cream
1½ cups rich chicken stock
1 teaspoon cornstarch, dissolved in 1 tablespoon water
Fresh, chopped parsley or cilantro for garnish, if desired

Wash mushrooms — do not soak. Toss mushrooms in lemon juice; dice into small cubes. Melt butter; lightly cook shallots. Add mushrooms, thyme and bay leaf. Cook until excess liquid disappears. Add salt and pepper, cream and chicken stock. Simmer for about 20 to 30 minutes. Thicken slightly with the cornstarch mixture. Garnish with fresh, chopped parsley or cilantro.

Serves 12

"This chowder is easy to make and very tasty with a sprinkling of mild Cheddar on top," writes Jan Brower from the family's Colorado vacation spot. "It's served a lot out here, and is a third-generation recipe." For fewer calories, use low-fat soup and cheese with skim milk. It will still taste great!

Pot o' Gold Chowder

¾ cup chopped onion
2 tablespoons margarine
1 cup diced, cooked potato
1 cup diced, cooked bacon
2 cups whole kernel corn
   (fresh, canned or frozen)

14-ounce can cream-style corn
10¾-ounce can condensed
   cream of mushroom soup
2½ cups milk
Salt and pepper to taste
Grated Cheddar cheese

Saute onion in margarine. Combine all ingredients except cheese in soup pot. Mix well and heat over low heat. Simmer for 30-45 minutes. Top each serving with grated Cheddar.

Serves 4 to 6

Corn and curry are a delicious duo in this made-in-minutes mini-meal. Most of the ingredients can be ready and waiting for times when dinner on the double is a necessity. Great with a green salad and hot French bread. Leftover cooked, diced ham can be added for extra heartiness.

Curried Corn Soup

2 tablespoons butter
1 teaspoon curry powder, or to taste
15-ounce can cream style corn
1 cup whole kernel corn, drained
1 cup milk
2 tablespoons chopped pimiento
Salt and pepper to taste
1 cup sharp Cheddar cheese, shredded
Paprika for garnish

Melt butter in 11-inch skillet. Add curry and cook briefly. Add creamed corn, whole kernel corn, milk and pimiento. Cook, stirring, until heated through. Fill soup dishes with hot soup and sprinkle with cheese and paprika.

Serves 3 to 4

"Coming across some great summer corn" inspired ECC Executive Chef Jerry Cegla to feature it in a recipe he hadn't used in a long time. Tester Terri Gulliford pronounced it "excellent," and said it took only 30 minutes to prepare. All the tastier if you can snip the fresh basil from a sunny windowsill herb garden so the subtle, distinctive flavor is in its prime.

Cream of Crab and Corn Soup

¼ cup olive oil
1 medium to large yellow onion, diced
2 medium to large peeled potatoes, diced
1 large clove garlic, minced
1 medium bay leaf
4 cups fresh corn kernels
¼ cup fresh basil leaves, shredded (no stems)
4 cups rich chicken stock
   (2 cans chicken broth may be substituted)
½ cup dry white wine
1 pound lump crab meat
1 cup heavy cream
Salt and pepper to taste

Heat oil in soup kettle. Saute onion, potatoes, garlic and bay leaf in oil. Add corn kernels, basil leaves chicken stock and wine; bring to a boil for 8-10 minutes. Add crab meat, cream, salt and pepper; simmer for about 10 minutes, stirring to prevent soup from sticking to the pan. Serve with your favorite white wine and a crisp loaf of French bread.

Serves approximately 8 to 10 portions

ECC Sous Chef Tim Cegla devised this stick-to-the-ribs soup, perfect for frosty Minnesota evenings. Tester Karen Remund served it to enthusiastic guests who "ate at least two bowlfuls apiece. It's just delicious!" she adds. Karen suggests that broccoli lovers might want to add even more — she used twice as much as called for with pleasing results.

Cheese-Broccoli Soup with Ham

½ pound butter
1 cup diced onion
1 cup diced celery
½ cup diced carrots
All-purpose flour
3½ quarts chicken stock
1 pound American cheese, diced
1 cup blanched broccoli buds
¾ cup diced ham
Salt and pepper to taste
Hot pepper sauce to taste
Worcestershire sauce to taste

Melt butter in large soup pot. Add onion, celery and carrots. Cook until tender. Add enough flour to soak up all butter. Cook for several minutes over low heat. Add cold chicken stock and let come to a boil. Stir with a wire whisk until thickened (like gravy). Add cheese and let it melt. Add broccoli and ham, then season with salt, pepper, hot pepper sauce and Worcestershire sauce to desired flavor.

Yield: 16 one-cup servings

"Traditionally, this is the first course for our Christmas Eve supper," says Terry Swanson. "It's wonderfully rich and makes a good meal by itself on cold nights. Taste is best when it is eaten the same day it is made," she adds. A psychiatric nurse, Terry enlisted her husband, Dr. John Eichten, and daughter, Alison, to assist with taste-testing a number of recipes for this book.

Cheesy Clam Chowder

6 slices bacon (reserve drippings)
½ cup diced carrots
½ cup minced onion
½ cup diced celery
½ cup flour
1 tablespoon cornstarch
½ teaspoon salt
¼ teaspoon pepper
Three 8-ounce cans minced clams, drained (reserve juice)
Two 6-ounce bottles clam juice
4 cups milk
1 cup pared, cubed potatoes
1 pound white Cheddar cheese, grated
Parsley for garnish

Cook bacon in dutch oven or stock pot until crisp. Remove bacon; drain and crumble. Sauté carrots, onion and celery in bacon drippings until onion is transparent. Stir in flour, cornstarch, salt and pepper. Cook until bubbly. Combine juice drained from clams and bottled juice to make 3½ cups. Stir juice and milk into vegetable mixture. Heat to boiling, stirring occasionally until mixture thickens. Add potatoes; cook until just tender. Add clams; heat 5 minutes. Add cheese, stir and cook over low heat until cheese melts. Serve hot; sprinkle with crumbled bacon and parsley.

Serves 10

The popularity of this colorful soup, developed by ECC's Sous Chef, Tim Cegla, has spread far beyond the confines of the Club dining rooms. It was featured in the TASTE section of the Star-Tribune, *was reprinted in* America's Best Loved Community Recipes *published by Better Homes and Gardens, and appeared in* The Global Gourmet, *a Concordia Language Village cookbook. Lower in calories than the milk-based version, the soup works well with fresh or canned clams, and leftovers freeze beautifully. The question is — what leftovers?*

Manhattan Clam Chowder

2 cups diced potatoes
4 cups chicken stock
2 tablespoons butter
2 tablespoons olive oil
1 cup diced carrots
1 cup diced celery
1 cup diced onions
¼ teaspoon dried leaf thyme
¼ teaspoon dried leaf oregano
½ teaspoon chopped garlic
½ teaspoon snipped fresh parsley
2 cups diced tomatoes, with juice
2 cups tomato sauce
6 cups chopped canned or fresh clams, with juice
Salt and pepper to taste

Cut potatoes into ½-inch pieces. Cook in chicken stock. Remove potatoes from stock when about ¾ cooked (about 15 minutes). Add butter and oil to stock; thoroughly heat. Cut carrots, celery and onions into ½-inch dice. Stir carrots, onions, thyme, oregano, garlic and parsley into butter-oil mixture. Cook until tender. Stir in tomatoes, tomato sauce, clams, potatoes, salt and pepper; heat thoroughly.

10 to 12 servings

Here's an ECC masterpiece that can be the soul of a meal or a richly satisfying first course to be followed by a light entrée. One secret to successful chowders is to refrain from overcooking the vegetables to retain a pleasant texture. And, notice the important final step which prevents the clams from overcooking as well. Tester Janet Markee said her husband expecially enjoyed the "thick, chunky consistency."

New England Clam Chowder

2 pounds white potatoes (or about 8 medium baking potatoes), peeled and diced into ½-inch cubes
1 tablespoon chicken bouillon
¼ pound bacon (8 slices), diced
1 cup diced white onion
½ cup diced celery
1 cup flour
½ gallon whole milk
2 bay leaves
1 teaspoon dried leaf thyme
Salt and white pepper to taste
1 quart chopped clams with juice

In large saucepan, cover potatoes with water. Add bouillon and simmer until potatoes are tender but not mushy.

In large kettle, partially cook bacon. Add onion and celery; cook until tender. Stir in flour to make a roux. Then, stir in milk, bay leaves, thyme, salt and pepper. Simmer chowder for 20 minutes without clams. Add potatoes and clams last 5 minutes and let clams steep. This prevents clams from overcooking.

Serves 12

This creation by ECC Sous Chef Tim Cegla was eagerly tested by Jan Collins after it appeared in the Club newsletter. "My husband loves bean soup and enjoyed the zingy flavor of this rendition. He had two helpings!" Jan appreciated the time-saving feature of using canned rather than dried beans. If "zing" isn't your thing, simply trim amounts of chili powder, paprika and cumin to please your palate.

Southwestern Chicken and Bean Soup

6 ounces clarified butter
1 cup diced onion
1 cup diced green pepper
1 cup diced red pepper
½ cup diced carrots
1 tablespoon diced garlic
1 cup diced green chilies
3 cups cooked, cubed chicken
2 quarts rich chicken stock
16-ounce can northern beans
2 cups cooked white and wild rice, combined half and half
16-ounce can diced tomatoes with juice
2 tablespoons cornstarch
2 tablespoons water

In clarified butter, saute vegetables. Add chicken, chicken stock, beans, rice, and tomatoes. Simmer and thicken slightly with 2 tablespoons cornstarch mixed with 2 tablespoons water.

SEASON SOUP WITH:
1 tablespoon fresh chopped cilantro
1 tablespoon chili powder
1 tablespoon paprika
½ tablespoon cumin
Salt and pepper to taste

Serves 9 to 12

Virginia Krusell, who lives in the Highland Park area of St. Paul, was blessed with this recipe from a Jewish neighbor "who tested and tested again until she had perfected the 'best' of matzo ball soups." Soup plays a diverse role in Jewish menus — from a starter course for holiday meals to a main course for casual suppers. Matzos are thin pieces of unleavened bread made of flour and water, and the meal is made from finely grinding the bread. Home Economist Ann Burckhardt suggests making soup ahead so flavors marry and fat can be skimmed from the top.

Matzo Balls and Chicken Soup

3 eggs, separated
¾ cup matzo meal
1 tablespoon chicken fat (can be skimmed from chicken soup)
1 teaspoon salt, or to taste
¾ teaspoon pepper, or to taste

CHICKEN SOUP
4 quarts water
1 large onion
4 celery stalks, cut in thirds
5 carrots, cut in thirds
Salt and pepper to taste
1 stewing chicken, cut in quarters
Water to cover chicken

For matzo balls, beat egg whites until stiff. In separate bowl, beat yolks until thick and creamy. Combine yolks and whites. Then slowly fold in matzo meal, chicken fat, salt and pepper. Let mixture rest for a few minutes. Moisten hands slightly for ease in handling mixture. Carefully form medium-sized balls, the size of small apple or smaller. Bring soup to simmering boil. Carefully drop balls into soup. Cover and let cook for 10 minutes. Turn balls over, re-cover and cook an additional 10 minutes. They will puff up and increase in size. When cover is removed they will deflate some, but will puff again when re-covered.

Serves 6 to 8

For soup, combine in 6-quart kettle vegetables, seasonings, chicken and the water. Simmer until chicken is tender, 1½ to 2 hours. Cool chicken, remove wings, detach meat from bone and return meat to broth.

Yield: 4 quarts

Unlike some Tex-Mex recipes, this soup is actually served in many of Mexico's finest restaurants. A colorful array of toppings is offered, representing a variety of textures and colors. Try crisp corn tortilla strips, shredded Cheddar, dollops of sour cream, sliced black olives, chopped scallions and/or diced green pepper. Another rave-winner from the ECC kitchen!

Tortilla Soup

2 tablespoons vegetable oil
2 cloves garlic, minced
1 small onion, chopped
Two 6-ounce cans chopped green chilies, drained
1 cup peeled, chopped tomato
1½ cups beef bouillon
1½ cups chicken broth
1½ cups water
1½ cups tomato juice
1 teaspoon cumin
1 teaspoon chili powder
1 teaspoon salt
⅛ teaspoon pepper
2 teaspoons Worcestershire sauce
1 tablespoon bottled steak sauce
Tortillas

Heat oil; sauté onions and garlic until transparent. Add chilies and tomatoes; simmer 10 minutes. Add beef and chicken stocks, water and tomato juice. Bring back to simmer for 10 minutes. Add remaining ingredients and heat thoroughly. For a garnish of crisp tortilla strips, cut corn tortillas into ½-inch pieces and fry until crisp. Drain on paper toweling.

Note: If soup seems to be too thin, thicken with 1 tbsp. of cornstarch mixed with 2 tbsps. water.

Serves 4 to 6

Preparation for this trendy treat from Pat Meyers begins the night before serving with the soaking of the beans. "Good flavor!" commented tester Pat Clemmer. A surprise addition of green chilies adds zip.

Santa Fe Black Bean Soup

1 pound dry black beans
¼ cup olive oil
3 large onions, chopped
4 cloves garlic, minced
1 medium green pepper, chopped
Four 14½-ounce cans beef broth
1½ pound ham hock
1 tablespoon cumin
1 tablespoon oregano
½ teaspoon thyme
Salt and pepper to taste
1 bay leaf
4-ounce can green chilies
2 tablespoons sherry
Garnishes as desired

Wash beans, cover with water and soak overnight. Drain beans. Heat oil in 3-quart saucepan. Add onions, garlic and green pepper. Saute about 3 minutes. Add beans and cover with broth; add ham hock. Cover pan and simmer 1 hour. Add remaining seasonings, chilies and sherry, and simmer 1½ hours. Take meat from ham hock, dice and add to mixture. Mash some of beans in the pot. Remove bay leaf before serving. Garnish soup bowls with lite sour cream, tomato, and/or sliced hard cooked egg.

Serves 8 to 10

This southern staple has been adapted from a Charleston recipe by Julian Plante, Ph.D. Although the lemon juice addition is optional, Julian likes the added zing. Okra, sometimes referred to as "the poor man's oyster," has interesting qualities. When cut and briefly simmered, it thickens the mixture and it provides fiber, Vitamin A and other nutrients. Okra and filé powder are essential gumbo ingredients.

Old South Okra Gumbo

2 cups diced stewing beef
4 cups stewed tomatoes, undrained
2 medium onions, quartered
1 quart chicken stock
1 quart water
2 beef bouillon cubes
8 or 10-ounce package frozen lima beans
8 or 10-ounce package frozen okra, cut up
½ cup cooked, diced ham
1 cup cooked, diced chicken
½ cup halved mushroom buttons
1 teaspoon filé powder
16-ounce can of whole kernel corn, drained
2 tablespoons lemon juice (optional)
Salt and pepper to taste

In large soup kettle, simmer beef, tomatoes, onions, stock, water and bouillon cubes for 1 hour. Add frozen lima beans. Simmer 20 minutes. Add okra, ham, chicken, mushrooms and filé. Cook an additional 20 minutes. Finally, add corn, lemon juice, salt and pepper; continue simmering 5 more minutes.

Serves 6 to 8

Salads, Dressings and Condiments

A chilled vegetable salad served with grilled meat or poultry makes an appealing warm-weather menu that's hassle-free. In season, use fresh green beans, cooked until tender-crisp. Or, fresh asparagus can be substituted. Thanks to Gretchen Pracht for this divine departure from the usual marinated vegetable salad.

Asian Green Bean Salad

1 tablespoon soy sauce
1 tablespoon dark Oriental
  sesame oil
1 teaspoon red wine vinegar
1½ teaspoons sugar
½ clove garlic,
  minced or crushed
Lettuce leaves

1 thin slice (nickel size) fresh
  ginger, minced, OR ¼ teaspoon
  powdered ground ginger
Salt and pepper to taste
16-ounce can green beans,
  drained

Combine all ingredients except green beans; mix with beans. Refrigerate at least several hours or overnight to meld flavors. Serve on lettuce leaves.

Note: If desired, substitute 1 pound thin asparagus stalks, cut into bite-sized pieces and cooked al dent for green beans.

Serves 4

Black beans, also known as "turtle beans," bring a rich, earthy taste to this simple, satisfying do-ahead salad from Eleanor Nelson of Edina. Tester Hille Kersten served it with chicken fijitas and "there were no leftovers," she reports. Cilantro, the Spanish name for coriander, is fairly intense. So, you may want to modify the amount to suit your personal preference.

Black Bean Salad

Two 15-ounce cans black beans,
  drained and rinsed
1 cup chopped red onion
1 cup chopped red bell pepper
4 tablespoons fresh lime juice

1 to 2 cloves garlic, minced
6 tablespoons chopped cilantro,
  or to taste
½ to 1 cup salsa

Combine all ingredients, chill and serve.

Serves 8

An appealing four-season salad combining readily-available ingredients with a garlic-sparked oil and vinegar dressing. Contributor Eleanor Nelson uses a whisk to mix dressing and allows flavors to blend for at least an hour before adding to vegetables. After combining all ingredients, she waits another hour before serving for peak flavor.

Broccoli-Mushroom Salad

1 bunch broccoli
   (2 pounds 2 large stalks)
   cut into florettes
1 bunch green onions, chopped
8 ounces sliced mushrooms

1 cup salad oil
½ cup sugar
¼ cup red wine vinegar
1 teaspoon minced garlic

Combine broccoli, onions and mushrooms. Whip salad oil, sugar, vinegar and garlic. Combine all ingredients. Allow to stand for one hour or longer!

Serves 6-8

No ordinary broccoli salad, this combines a fetching array of colors, textures and flavors with a quickly-mixed dressing. Pauline Anderson, the enthusiastic tester for Allison Gaasedelen's recipe, says simply, "It's wonderful!" And, it can be prepared well ahead of serving.

Broccoli Salad Supreme

4 stalks broccoli florettes
   (3 to 4 pounds)
½ cup chopped green onion
½ cup diced celery
3 cups seedless red grapes
3-ounce package sliced almonds
1 cup raisins
1 pound bacon, cooked, drained and diced or crumbled

DRESSING
1 cup salad dressing
½ cup sugar
1 tablespoon vinegar

Combine all salad ingredients in large bowl. Combine dressing ingredients in small bowl. Gently toss and serve.

Serves 8

Tester Linda Johnson of Woodbury offers kudos for this colorful combo from Jaye Vaaler of Golden Valley. "It's a beautiful salad to serve with almost any entree," says Linda. Jaye suggests doubling or even tripling ingredient amounts to serve a crowd. Be sure to combine salad and dressing at least several hours ahead of serving.

Carnival Coleslaw

3 cups shredded green cabbage
2 cups shredded red cabbage
½ red pepper, diced
½ green pepper, diced
½ yellow pepper, diced
½ cup chopped onion
1 carrot, grated

DRESSING
2 tablespoons fresh dill, chopped,
   or 1 teaspoon dried
1 clove garlic, minced
½ teaspoon salt
½ teaspoon dry mustard
2 tablespoons honey
3 tablespoons vegetable oil
¼ cup cider or red wine vinegar

Combine all the vegetables. Whisk dressing ingredients together and drizzle over the vegetables. Toss to mix well. Refrigerate at least several hours before serving.

Serves 6 to 8

Tester Shirley Bard has high praise for Gretchen Pracht's perky pepper and pineapple slaw. "This is a real crowd-pleaser — the flavor is addictive!" says Shirley. Only 30 minutes of preparation time results in a salad which has guests clamoring for seconds.

Company Best Coleslaw

1 head cabbage
1 cup mayonnaise
1 cup sour cream
¼ cup (or less) diced canned
   mild jalapeño peppers
3 tablespoons Dijon mustard

3 tablespoons sugar
2 tablespoons lemon juice
½ teaspoon salt
½ teaspoon cumin
5½-ounce can
   pineapple chunks, drained

Shred cabbage; set aside. Combine mayonnaise, sour cream, diced peppers, mustard, sugar, lemon juice, salt and cumin. Add cabbage and pineapple; toss thoroughly. Cover and refrigerate for an hour or more before serving.

Serves 10 to 12

This salad from Gene Gaasedelen of Edina has all the "right stuff!" Low in calories and fat, it may be readied ahead except for the dressing addition. Tester Mary Mulheran found it "quick and easy to assemble" and commented on the "peppy flavor." "Expect requests for second helpings," she adds.

Cabbage-Parsley Toss

2 cups crisp shredded or
  finely-chopped cabbage
½ cup chopped parsley
1 medium onion,
  finely chopped or sliced
  and separated into rings
2 tablespoons salad oil (canola)

DRESSING
3 tablespoons sugar
½ teaspoon salt
3 tablespoons white wine vinegar

Combine prepared vegetables; chill. Combine dressing ingredients, stirring to dissolve sugar. Pour over vegetables and toss lightly. Garnish with additional onion rings.

May be prepared in part the day before, but do not combine vegetables and dressing until serving time.

Serves 4

Don Stork, formerly on ECC's culinary staff, developed a big-batch cucumber salad which is party perfect. Tester Terry Swanson suggests it for your next family reunion, block party or picnic buffet. For her family, she used one-fourth of all ingredients and light sour cream with excellent results.

Overnight Cucumber Salad a la Stork

8 cucumbers
2 red onions
2 cups apple cider vinegar
1 cup water

1 teaspoon salt
2 cups sour cream
½ cup sugar

Peel, seed and slice cucumbers. Peel onions; cut into julienne strips. In large non-metallic bowl, combine cucumbers, onions, vinegar, water and salt. Cover and refrigerate overnight. Drain all liquid from cucumber and onions. Combine sour cream and sugar. Add to vegetables and chill until serving time.

Yield: 18 to 24 serving

Hearts of palm, a velvety-textured vegetable gleaned from palmetto trees of Florida and South America, star in this elegant salad from Pat Stark. Tester Mary L. Miller, eloquently describes it as "an eat-your-heart-out, Martha Stewart" sensation. "One of the prettiest and most satisfying salads I've tried," says Mary. Dressing may be made ahead and refrigerated until serving time.

Hearts of Palm Salad

Two 14-ounce cans hearts of palm, chilled
1 large head Boston lettuce

DRESSING
½ cup salad oil
2 tablespoons finely-chopped parsley
2 tablespoons finely-chopped onion
2 tablespoons white wine vinegar
2 teaspoons lemon juice
½ teaspoon salt
¼ teaspoon dried mustard
2 hard-cooked eggs, finely chopped
2 tablespoons chopped pimiento

Rinse and drain hearts of palm; cut into strips. Cover and refrigerate. Combine dressing ingredients in a jar with a tight-fitting lid. Shake well to blend. To assemble salad: Line chilled plates with lettuce leaves. Arrange palm strips over lettuce. Drizzle with dressing just before serving.

Serves 8

Jicama is a mild, white root vegetable that marries well with Southwestern cooking. And, it is low in calories and abundant in Vitamin C. Marde Olson pairs this salad with Mexican entrées and finds the refreshing crunch of the vegetables a pleasing contrast to hearty, spicy dishes.

Sun Country Salad

1 large jicama, peeled
1 red pepper
1 carrot, peeled
¼ cup chopped fresh cilantro

2 green onions, chopped finely
1 tablespoon fresh lime juice
1 teaspoon sugar
½ teaspoon coarse salt

Cut jicama, pepper and carrot into julienne strips. Combine with remaining ingredients. Cover and refrigerate until serving time. Can be made ahead; keeps well in refrigerator.

Serves 4

The tantalizing fragrance of fresh mint permeates this summery salad. Contributor Liana Peterson cuts the snow peas into julienne strips for easier eating and a delicate appearance.

Minted Pea Salad

10-ounce package frozen peas, thawed and well drained
8 ounces fresh or frozen snow peas, thawed and well drained
8 slices bacon, cooked and crumbled
½ cup fresh mint leaves, snipped into slivers
¼ cup mayonnaise
¼ cup sour cream

Combine well-drained peas with crumbled bacon, mint leaf slivers, mayonnaise and sour cream. Add more mayonnaise and sour cream, if desired. Cover and refrigerate until serving.

Serves 4 to 6

Mildly-flavored mushrooms are pepped up with snipped chives and combined with a creamy dressing. A favorite of Gretchen Pracht's for year-around serving. Allow ample time to chill the mushrooms before completing preparation.

Fresh Mushroom Salad

½ teaspoon salt
1 cup water
1 pound fresh mushrooms, sliced
2 tablespoons chives, finely snipped
¼ cup whipping cream or half & half
2 teaspoons sugar
Dash of pepper
Fresh dill, if desired
Lettuce cups

Add ½ teaspoon salt to 1 cup water. Heat in medium saucepan to boiling. Add mushrooms. Bring to a boil; reduce heat and simmer 1 minute. Drain and chill. Add chives. Mix remaining ingredients. Pour over mushrooms and chives. Toss and spoon into lettuce cups. Garnish with fresh dill if desired.

Serves 4

This recipe, developed by De Evenson, ECC Banquet Pantry Supervisor, makes great picnic fare and can be prepared the night before serving. Because of the mayonnaise in the dressing, be sure to keep salad well chilled until serving time.

Peas 'n Peanuts

16 ounces frozen green peas, thawed and drained
¼ cup diced celery
¼ cup diced onion

2 cups salted Spanish peanuts
¾ cup mayonnaise
1 tablespoon sugar

Combine thoroughly drained peas with celery, onion and peanuts. Combine mayonnaise and sugar. Toss with remaining ingredients. Chill until serving time.

Serves 6 to 8

A savory salad with old-world overtones from the ECC kitchen. It's a marvelous make-ahead (note 8-hour refrigeration step) to team with grilled entrées. Or, mound it in the center of a platter of cold cuts with sandwich buns near by.

Russian Potato Salad

2 to 2-½ to 2-½ pounds baby red potatoes, cooked

8 slices cooked bacon, cooked and crumbled

2 tablespoons chopped green onions (with tops)

2 tablespoons yellow onions,

1 tablespoon fresh chives, chopped

2 tablespoons medium diced celery

2 tablespoons diced red pepper

DRESSING

1 cup mayonnaise

1 cup sour cream

½ cup prepared mustard-mayonnaise dressing,
   like Durkee's Famous Sauce

1 tablespoon fresh chives

Cut potatoes into bite-sized pieces if necessary. Lightly combine salad ingredients in large bowl. In another bowl, combine dressing ingredients. Fold dressing gently into salad until well mixed, taking care not to crumble potatoes. Chill, covered, overnight or at least 8 hours before serving. (Potatoes will absorb much of the dressing during refrigeration.)

Serves 6 to 8

Nothing ho-hum about this potato salad. Shirley Bentdahl suggests this European variation sans mayonnaise and subtly seasoned with fresh herbs. Tester Jacqui Jarnes appreciated the attractive, colorful presentation as well as the flavor and texture. Take care not to overcook potatoes to retain a pleasing consistency.

Veggie Salad Vinaigrette

8 small new potatoes
2 medium tomatoes, cut into wedges
½ red onion, sliced
¼ cup sliced green onion
½ cup pea pods, cut into bite-sized pieces

DRESSING
¼ cup plus 3 tablespoons extra virgin olive oil
2 tablespoons balsamic vinegar
2 tablespoons finely-chopped fresh tarragon or Italian parsley
¼ teaspoon salt
⅛ teaspoon pepper

Cook the potatoes in salted water just until tender. Drain, cool slightly and halve or quarter, depending on size. In a small jar with a tight fitting lid combine the dressing ingredients. Shake to mix well. When ready to serve, combine the veggies; toss lightly with dressing. May be served at room temperature.

Serves 4 to 6

Trish Ura of Edina proudly presents her husband's specialty. "No other oil but olive oil will do," she warns, and adds, "the great garlic flavor is loved by all but the weak of heart!" Also note that Bob insists on fresh, not bottled, lemon juice and specifies freshly-grated Parmesan. Tester Peggy Dodge liked the "unique tang of the Worcestershire sauce," and found the salad could be prepared in just 20 minutes.

Bob's Sensational Caesar Salad

4 anchovy fillets, soaked in milk
1 head romaine lettuce, washed and torn
1 coddled egg
⅓ cup olive oil
2 tablespoons Worcestershire sauce
3 to 4 cloves fresh garlic, pressed
Juice of 1 lemon, or ¼ cup
1 cup freshly-grated Parmesan cheese
Croutons as desired

Place anchovy fillets on small plate; cover with milk and set aside. (The milk bath removes oils and salt from the anchovies. If you want more anchovy flavor, simply mash the fillets right out of the can.) Prepare romaine; wrap in towel and return to refrigerator to crisp. To coddle egg, boil for 1½ minutes.

In large salad bowl, combine olive oil, Worcestershire sauce, pressed garlic and the still warm egg. When breaking egg into bowl, do not scrap out the albumin still clinging to the shell. Rinse anchovy fillets under water, dry with paper towel and mash into small pieces with back of fork. Add anchovy bits to the mixture. Add romaine to bowl, drizzle on lemon juice and sprinkle on Parmesan. Add croutons and toss.

Serves 4 to 6

Toasting nuts brings out even more flavor as you will find when you sample Judy Tucker's creative combination. The unpeeled apple sections provide color and additional texture, and the Dijon-infused dressing is the crowning touch. Tester Marlys Wahlberg had this table-ready in just 20 minutes!

Apple-Walnut Salad

½ cup walnuts
1 head Boston or Bibb lettuce, torn into bite-sized pieces
1 unpeeled Granny Smith apple, sliced
3 (or more) tablespoons crumbled Roquefort cheese

DRESSING
3 tablespoons extra virgin olive oil
1 tablespoon white wine or peach-flavored vinegar
½ teaspoon Dijon mustard
¼ teaspoon salt
Freshly ground pepper to taste

Preheat oven to 250°. Spread walnuts in shallow pan. Bake 15 minutes. Combine dressing ingredients thoroughly; set aside. Place walnuts, lettuce, apple slices and Roquefort in large bowl. Just before serving, toss with dressing.

Serves 4

Recipe contributor Charlotte Tudor and tester Sheran McNulty agree that this is a terrific special-occasion salad. Mix and match choice greens with an eye to contrasting colors, textures and flavors. Dry washed greens gently but thoroughly so excess moisture doesn't dilute dressing.

Mandarin Orange-Almond Salad

Mixed greens of choice to serve four
11-ounce can mandarin oranges, drained
⅓ cup slivered almonds
2 tablespoons sugar

SWEET DRESSING
¼ cup salad oi
2 tablespoons sugar
2 tablespoons tarragon vinegar
½ teaspoon salt
Dash pepper

Prepare greens; refrigerate. Combine almonds and 2 tablespoons sugar in small sauté pan. Cook over high heat until golden brown, stirring constantly and watching carefully. (This step takes only a few minutes.) Empty almonds onto waxed paper. Cool, then break up into pieces. Combine dressing ingredients thoroughly. At serving time, combine greens with oranges, almonds and dressing. Mix lightly to keep greens from bruising.

Serves 4

Louise Saunders, who with her late husband, operated the famous Charlie's Cafe Exceptionale in downtown Minneapolis, shares one of their most popular salad recipes. Tester Gene Gaasedelen comments, "This is as exceptional as the restaurant name implies. And the dressing is just right — light and tangy!"

Salad Bowl du Chef

Crisp greens of choice for two
1 tomato, quartered
4 slices avocado
6 red onion rings
4 marinated artichoke hearts
6 rolled anchovies
4 sliced ripe and green olives
2 ounces crumbled Roquefort cheese

FRENCH DRESSING
4 tablespoons salad oil
2 tablespoons lemon juice
2 tablespoons red wine vinegar
¼ teaspoon leaf oregano
Salt and pepper

In a large bowl, gently combine greens with remaining salad ingredients. In a separate bowl or jar, mix dressing ingredients. At serving time, toss salad with dressing. Serve immediately in two chilled salad bowls.

Serves 2

Eating alone? All the more reason to prepare a fine salad to entice you to the table. This Scott Rochat specialty features colorful fruit and vegetables plus a favorite Italian blue-veined, semi-soft cheese. Gorgonzola, which originated over 1,000 years ago in a village near Milan, is frequently served with pears.

Milan Medley for One

Baby mixed greens,
    including Romaine
2 slices fresh, ripe pear
2 slices Roma tomato
2 green olives

3 pea pods
1 ring yellow pepper
1 ounce Gorgonzola cheese,
    crumbled
Raspberry vinaigrette

Combine greens and place on a chilled salad plate. Arrange pear and tomato slices, olives, pea pods, pepper ring and cheese on greens. Drizzle with raspberry vinaigrette.

Serves 1

"Attractive, unique and easy" is how Diane Lacy Harr describes this salad after testing it on her family. Contributor Jan Winters Keprios wisely uses skin-on apples for added color and fiber. Spinach leaves are best washed in several changes of water to eliminate any traces of soil. And, any tough central ribs should be removed before spinach is torn.

Autumn Apple-Spinach Toss

1 bunch fresh spinach
½ pound bacon
3 medium apples

DRESSING
⅔ cups mayonnaise
⅓ cup orange juice concentrate

Wash and dry spinach; tear into bite-sized pieces. Cook and drain bacon; cut into 1-inch pieces. Core apple and dice. Combine spinach, bacon and apple in large bowl. In small bowl, combine mayonnaise and orange juice concentrate. Just before serving, toss spinach mixture with dressing.

Serves 6 to 8

Sunny orange sections brighten Julie Waychoff's favorite spinach salad. What a delectable way to consume Vitamins A and C! Tarragon vinegar is a congenial addition to the dressing because of its subtlety and universal appeal.

Spinach-Orange Salad

1 bunch fresh spinach
1 orange, peeled and sectioned
1 red onion,
  separated into rings
½ pound bacon cooked
  until crisp and crumbled
¼ cup slivered almonds

DRESSING
¼ cup salad oil
2 tablespoons sugar
2 tablespoons tarragon vinegar
½ teaspoon salt
Dash tabasco sauce

Wash and dry spinach; tear into bite-sized pieces. In large bowl, combine spinach with orange sections, onion rings, crumbled bacon and slivered almonds. In glass jar, combine all dressing ingredients. Shake until well blended. Just before serving, add dressing to salad ingredients. Or, serve dressing on the side.

Serves 6 to 8

When Jan Collins spies the first fresh spring strawberries, she is inspired to prepare this pretty salad. The dressing has just enough "bite" to add character. Choose tender, young spinach leaves, deep green in color, and use as soon as possible after purchasing or picking.

Spinach-Strawberry Salad

10 ounces spinach, washed and torn
1 pint strawberries, sliced
1 bunch green onions, thinly sliced

DRESSING
½ cup oil
½ cup vinegar
¼ cup sugar
⅛ teaspoon pepper
½ teaspoon salt
½ teaspoon tabasco sauce, or to taste

In large bowl, combine spinach, berries and onions. In small bowl or glass jar, blend dressing ingredients. Just before serving, toss salad with just enough dressing to moisten spinach. Refrigerate leftover dressing.

Serves 4 to 6

Scott Rochat's designer spinach salad features an intriguing dressing with a mayonnaise consistency. Tester Betty Bajwa commented on "the unusual texture supplied by the vegetables and the unique flavor of the dressing." The cheese adds heartiness and makes this a candidate for a light main dish as well as a first course or side salad.

Spinach Salad with Chutney-Mustard Dressing

1 pound spinach
8 ounces mushrooms, sliced
1 cup sliced water chestnuts
¾ fresh cup bean sprouts
1 cup shredded Swiss or Gruyère cheese
¼ cup sliced red onion

DRESSING
½ cup red wine vinegar
3 tablespoons mango chutney
1 clove garlic, minced
2 tablespoons Dijon mustard
2 teaspoons sugar
½ cup salad oil

Wash and dry spinach; tear into bite-sized pieces. In large bowl, combine spinach with mushrooms, water chestnuts, sprouts, cheese and onion. In blender container, combine vinegar, chutney, garlic, mustard and sugar. Blend until sugar is dissolved. Slowly pour in salad oil until mixture takes on a mayonnaise consistency. Just before serving, toss salad ingredients with dressing.

Serves 8 to 10

Although the salad itself calls for traditional ingredients, the robust dressing with its spicy accents gives the final presentation a distinct personality. Contributor Gretchen Pracht suggests making the dressing in advance so the myriad of flavors has time to meld.

Spinach Salad Internationale

1 bunch fresh spinach
5 slices bacon, cooked,
   drained and crumbled
2 hard-cooked eggs,
   finely chopped
DRESSING
⅔ cup salad oil
¼ cup red wine vinegar

1 clove garlic, minced
2 teaspoons soy sauce
1 teaspoon sugar
1 teaspoon dry mustard
½ teaspoon curry powder
½ teaspoon salt, or to taste
½ teaspoon seasoned pepper

Wash and dry spinach; tear into bite-sized pieces. In large bowl, toss spinach with crumbled bacon and chopped eggs. In small bowl, combine all dressing ingredients. At serving time, toss salad with dressing.

Serves 8

"When it's a potluck gathering, I'm always asked to bring this," says contributor Judy Tillson of Edina. "Everyone seems to enjoy it, and it can be made ahead." Orzo is a rice-shaped pasta which, like all other varieties, should be timed carefully during cooking to retain firm texture.

Orzo and Olive Salad

¾ pound (1¾ cups) orzo
1 cup pitted ripe olives, sliced
1 cup pimiento-stuffed
   green olives
⅓ cup minced fresh parsley
   or more

½ cup chopped green onion,
   including tops
5 tablespoons
   extra virgin olive oil
2½ tablespoons
   fresh lemon juice (or to taste)
Salt and pepper to taste

Cook orzo according to package directions until al dent. Rinse in cold water; drain. Place well-drained orzo in large serving bowl. Add olives, parsley and onion. Combine lemon juice and oil. Add salt and pepper to taste. Toss with orzo mixture and chill until serving.

Serves 6

Although this recipe is completed in several stages, the preparation is really quite stream-lined. Furthermore, the result is a make-ahead side dish which eliminates any need for another vegetable or starch on the menu. Another bonus? It is easily transformed into a main dish salad with the addition of cooked meats, poultry, seafood and/or cheese.

ECC Pasta Salad with Dill Dressing

2 pounds bow tie or spiral pasta
½ pound carrots (about 7)
½ pound broccoli (about 1 large stalk)
½ pound cauliflower (about 1/4 head)

DILL DRESSING
¼ cup white vinegar
2 tablespoons sugar
2 cups mayonnaise
6 tablespoons fresh dill, snipped
Salt to taste
White pepper to taste

Slice carrots and cut up broccoli and cauliflower into bite-sized pieces. Blanch vegetables; set aside to cool. Cook pasta according to package directions; rinse, drain and cool. While pasta and vegetables are cooling, combine vinegar and sugar for dressing in saucepan. Heat and stir until sugar is dissolved; set aside to cool. In large bowl, toss pasta with vegetables. Combine vinegar-sugar mixture with remaining dressing ingredients. Combine dressing with salad ingredients. Cover and chill thoroughly before serving.

Serves 8 to 10

Block parties are a great way to meet neighbors, especially when everyone requests the recipe for your popular contribution. That happened to Mary L. Miller when she brought this salad to the potluck gathering on her street. "It's unique, attractive and should be prepared at least 8 hours ahead of serving," she says. Pretty in a lettuce-lined bowl.

Barley Salad with Vinaigrette Dressing

2 cups water	3 tablespoons fresh parsley,
Dash salt	chopped
1 cup quick-cooking barley	⅓ cup olive oil
⅔ cup chopped red pepper	¼ cup white wine vinegar
⅔ cup chopped green pepper	¼ teaspoon salt
16-ounce can	¼ teaspoon pepper
whole kernel corn, drained	⅛ teaspoon paprika

Combine water and dash of salt in medium saucepan; bring to a boil. Stir in barley; return to a boil, stirring several times. Cover, reduce heat and simmer about 12 minutes or until barley is tender but still firm, stirring several times during cooking. Drain barley and cool. Combine barley with red and green pepper, corn and parsley. Combine oil, vinegar, salt, pepper and paprika. Pour over barley mixture and toss. Cover and chill at least 8 hours before serving.

Serves 10

A fuss-free fruit salad which Mary Morton whips up upon request for her son, Jeff. Save out a few of the orange segments and add some maraschino cherries for a bright garnish. Definitely a kid-pleaser for birthday parties, teen gatherings and potlucks.

Creamy Fruit Salad

32 ounces low-fat cottage cheese (small curd)
6-ounce package orange-flavored gelatin
20-ounce can crushed pineapple, drained
15-ounce can mandarin oranges, drained
8-ounce container whipped topping

In a large bowl, stir the dry gelatin into the cottage cheese. Fold in well-drained fruit. Finally, fold in whipped topping. Cover and refrigerate several hours before serving.

Serves 8

We've all had tomato aspic, but probably not with the splendid surprise of nut-coated cream cheese balls tucked inside. Dianne Safley, who tested Pat Clemmer's recipe, found it "pretty as well as fun to make. Kids could help," she adds.

Tomato Aspic Surprise

1 small package lemon gelatin
1 cup boiling water
1 cup tomato juice

3-ounce package cream cheese, softened
¼ pound chopped pecans

Dissolve lemon gelatin in water; add tomato juice. Pour into 6 individual molds, or custard cups; refrigerate. Shape softened cream cheese into balls, using 1 level teaspoon for each. Roll cheese balls in crushed pecans. Press into gelatin when it is almost set.

Serves 6

"So good, it could be considered a dessert!" says Pat Clemmer about this make-ahead salad with a gelatin base and old-fashioned cooked topping. And, you can vary the color and flavor of gelatin to suit the season — green for St. Pat's Day, red for Christmas and Valentine's Day parties, orange for autumn, yellow for Easter, etc. Go for it!

Frosted Apricot Salad

6-ounce package
  apricot-flavored gelatin
2 cups diced banana
1 cup crushed pineapple,
  well drained (reserve syrup)
1 cup miniature marshmallows
½ cup chopped
  walnuts or pecans

½ cup reserved pineapple syrup
½ cup sugar
1 egg
8-ounce package
  cream cheese, softened
1 cup whipped topping

Prepare gelatin according to package directions. Cool slightly and fold in fruit, marshmallows and nuts. Pour into a 2 x 13-inch glass dish. Refrigerate until set. Beat pineapple syrup, sugar and egg until thoroughly blended. Pour mixture into saucepan; cook until slightly thickened, stirring constantly. While hot, stir in cream cheese until mixture is smooth. Refrigerate until chilled. Fold in whipped topping and "frost" gelatin. Cut into squares and serve on lettuce leaves, if desired.

Serves 12

Cozily housed in a 100-year-old schoolhouse in the center of Grand Rapids, this restaurant actually began in the former first grade classroom. Owner Mary Jo Hendricks, who grew up in Minneapolis, shares just one of the recipes for which her establishment is famous. When she was invited to provide meals for visiting country music star Johnny Cash and his entourage, this salad was served with Minnesota walleyed pike. Tester Bonnie Damkroger suggests bright pimiento strips as a garnish if tomatoes aren't in season.

The First Grade Restaurant Wild Rice Salad

½ to ¾ cup uncooked white rice(to make about 2 cups)
1 cup uncooked wild rice
Water
4 hard-cooked eggs, chopped
1 small onion, chopped
¾ cup chopped celery
Tomato wedges

DRESSING
⅓ cup brown sugar
¼ cup oil
1 teaspoon salt
½ teaspoon pepper
½ cup mayonnaise
2 teaspoons prepared mustard
1 tablespoon vinegar

In a small saucepan, cook white rice according to package directions. In a separate saucepan, pour cold water over wild rice to cover by 1 inch, bring to a boil and simmer for 45 minutes, or until all liquid has been absorbed. Set aside to cool. Combine cooked rices. When rice mixture has cooled, add the chopped eggs, onions and celery.

To make dressing, combine brown sugar, oil, salt, pepper, mayonnaise, mustard and vinegar. Toss the dressing mixture with rice mixture. Garnish with tomato wedges.

Yield: 5 cups

Jan Winters Keprios contributes a Minnesota-hearty main dish salad ideal for luncheon or supper serving. Tester Shirley Bard calls it "a must for the buffet table — delicious and refreshing with the addition of mandarin oranges." Jan's husband, John, is Edina's Director of Parks and Recreation.

Wild Rice Chicken Salad

1 cup wild rice
4 chicken bouillon cubes
4 cups water
1 can sliced water chestnuts
1 small onion, finely chopped
1½ cups chopped celery
1½ cups cooked, cubed chicken
15-ounce can mandarin oranges, drained
1 cup cashews

DRESSING
1 cup mayonnaise
1½ tablespoons milk
1 teaspoon lemon juice
Dash pepper

Combine cleaned rice with bouillon and water in saucepan. Cook until water is absorbed. Cool rice. Add water chestnuts, onion, celery and cubed chicken to cooled rice. Combine dressing ingredients; add to rice. Chill. Just before serving, fold in drained oranges. Garnish with cashews.

Serves 10 to 12

This healthful, low-fat salad from Marianne Jasper of Edina is served warm, which brings out the distinctive flavor of the cumin in the dressing. "The bow tie pasta makes it especially attractive for bridal showers," says Marianne. "Feel free to assemble salad ingredients ahead and add the dressing just before baking." "Great flavor and texture," praised Jan Collins, tester.

Palm Beach Chicken Salad

½ cup chicken broth
2 whole chicken breasts, boned and skinned
1½ cups uncooked bow tie pasta
1 cup peas, cooked and drained
½ cup sliced pimiento
½ pound asparagus, cut up (optional)
2 cups grapefruit sections
⅓ cup grapefruit juice drained from sections

DRESSING:
¼ cup salad oil
2 tablespoons wine vinegar
1 clove garlic, minced
½ teaspoon ground cumin
½ teaspoon salt
⅛ teaspoon white pepper

Preheat oven to 300°. Bring broth to boil in a medium skillet. Arrange chicken in single layer in pan; return broth to boiling. Cover and simmer until chicken is thoroughly cooked. Drain and cool; cut chicken into strips. Meanwhile, cook pasta according to package directions; rinse and drain. Cook peas and asparagus until just tender. Combine all salad ingredients in a large bowl.

Combine dressing ingredients in a jar. Shake and pour over chicken mixture; toss lightly. Place mixture in oven-to-table baking dish. Heat about 20 minutes, or until mixture is warmed. Serve immediately.

Serves 4

A stellar suggestion from ECC chefs — next time you are barbecuing chicken or beef, prepare extra to serve salad-style for another meal. The unique Asparagus Dressing is one you will want to try with other salads as well.

Grilled Chicken Salad with Asparagus Mayonnaise

Grilled poultry or meat, sliced
Fresh tomatoes, diced
Fresh mushrooms, sliced
Summer squash, sliced and blanched
Sliced black or green olives
Mixed greens of choice

DRESSING
1 cup chopped, cooked asparagus (use only tender portions)
1 cup olive oil
1 pasteurized egg
Salt and pepper to taste

On a bed of mixed greens, arrange meat or poultry slices and vegetables. In blender, combine all dressing ingredients. Blend until well mixed and thickened. Pour over salad or serve on the side.

Yield: 1½ cups Dressing

This recipe travels well — all the way from Doreen O'Toole of Merrill, Michigan (mother of Michelle Lass and mother-in-law of Marty, PGA golf professional). Doreen advises making the dressing well ahead to allow for necessary cooling step. She serves this on hot days with wedges of corn bread or sliced nut bread. Tester Mary Miller dubbed it "a great summer supper" and served it with cups of Egg Flower Soup.

Chinese Chicken Salad

3 chicken breasts, cooked
¼ cup sesame seed
1 head lettuce
6 green onions, chopped
2-ounce package almonds
Half of a 2½-ounce can chow mein noodles

DRESSING
4 tablespoons sugar
2½ teaspoons salt
1 teaspoon monosodium glutamate
¼ teaspoon pepper
4 tablespoons vinegar
½ cup olive oil

Cut cooked chicken into strips. Toast almonds and sesame seed by baking in a 350° oven for about 10 minutes; cool. Tear lettuce into bite-sized pieces. Combine lettuce with chicken strips, onion, almonds, sesame seed and chow mein noodles.

For dressing, combine sugar, salt, monosodium glutamate, pepper and vinegar in small saucepan. Heat and stir over low heat until sugar dissolves. Remove from heat; cool com-pletely. Whisk in oil. Combine dressing with salad ingredients and serve.

Serves 8

Mary Morton has aptly named this recipe for her daughter, who requests it for her "coming-home-from-college" meal. The Mortons enjoy it spooned onto a bed of shredded lettuce with a parsley garnish, accompanied by freshly-baked muffins. All we can add is, "Who wouldn't?"

Jacquie's Fruited Chicken Salad

5 cups cooked, cubed chicken
3 cups cooked rice or orzo
1½ cups red and/or green grapes, halved
1½ cups diced celery
20-ounce can pineapple tidbits, drained
15-ounce can Mandarin oranges, drained
6 ounces slivered almonds, toasted

DRESSING:
1½ cups mayonnaise
2 tablespoons orange juice
2 tablespoons vinegar

Cook the chicken; cool and cut it into bite-sized pieces. Prepare rice according to package directions. Combine all salad ingredients. Mix dressing ingredients. Fold into chicken mixture. Refrigerate several hours before serving.

Serves 12

Chef David Kennedy of Chanhassen's Thyme to Spare Personal Chef Service, shares a main dish salad brimming with colorful vegetables as well as chicken and couscous, a staple of north African cuisine. Although it is considered a pasta, it more closely resembles rice or grits. This recipe is a real host-pleaser because it must be made ahead of serving — no last minute details. Tester Marie Lacy found it "easily prepared and very attractive. Great for a group!" she adds.

Couscous Chicken and Vegetable Salad

6 ounces couscous
8 ounces cooked skinless, boneless chicken
1 ear fresh corn, cooked
  (1 cup canned or frozen may be substituted)
1 ripe medium-size tomato
3 to 4 chopped green onions
1 medium red pepper, diced
1 medium zucchini squash, diced
7½ ounces canned garbanzo beans (chickpeas), drained
½ cup raisins

<u>DRESSING</u>
3 tablespoons extra virgin olive oil
1 tablespoon vinegar
1 teaspoon Dijon mustard
½ teaspoon hot pepper sauce, or to taste
½ teaspoon cumin seed
¼ teaspoon curry powder
⅛ cup minced fresh parsley

Cook couscous according to package directions; drain and cool. Cut chicken into bite-sized pieces. When couscous is sufficiently cooled, transfer it to a large bowl. Mix in corn, diced vegetables, drained beans, cut-up chicken and raisins.

Combine oil, vinegar, mustard, hot pepper sauce, cumin and curry powder. Pour dressing slowly over the vegetable mixture; toss well. Garnish with parsley. Cover and let stand in the refrigerator for several hours to meld flavors.

Serves 10

From the ECC kitchen comes a versatile, make-ahead salad, as easy as it is elegant. Use your favorite rice or a blend for variety. Substitute cooked, flaked crab or white fish for the lobster if you wish. Serve from a lettuce-lined bowl or press salad into individual molds, if desired. Lots of options, and all are winners!

Lobster-Rice Salad

¾ cup cooked, diced lobster meat
2 cups cooked rice
1 cup finely-diced celery
¼ cup finely-diced green pepper
½ cup crushed pineapple, well drained
⅓ cup mayonnaise
1 tablespoon lemon juice
1 teaspoon salt
½ teaspoon pepper

In large bowl, combine lobster, rice, celery, green pepper and pineapple. In small bowl, mix mayonnaise, lemon juice, salt and pepper. Stir dressing into seafood mixture. Cover and refrigerate at least 4 hours before serving.

Serves 4

We're "puttin' on the Ritz" with this ambrosia for shellfish lovers. A first class entrée for a VIP luncheon or light supper. Compliments to ECC chefs for another stunning selection! They serve it with pita bread wedges.

Crab, Lobster and Hearts of Palm Salad

¾ pound fresh lump crab meat, cooked
½ pound cooked lobster
14-ounce can hearts of palm, drained
Mixed greens of choice

DRESSING
⅔ cup mayonnaise
¼ cup chili sauce
¼ cup thinly-sliced scallions

¼ cup diced green and red bell peppers
1 tablespoon chopped fresh parsley
1 tablespoon fresh lemon juice
1 tablespoon prepared horseradish
Dash Worcestershire sauce
Salt and pepper to taste

Remove all shell bits from crab and lobster. Slice hearts of palm into "sticks." Whisk dressing ingredients until well blended. Fold crab and lobster into dressing. On chilled plates, arrange greens. Top with portion of crab mixture. Arrange hearts of palm for a garnish.

Serves 4

"If you can't stand the heat," toss together Mary Schrock's salad, tuck it in the refrigerator and head out to the Club for a dip in the pool. Lunch or dinner will be ready and waiting when you get home. It took tester Angie Fox only minutes to prepare once the eggs were cooked. Round out the meal with toasted pita crisps, bagels or crusty rolls.

Mandarin Tuna Salad

Two 9¼-ounce cans water-packed tuna, drained
2 tart apples, cored and chopped
2 large onions, chopped (or to taste)

2 large pickles, chopped
2 hard-cooked eggs, chopped
One 15-ounce can mandarin oranges, drained
Mayonnaise to taste

Combine tuna, apples, onions, pickles and egg in a large bowl. Add mayonnaise to taste. Fold in mandarin oranges, saving a few for garnish, if desired.

Serves 8 to 10

Tester Peggy Dodge especially enjoyed the "light, fresh-tasting dressing which complements the shrimp beautifully." Feta cheese, a main character of Greek cooking, exudes a salty taste. So, you may want to try the prepared salad before deciding whether or not to add salt. Peggy chose to add ½ teaspoon. She also sprinkled the crumbled Feta over the salad rather than mixing it in.

ECC's Dilled Shrimp and Feta Cheese Salad

1 pound large shrimp, cooked, peeled and deveined
3 Spring onions, thinly sliced (with tops)
1 small cucumber, peeled, seeded and sliced
1 small red pepper, diced
2 tablespoons fresh snipped dill
1 cup crumbled Feta cheese

DRESSING
3 tablespoons lemon juice
3 tablespoons olive oil
2 tablespoons white wine vinegar
2 teaspoons Dijon mustard
1 clove garlic, minced
¼ teaspoon black pepper

In large bowl, combine shrimp, onion, cucumber, red pepper, dill and cheese. In a small bowl, whisk together lemon juice, olive oil, vinegar, mustard, garlic and pepper. At serving time, toss shrimp mixture with dressing. Serve over mixed greens, if desired.

Serves 4

A marvelous ECC salad medley for warm days spring through early fall when fresh asparagus and tomatoes are still available. Although fennel resembles celery, it dries out much more quickly and has a very distinctive anise flavor. It's low in calories and adapts well to eating raw or cooking. So, don't be shy about giving it a try.

Mediterranean Rice and Shrimp Salad

1½ cups long-grain white rice
¼ cup lemon juice
12 to 16 large shrimp, shelled and deveined
1 teaspoon lemon juice
5 tablespoons olive oil
4 large tomatoes, peeled, seeded and diced
1 cup diced fennel bulb
4 green onion stems, thinly sliced
¼ cup minced fresh dill
1 teaspoon minced garlic
4 medium fresh asparagus spears, blanched slightly and diced
  (to make ½ cup)

Cook rice in 6 cups boiling, salted water until rice is done. Drain and rinse immediately. Cook shrimp in lightly salted water to which lemon juice has been added. (Total cooking time should be approximately 3 minutes; do not overcook.)

At this point you have the option to coarsely chop the shrimp or leave whole for two different looks. If shrimp is chopped, add to rice at this time.

Add all remaining ingredients and chill well for about 1 hour. Salad may be served at room temperature if you prefer.

Serves 4 to 6

NOTE: If being used as an entrée, arrange whole shrimp over top of salad

Tester Mary L. Miller served Allison Gaasedelen's sublime salad to dinner guests, and "they all gave it a '10'!" Mary describes the colorful combination as "easy, different and delicious." She served it on a summer evening with rolls and a simple side of fresh fruit.

Zesty Tortellini and Shrimp Salad

2 pounds frozen cheese tortellini
1 pound frozen cooked salad shrimp, thawed
14-ounce can artichoke hearts, drained and cut into small pieces
1 medium red pepper, chopped
⅓ cup pitted and sliced black olives

HONEY-MUSTARD DRESSING
⅓ cup vinegar
¼ cup honey
2 tablespoons minced onion
1 teaspoon dry mustard
¾ teaspoon salt
1 cup salad oil

Cook and drain tortellini according to package directions. Drain shrimp thoroughly. Combine all salad ingredients in large bowl. Toss tortellini mixture with dressing and chill before serving.

Place first five dressing ingredients in blender. Slowly add oil until thoroughly blended.

Serves 8 to 10

Lighten up with this salad or sandwich spread. Each serving is only about 170 calories when low-fat yogurt and mayonnaise are used. Norine Ahmann of Eden Prairie tried it out on a warm August day and appreciated the "ease of preparation. My husband and I found it to be just as delicious the second day after flavors had blended even more."

Country Club Crab Salad

¼ cup plain low-fat yogurt
2 tablespoons
  low-fat mayonnaise
⅓ cup chopped green pepper
¼ cup red onion,
  finely chopped
1 tablespoon Dijon mustard

1 tablespoon
  finely-minced parsley
2 tablespoons fresh minced dill,
  or to taste
Dash white pepper
¾ to 1 pound fresh
  lump crab meat

Combine yogurt and mayonnaise with chopped vegetables and seasonings. Cover and refrigerate for at least 30 minutes. When thoroughly chilled, fold in crab meat. Serve as a salad in lettuce cups or as a sandwich filling.

Serves 6

Definitely deluxe! When a celebratory menu is in order, serve this with a flourish — ECC style. By the way, when was the last time you had tequila in a salad dressing? Not a bad idea, as your taste buds will tell you.

ECC Seafood Salad with Tequila Dressing

2 pounds cooked lobster,
  cut into ½-inch pieces
12 to 15 medium shrimp,
  cooked, shelled and chilled
3 heads Boston or Bibb lettuce
1 seedless orange,
  peeled and sectioned
1 teaspoon fresh chives,
  finely-chopped

TEQUILA DRESSING
1 cup fresh lime juice
1 cup fresh orange juice
2 tablespoons virgin olive oil
1 tablespoon tequila
2 teaspoons sugar
Pinch of salt

Place seafood in large glass bowl. Combine dressing ingredients; pour evenly over lobster and shrimp. Let mixture stand for 5 minutes. Arrange seafood on a bed of lettuce leaves, alternating with orange sections for an attractive presentation. Spoon dressing over salad; top with chives. Serve thoroughly chilled.

Serves 6

From Scott Rochat of the ECC culinary staff comes a Calypso combo to mix with greens or combine with leftover cooked poultry or pork, cut into julienne strips. Remember to protect your hands with gloves when chopping the peppers.

Jamaican Jerk Dressing

2 onions, chopped
½ cup chopped green onions
4 garlic cloves, minced
1½ teaspoons leaf thyme
2 teaspoons salt
2 teaspoons allspice
¾ teaspoon nutmeg
1½ teaspoons cinnamon
2 jalapeño peppers,
    seeded and finely-chopped
    (do not substitute)

2 teaspoons black pepper
12 drops tabasco sauce
4 tablespoons soy sauce
1 cup salad oil
¼ cup lime juice
¾ cup honey

Combine all ingredients. Store in refrigerator in covered non-metallic container. Garnish salad with pepperonicini peppers and assorted olives and diced tomato, if desired.

Yield: 3 cups

This old-timer, so named because of the consistency, is almost as easy to make as it is to buy, and so much tastier. You may want to double Liana Peterson's recipe to keep on hand for more than one occasion. For variety and more "islands," try adding chopped fresh parsley, minced green and red pepper and finely-diced celery. A dash of cayenne promises a bit of "bite."

Thousand Island Dressing

1 cup mayonnaise (low-fat, if desired)
1 hard-cooked egg, chopped
1 teaspoon chopped onion
1 tablespoon chili sauce
1 teaspoon chopped dill pickle or pickle relish

Combine all ingredients. Cover and store in refrigerator.

Yield: 1¼ cups

What to do with leftover beef?* Just cut into julienne strips and toss with assorted greens (lettuce bok choy, spinach, sprouts and perhaps pea pods). Then, add just enough of the lively dressing to coat ingredients. ECC tops this inviting salad with orange cartwheels, strawberries and a sprinkling of toasted sesame seed.

Oriental Salad Dressing

1 cup bottled teriyaki sauce
1 cup orange juice
¾ cup honey
½ cup soy sauce
½ cup dry red wine
¼ cup dark Oriental sesame oil
½ cup Dijon mustard

1 teaspoon oregano
1 teaspoon thyme
½ teaspoon garlic salt
⅛ teaspoon ginger
2 tablespoons toasted
   sesame seed for garnish

Combine all ingredients except sesame seed. Stir, shake or beat until honey is completely dissolved. Store in tightly-sealed non-metallic container. Combine with salad ingredients at serving time. Top with toasted sesame seed.

Yield: 4 cups

*Beef tenderloin is particularly appropriate. However, any cooked lean and tender beef will suffice.

Jack Bucklin has a multitude of uses for this recipe — as a traditional salad dressing, a topping for pasta and hot vegetables and combined with new potatoes and Vidalia onions for a unique potato salad. Tester Marianne Jasper tried it as a dip for crudites and pronounced it "very flavorful and quick to fix."

Bucko's Bleu Cheese Dressing

½ cup canola oil
⅛ cup lemon juice
Dash of Worcestershire sauce
2 ounces crumbled bleu cheese

1 large garlic clove, minced
½ teaspoon salt
⅛ teaspoon dry mustard

Pour all ingredients into small container with lid. Shake well. Pour over greens of your choice and toss.

Yield: 1 cup

The rich nutty flavor and aroma of sesame seed and oil are particularly favored in Asian and the Middle Eastern fare. A plus is a substance contained in the oil which allows it to keep quite well for several weeks without refrigeration. ECC chefs and tester Mary Morton find this recipe does delicious double duty as a salad dressing and as a golden glaze for poultry, pork or shrimp.

ECC Honey-Sesame Dressing

1 cup dark Oriental sesame oil
1 cup honey
⅛ cup lemon juice
Pinch of ground cinnamon
½ cup toasted sesame seed
Combine all ingredients. Store in sealed jar; do not refrigerate.

Yield: 2 cups

Easy as one-two-three, and that's the number of ingredients in this dandy dressing to drizzle over your favorite in-season fruits. Contributor Marian Clay says "It's particularly pleasing with citrus salads. Just mix up the amount you need and keep leftovers on hand in the refrigerator."

Fast Fruit Dressing

Salad oil
Honey
Frozen limeade concentrate, thawed
Fresh fruits
Lettuce
Combine equal parts of oil, honey and limeade concentrate. Blend well and drizzle over fresh fruits arranged on a bed of lettuce, if desired.

"Let the blender do the work at least several hours before serving so the flavor bouquet can develop," says contributor Liana Peterson. Interesting to note that "French Dressing" is the name given by the English for mixture of oil, vinegar and seasonings the French use on greens.

Blender French Dressing

1 cup salad oil	¼ cup vinegar
½ cup sugar	1 teaspoon celery seed
½ teaspoon salt	1 teaspoon dry mustard
1 small onion, diced	¼ teaspoon oregano
½ cup ketchup	⅛ teaspoon paprika

Combine all ingredients in blender. Blend until well mixed. Store in refrigerator in tightly-covered non-metallic container.

Yield: About 2 cups

Marjorie Kugler of North Oaks, owner of the interior design firm Interspace, Inc., has relied on this recipe since the '70's. "Our family has vacationed in Colorado for years, and after tasting this at Baxter's Restaurant in Vail I wanted to be able to make it at home." Conveniently, the main ingredient is a commercially-prepared dressing embellished with a blend of seasonings, wine and just a "tot" of licorice liqueur. Marjorie is especially fond of it combined with cooked wild rice, chopped green onions and diced pimiento.

Creamy Italian Dressing

8 ounces bottled zesty Italian salad dressing	½ teaspoon lemon juice
	1 teaspoon brandy
½ tablespoon mayonnaise	2 ounces dry white wine
¼ tablespoon prepared yellow mustard	1 teaspoon Pernod liqueur
	1 tablespoon parsley flakes
1 tablespoon Dijon mustard	1 tablespoon Italian seasoning
½ teaspoon Worcestershire sauce	Dash of salt

Combine all ingredients in blender and whip until creamy. Great on lettuce greens and onion rings with garnish of sliced mushrooms, green grapes, and goldfish crackers.

Yield: 1½ cups

ECC Members appreciate Chef Jerry Cegla's generosity in sharing Club recipes. Here's an oft-requested hit which has been "downsized" for the home chef. Black pepper is always more flavorful when freshly and coarsely ground.

Edina Country Club Peppercream House Dressing

2 cups mayonnaise
½ tablespoon Worcestershire sauce
½ tablespoon A-1 steak sauce
2 splashes tabasco sauce
⅛ cup lemon juice
½ teaspoon cracked black pepper
¼ teaspoon salt
⅛ cup liquid Maggi seasoning
1 tablespoon grated Parmesan cheese

Blend all ingredients except for Parmesan until smooth. Fold in cheese; do not overmix. Cover and refrigerate.

Yield: About 3 cups

Mary Alice Bell and her husband were served this recipe about 20 years ago at 3M's Wonewok Lodge in Park Rapids. "Everyone loved it and I've been making it ever since," she says. Tester Pat Clemmer was equally enthusiastic, adding that she would definitely make it again for her own family.

Piquant Slaw Dressing

1 cup sugar
1 cup oil
1 teaspoon salt
1 teaspoon dry mustard
1 medium onion, quartered
½ cup apple cider vinegar
1 teaspoon celery seed

Blend all ingredients well in blender. Refrigerate in tightly-covered glass jar.

Yield: About 2½ cups

This lovely light dressing created by former Pub cook David Striefel spells springtime in no uncertain terms. He particularly enjoyed it with chilled grilled chicken served with greens and fresh berries. Recipe is easily reduced for fewer servings.

Strawberry-Kiwi Vinaigrette

2 cups sliced strawberries
½ cup white granulated sugar
2 cups salad oil
3 cups white wine vinegar
2 kiwi, peeled and diced

Combine strawberries and sugar; let stand 15 minutes. Combine oil and vinegar in a mixer, combining thoroughly. Add strawberry-sugar mixture and kiwi to oil and vinegar. Mix until fruit pieces are blended into dressing. Store in refrigerator.

Yield: About 8 cups

When Evie Teegen, formerly of Edina, served as U.S. Ambassador to Fiji, Tuvalu, Kiribati and the Kingdom of Tonga she became very fond of tree-ripened mangoes. "This is a delightful accompaniment for pork, duckling, chicken and turkey," she says. Key to the success of this chutney is using pears and mangoes which are fully ripe and at their peak of flavor and texture. You may have to purchase the fruit well in advance to achieve this, but you will be rewarded for your patience.

Mango Chutney

4 cups cider vinegar
3 cups white sugar
3 cups brown sugar
2 tablespoons salt
4 tablespoons pickling spice
4 pears, peeled and chopped
6 ripe mangoes, peeled and chopped
8 apples, peeled and chopped
8 ounces dates, chopped
6 ounces dried apricots
8 ounces golden raisins
8 ounces raisins
½ cup grated fresh ginger
2 medium onions, chopped
3 cloves garlic, chopped

In dutch oven or large kettle, combine vinegar, sugars, salt and pickling spice. Bring to boil; simmer for 20 minutes. Add remaining ingredients. Continue simmering 30 minutes or until thickened. Pour or spoon into hot sterilized jars, leaving ¼-inch headspace, and seal. Process in boiling water bath 10 minutes. Serve at room temperature. Opened jars should be refrigerated.

Yield: 5 to 6 pints

Triple-Fruit Chutney

1 mango, peeled
1 papaya, peeled
3 fresh peaches peeled, or 3 cups frozen
1 medium red pepper
1 small red onion
2 tablespoons olive oil
1 clove garlic, pressed or minced
1 tablespoon freshly-grated ginger
¼ cup white wine vinegar
2 cups brown sugar
½ cup honey
1 teaspoon nutmeg
1 teaspoon cinnamon
1 teaspoon allspice
¼ teaspoon cayenne pepper
½ teaspoon freshly-ground pepper
1 teaspoon kosher salt
¼ cup cilantro (optional)

Cut mango, papaya and peaches into ½-inch cubes. Dice red pepper and red onion into ½-inch pieces. Heat olive oil in large saucepan over medium heat. Add garlic, ginger, peppers and onion. Cook until onion softens, about 5 minutes. Add peaches, mangos, papayas, brown sugar, vinegar and honey. Cook, stirring often, about 15 minutes. Stir in seasonings and cilantro; cook an additional 15 minutes. Seal in jars and store in refrigerator.

Yield: 1 quart

When fresh peaches are in season, Marjorie Connelly of Edina wastes no time "putting up" this ginger-sparked chutney. "It's delicious with pork and poultry and keeps several weeks in the refrigerator," she says. It also can be frozen in plastic containers for a midwinter treat.

Fresh Peach Chutney

3 cups (5 medium) peeled, chopped peaches
½ cup golden raisins
¼ cup chopped onion
1 tablespoon grated ginger root
½ cup brown sugar, packed
⅓ cup cider vinegar
¼ teaspoon salt

Combine all ingredients in large saucepan. Cook over low heat 20 minutes or until mixture thickens, stirring frequently. Spoon into 3 sterile jars, 8 ounces each. Cover tightly. Store in refrigerator.

Yield: 2⅔ cups

What host doesn't appreciate a thoughtful homemade gift from a guest's kitchen? Liz Krezowski of Minneapolis finds her special herb butter is greatly appreciated, and it totes well in "recycled plastic butter or margarine containers." Fresh grey-green thyme leaves offer distinctive flavor and aroma to this savory medley.

Blender Herb Butter

1 pound butter, softened*
6 ounces sun dried tomatoes, packed in oil
1 tablespoon shallots or green onion, minced
1 tablespoon chopped fresh thyme, or to taste
1 tablespoon minced garlic, or to taste
1 tablespoon plus 1 teaspoon lemon juice
*Variation: Use 8 ounces light margarine and 8 ounces fat-free cream cheese in place of butter.

Drain and dice sun dried tomatoes. Place all ingredients in blender or food processor; blend thoroughly. Spoon into plastic containers. Cover and store in refrigerator.

Yield: About 1½ pounds spread

Gardener alert! Don Stork, formerly of the ECC staff, developed a recipe just for you! "This mixture can be served chilled over mixed greens or hot over pasta, seafood, chicken and pork. It also serves as a salsa," he explains. Fennel, which looks like a stubby stalk of celery, should be eaten in its freshest possible state. Toss any extra into soups or salads for a unique aniseed flavor.

Tomatoes Provencale

2½ cups peeled, seeded and chopped tomatoes
½ cup chopped fresh shallots
½ cup chopped fresh basil leaves
¼ cup chopped fresh fennel root
½ cup chopped fresh garlic, or to taste
White wine enough to cover mixture
Salt and pepper

Combine first five ingredients in glass jar or bowl. Cover with white wine. Add salt and pepper to taste.

Yield: About 4 cups

Especially when tomatoes are at their best, try this versatile sauce from Gene Gaasedelen. She highly recommends it with Marian Hamilton's Chicken Florentine recipe and other poultry entrées.

Yogurt-Tomato Sauce

1 cup plain low-fat yogurt*
1 large ripe tomato, peeled, seeded and finely chopped
4 large basil leaves, thinly sliced or 1 teaspoon dried sweet basil
1 tablespoon red wine vinegar
¼ teaspoon salt
Freshly-ground black pepper to taste
*Low-fat sour cream may be substituted for yogurt

Combine all ingredients. Cover and refrigerate.

Yield: About 1½ cups sauce

As a condiment, salsa seems here to stay. So, add this refreshing ECC rendition to your collection. The Chef suggests it as a colorful side to grilled seafood and poultry. Tester Susan Flynn reminds us not to overcook so fruits retain their inherent texture.

Watermelon Salsa

2 tablespoons fresh butter
½ cup sugar
2 cups diced watermelon
1 cup diced fresh pineapple
Juice of 1 orange (½ cup)

Juice of 1 lime (3 tablespoons)
¼ cup diced red onion
1 tablespoon chopped cilantro
⅛ teaspoon cumin

In large saucepan, combine butter and sugar. Simmer and stir over low heat just until sugar is dissolved. Add remaining ingredients; cook just until fruit is transparent. Spoon over grilled seafood or poultry.

Yield: About 4 cups

Whether Gretchen Pracht is entertaining at her Edina or Bay Lake home, she is likely to include these on the buffet table. The 12-hour soaking time contributes to a "super crisp" texture and the spice combo adds up to fantastic flavor.

Watermelon Pickles

4 quarts watermelon rind,
  cut into 2-inch squares
2 quarts cold water
2 tablespoons slacked lime*
1 quart white distilled vinegar
2 cups water

6 cups white sugar
2 teaspoons whole cloves,
  crushed
2 teaspoons allspice
2 teaspoons cinnamon
1 teaspoon mace

*Slacked lime can be purchased at drug and garden stores.

Trim all red fruit and green skin from melon. Add lime to 2 quarts of water. Soak squares in lime mixture for 12 hours. Drain; combine remaining ingredients for a syrup. Cook rind over low heat in syrup for 30 to 60 minutes or until squares are transparent. Place rind squares in hot, sterilized jars leaving 1/8-inch headspace; seal. Process in boiling water bath 10 minutes.

Yield: 5 to 6 pints

Shirley Bard describes these "gussied up" dills as "super crisp." Tester Pat Meyers urges very thorough draining of pickles before adding boiled mixture. "A unique recipe for pickle lovers," adds another tester, Mary L. Miller. "Expect a 'pucker' from this adaptation."

Crispy Sweet Dills

1 quart non-kosher dills
2 cups sugar
½ cup white distilled vinegar
½ cup water

Drain, rinse, and cut pickles into bite-sized pieces. Return pickle pieces to jar. Boil sugar, vinegar and water 5 minutes. Pour over pickles. Let set at least 24 hours before serving.

Yield: 1 quart

Rochester resident Gwen Ladner provides the perfect go-along for your favorite pork recipes. Or, try as a welcome addition to a brunch buffet. She prefers using Jonathan or McIntosh apples — both are juicy, slightly tart and well suited to cooking. Tester Pauline Anderson suggests teaming the warm apples with vanilla or cinnamon ice cream for a deliciously different sundae.

Sautéed Apple Slices

¼ cup (½ stick) butter or margarine
6 cups sliced, unpeeled cooking apples
2 tablespoons granulated sugar
2 tablespoons brown sugar

Melt butter in a large, heavy skillet. Add remaining ingredients. Cook over low to medium heat, uncovered, for 10 minutes. As they cook, turn apples carefully with a spatula without breaking them.

Serves 4 to 6

ECC's creative chefs enjoy the challenge of developing new recipes for special culinary events. This sauce was stirred up by Scott Rochat to accompany marinated chicken on skewers. With Thai cuisine becoming increasingly popular (yes, even in the heartland), this is a dandy recipe to have in your international repertoire.

Thai Peanut Sauce

1 tablespoon olive oil
2 tablespoons shallots, minced
½ tablespoon garlic, mashed
1 cup peanut butter
1 cup honey
½ cup red hot sauce
½ cup white wine
1 cup chicken stock
½ tablespoon chicken bouillon granules
1 tablespoon red pepper flakes
½ tablespoon granulated onion
½ tablespoon kosher salt
1 tablespoon cornstarch dissolved in 1 tablespoon water

In small saucepan, heat olive oil. Add shallots and garlic; sauté until tender. Add white wine; reduce slightly. Add remaining ingredients except cornstarch and water mixture. Cook 10 minutes, stirring frequently. Add cornstarch-water paste to thicken if needed.

Yield: Approximately 1 quart

Helen Waldron of Edina "loves to try new recipes and pore over cookbooks looking for innovative ideas." This Scandinavian sauce is her favorite to serve with grilled or baked salmon. "You don't need much with each serving, so this amount would serve 4 to 6 people," she advises.

Swedish Mustard-Dill Sauce

4 tablespoons dark, highly-seasoned prepared mustard
1 teaspoon ground mustard
3 tablespoons sugar
2 tablespoons white vinegar
⅓ cup vegetable oil
1 tablespoon dill weed, or to taste*
*If using fresh dill, add 2 to 3 tablespoons finely chopped.

In a small, deep bowl, thoroughly mix the two mustards, sugar and vinegar. With a wire whisk, slowly beat in the oil until it forms a thick mayonnaise-like emulsion. Stir in the dill. The sauce may be kept refrigerated in a tightly-covered jar for several days. Shake vigorously or beat with a whisk to re-mix the ingredients before serving, if necessary

Yield: About ¾ cup

During ECC's grand reopening celebration, a sushi bar was a highlight —
complete with an ice carving and fish aquarium. "It was a memorable food
buffet display," recalls Executive Chef Jerry Cegla, CFBE. "And, this was the
most talked-about dipping sauce." Tester Peggy Bishop loved it with shrimp.

Japanese Ginger Sauce

¼ cup chopped onions (Spring and green)
1 tablespoon garlic
2 tablespoons dark oriental sesame oil
¼ cup rice wine vinegar
2 tablespoons soy sauce
¼ cup sugar
1 cup sake
1 teaspoon fresh ginger root
2 tablespoons hondashi*
*Hondashi is a fish paste made from white tuna and may be found in
  Asian markets and at other specialty grocers.

Sauté onion and garlic with sesame oil until onions turn transparent.
Add vinegar, soy sauce, sugar, sake and ginger; simmer for 15 minutes.
Add hondashi. If you desire a thicker sauce, add 1 tablespoon
cornstarch and 1 tablespoon sake.

Serve as a dipping sauce for deep-fried shrimp, chicken strips or beef
tenderloin.

Yield: 1 cup

This makes a party-sized portion which is easily reduced to one or two cups depending on your needs. Just the sauce for dipping crisp, deep-fried won ton skins, egg rolls, tempura and other Asian delicacies.

Mustard Sauce for Won Tons

1 cup Dijon mustard
1¼ cups honey
5 teaspoons dried onion
⅓ cup dark oriental sesame oil
½ cup Pommery mustard (with seeds)
Combine all ingredients. Cover and refrigerate

Yield: Approximately 3 cups

Pat Clemmer introduces us to a delicate and unusual side dish for ham and poultry. She finds it attracts a lot of attention on a buffet table and points out that it is "easily doubled for a larger mold." The bright cranberry sauce or beets is a striking contrast to the pale cream-colored ring.

Creamy Mustard Mold

4 eggs
¾ cup sugar
1 tablespoon dry mustard
Dash of salt
1 envelope unflavored gelatin
½ cup white distilled vinegar
½ cup water
½ pint whipping cream, whipped stiff
Cranberry sauce or pickled beets, optional

Beat eggs and sugar in double boiler. Add dry mustard, salt, gelatin, white vinegar and water. Cook 5 to 10 minutes or until thick. Cool mixture. Then fold in ½ pint whipping cream, whipped stiff. Put into small ring mold and refrigerate until set, at least 3 hours. If desired, serve cranberry sauce or pickled beets in center of ring.

Serves 8

Breads and
Brunch Dishes

Popular in middle-European and Scandinavian cooking, poppy seeds bring a sweet nut-like flavor to Judy Tucker's bread recipe. The delicate almond and vanilla flavorings are repeated in the glaze which is poured over the loaves hot from the oven. Tester Karen Remund sprinkled some poppy seeds over the glaze for a decorative touch.

Poppy Seed Bread

3 eggs, beaten
2½ cups sugar
1½ cups milk
1 cup + 2 tablespoons oil
1½ teaspoons almond extract
1½ teaspoons vanilla extract
1½ teaspoons butter flavoring
3 cups flour
1½ teaspoons salt
1½ teaspoons baking powder
2 tablespoons poppy seeds

GLAZE
¾ cup sugar
¼ cup orange juice
½ teaspoon almond extract
½ teaspoon vanilla extract
½ teaspoon butter flavoring

Preheat oven to 350°. Mix all bread ingredients in order given. Pour batter into greased bread pans, two 9 x 5 x 3-inch or four 8 x 4 x 2-inch. Bake 40 to 50 minutes or until loaves test done.

For glaze, combine all ingredients in sauce pan. Heat and stir until sugar dissolves. Pour over loaves while they are hot and still in pans.

Yield: Two large loaves or four small loaves

Oven pancakes like this one from Pat and Jim VanValkenburg are versatile enough to be enjoyed for breakfast, brunch, lunch, supper and even dessert. Tester Sabra Otteson had it oven-ready in only 20 minutes. Do use cooking rather than eating apples so they hold an attractive shape even after sautéing and baking steps.

Dutch Apple Raisin Pannekoeken

2 tablespoons butter
2 large cooking apples, peeled, cored and cut into thin wedges
1½ cups golden or dark raisins
¼ cup firmly-packed brown sugar
½ teaspoon ground cinnamon
4 eggs
1 cup milk
1 cup flour
1 tablespoon granulated sugar
⅛ teaspoon salt
1 tablespoon grated lemon or orange rind
Lemon juice (optional)
Powdered sugar (optional)

Melt butter in large skillet. Add apples, raisins, brown sugar and cinnamon; sauté until tender. Set aside. Preheat oven to 425°. Combine eggs, milk, flour, granulated sugar, salt and rind in blender. Blend until smooth. Butter inside of 10 to 12-inch skillet with oven-proof handle. Pour in batter. Spoon apple-raisin mixture evenly over top. Bake 20 minutes or until pannekoeken is puffy and golden brown. Sprinkle with lemon juice and powdered sugar if you wish. Cut into wedges. Serve warm.

Serves 4 to 6

Maybe garlic bread used to be your favorite. But wait until you try this golden goodie from Rebecca Walser. Just the thing with Italian fare, soups and grilled entrées. Watch carefully during broiling step to avoid over cooking.

Three-Cheese French Bread

1 loaf French bread
10 ounces grated
   Monterey Jack cheese
5 ounces grated
   Mozzarella cheese
Paprika

5 ounces grated
   Cheddar cheese
1½ cups real mayonnaise
½ to 1 teaspoon
   garlic powder

Preheat oven to 350°. Halve bread loaf lengthwise. Combine cheeses, mayonnaise and garlic powder. Spread mixture evenly over each half of bread; sprinkle with paprika. Bake 20 minutes; broil 1 minute. Cut into thick slices.

Serves 8 or more

Those "summer sapphires" we all relish are featured in Judy Tucker's recipe for mini-loaves. Tester Shirley Bard found the smaller loaves useful as hostess gifts and said it took only 20 minutes to have batter oven-ready. Remember to fold in berries rather than mix for prettier appearance.

Blueberry Hill Bread

4 eggs
¾ cup oil
½ cup melted butter
3 cups flour + 2 tablespoons
1 teaspoon salt

1 teaspoon soda
1 tablespoon cinnamon
2 cups sugar
2 cups fresh blueberries

Preheat oven to 350°. Mix eggs, oil and butter. Gradually add sugar and other dry ingredients. Fold in blueberries. Batter will be thick. Pour into 4 small greased loaf pans. Bake for 40 minutes or until done.

Yield: 4 small loaves

Why not make your own breadsticks when it's this easy? Then wrap, sprinkle and bake just like they do in the ECC kitchen. You will have an impressive, ingenious hors d'oeuvre or meal accompaniment to tease the tastebuds.

Grissini Breadsticks

3½ cups all-purpose flour
½-ounce package fast-rising yeast
2 tablespoons sugar
¾ teaspoon salt
1 egg white
Ice water, 1 tablespoon at a time

Combine all ingredients; add water until dough forms into a ball. Place in a greased bowl. Cover and allow to rise until dough doubles in size, about 40 minutes. Preheat oven to 400°.

Divide dough into 30 portions. Roll each piece until thin and long, about ½-inch in diameter. Place on ungreased baking sheets. Combine 1 egg white with equal amount of water. Brush sticks with egg mixture. Bake for 11 to 13 minutes or until nicely browned. Remove from pan and let cool.

Makes 30 Breadsticks

Chili Bacon Breadsticks

30 baked Grissini Breadsticks (recipe above)
30 very thin slices of lean bacon, partially cooked
⅓ cup brown sugar
3 tablespoons chili powder

Preheat oven to 350°. Wrap each breadstick in one piece of bacon. Place in single layer in one or more jelly roll pans. Combine sugar and chili powder. Sprinkle sticks evenly with this mixture. Bake 10 to 15 minutes or until bacon is crisp, turning once.

Yield: 30 Breadsticks

Savory sticks from ECC's Executive Chef to serve as a handsome snack or menu embellishment. "Substitute other cheeses if you wish," says Chef Jerry Cegla. Basil's flavor and scent do wonders for absolutely anything with tomatoes, and shredding the leaves by hand brings out its attributes more keenly.

Tomato Basil Sticks

One 14 x 9½-inch puff pastry sheet
Tomato paste
½ cup chopped fresh basil
Garlic salt
Egg wash (1 egg mixed with ¼ cup water)
½ cup shredded Mozzarella cheese

Preheat oven to 400°. Sprinkle surface of pastry sheet with flour. Flatten pastry sheet slightly with rolling pin. Spread tomato paste in thin, even layer on half of pastry; sprinkle with garlic salt and basil. Fold pastry in half with tomato basil in middle and flatten slightly. Brush with egg wash. Sprinkle cheese on one-half of pastry. Fold pastry in half with cheese in middle; flatten slightly. Cut into 32 pieces (cut in half, then cut each piece in half until you have 32 strips). Twist and bake on sprayed sheet pan for 10 minutes, or until crisp and golden.

Yield: 32 sticks

If you're the "short-order" breakfast cook at your house, you will appreciate this simply-prepared treat from the Prairie Farm Bed and Breakfast. Have the egg mixture mixed and ready so you can offer the toast piping hot to both early risers and sleepy heads.

Saturday Morning French Toast

1 cup orange juice
3 eggs
¼ teaspoon cinnamon
2 teaspoons margarine, divided
8 slices cinnamon-swirl raisin bread
Powdered sugar
Pancake syrup, warmed

In small bowl, combine orange juice, eggs and cinnamon. In large non-stick skillet, melt 1 teaspoon margarine over medium heat. Dip both sides of 4 slices of bread into egg mixture. Brown bread over medium heat, about 2 minutes on each side. Repeat with remaining margarine and bread. Sprinkle with powdered sugar and serve with warmed syrup.

Serves 4

"My mother developed this recipe especially for entry in the very first Pillsbury Bake-Off," relates Virginia Bodine. "She wasn't a winner, but the recipe certainly is!" And, it's versatile enough to produce a variety of roll shapes plus an old-fashioned sugar-cinnamon coffee cake. It was Virginia's idea to add the touch of vanilla.

Mother's Rolls

Two ¼-ounce packages   2 eggs
   active dry yeast   ½ cup sugar
½ cup warm water   ½ teaspoon vanilla
2 cups milk, divided   7 cups flour (approximately),
¾ cup butter   divided
2 teaspoons salt   Additional butter to top dough

Mix yeast and water. (Yeast will work faster if a tiny pinch of sugar is added with water.) Put 1 cup of the milk in pan; bring to simmer while adding ¾ cup butter and salt. When butter is melted, allow to cool a bit. Put another cup of milk in bowl. Add eggs, sugar and vanilla. Beat thoroughly with mixer. Add warmed milk mixture and 3 cups of the flour. Mix with beater for 3 minutes. Add another 1½ cups of flour and continue beating. Add remaining flour gradually, mixing by hand. (Dough will be slightly sticky.) Let rise until doubled in size.

To make about 3 dozen rolls, take ⅓ of dough and roll into a circle. Lightly butter top of dough and cut into wedges. Roll each wedge into a crescent starting with the wide end. Continue with remaining dough. Let rise until doubled in size. Bake in 375° oven for 20 minutes.

NOTE: The same dough can be made into cocktail rolls by taking a piece the size of an egg and rolling in hand. Place rolls on pan, leaving room between pieces of dough for rising.

To make a delicious coffee cake, take ⅓ of dough, roll into rectangle, butter liberally and sprinkle with mixture of sugar and cinnamon. Roll dough and cut pieces about 1½ inches thick. Can be baked and topped with frosting made from 2 tablespoons softened butter, 3 cups powdered sugar, 2 tablespoons cream and 1 teaspoon vanilla. The same roll of dough can be put into a round mold. Cut slits in top and bake at 375° for 25 minutes. Use the same frosting and decorate with pecans or maraschino cherries.

Yield: 3 dozen rolls

The name means "lost bread" in French, and the make-ahead recipe is popular in New Orleans as well as in ECC dining rooms. For this and any other recipe where you are deep fat frying, be sure oil is heated to the proper temperature before immersing the food. This will help avoid excess absorption of oil.

Pain Perdu

1 loaf day-old French bread, cut into ¼-inch slices
Oil for deep-fat frying
Batter:
5 eggs
2½ cups light cream
¾ cup sugar
1 teaspoon vanilla
2½ tablespoons orange zest
5 ounces orange liqueur

TOPPINGS:
Powdered sugar
Creme frâiche
Strawberries or other fresh fruits
Maple syrup

The day before serving, combine batter ingredients in bowl. Pour into a shallow glass pan. Add French bread slices in a single layer. Cover and refrigerate overnight. To cook, heat oil in deep fat fryer to 360°. Using tongs, place a few slices at a time in hot fat; turn for even browning on both sides. Serve hot with toppings of choice.

Serves 6

NOTE: May also be pan fried on top of stove in small amount of cooking oil, if preferred.

"This was a huge hit with my Bible study group," says tester Terri Gulliford. "In fact, it could be renamed 'Manna from Heaven!'" Pat Clemmer, who contributed the tart, moist recipe, notes that it "freezes beautifully."

Lemon Bread

½ cup shortening, softened
2 eggs
1 cup sugar
1½ cups flour
½ teaspoon salt
1 teaspoon baking powder
½ cup milk
¼ cup chopped nuts
Grated rind of 1 lemon (1 to 2 tablespoons)

TOPPING
Juice of 1 lemon (2 to 3 tablespoons)
¼ cup sugar

Preheat oven to 350°. Mix shortening, eggs and sugar until creamed. Add remaining ingredients. Bake in greased 9 x 5 x 3-inch loaf pan 50 to 60 minutes, or until toothpick inserted in center comes out clean. When done, cover with ¼ cup sugar dissolved in juice of 1 lemon. (Leave in loaf pan as you are doing this.) Cool before removing loaf from pan.

Yield 20 to 24 slices

Spices and a hint of citrus add personality to Dr. John Eichten's favorite way to feast on excess zucchini. A psychiatrist who "loves to garden," he makes up to 15 small loaves at a time for on-the-spot enjoyment and to freeze for those months when the soil is blanketed with snow.

Gardener's Zucchini-Nut Bread

2½ cups flour
2 teaspoons baking powder
1 teaspoon baking soda
¾ teaspoon salt
½ teaspoon ground cinnamon
¼ teaspoon ground ginger
1 teaspoon shredded lemon zest
2 eggs, beaten
½ cup cooking oil
1¼ cups sugar
¼ teaspoon orange extract
2 cups finely-shredded zucchini
1 cup chopped pecans or walnuts

Preheat oven to 350°. In a large bowl, combine dry ingredients; set aside. Beat lemon zest, eggs, oil, sugar and orange extract. Add zucchini and nuts. Add flour mixture in 3 batches. Pour batter into greased 9 x 5 x 3-inch loaf pan. Bake 50 to 60 minutes, or until skewer inserted in center comes out clean. When cool, wrap in foil to store.

NOTE: This amount of batter can also be baked in two 7½ x 3½ x 2-inch loan pans 45 to 50 minutes.

Yield: 1 loaf

After some experimenting, Pat Clemmer reports, "This is the best zucchini bread recipe I've found!" If you like a more intense molasses flavor, use dark brown sugar. Light brown, which contains less molasses, gives a milder, less distinctive taste.

Zucchini-Cinnamon Bread

3 eggs, beaten
1 cup salad oil
1 cup white sugar
1 cup brown sugar
2 cups zucchini, peeled and grated
1 teaspoon vanilla
3 cups flour
1 teaspoon baking soda
1 teaspoon salt
1 tablespoon ground cinnamon
Nuts or raisins, if desired

Preheat oven to 325°. In large mixer bowl, combine beaten eggs with salad oil, sugars, zucchini and vanilla; mix well. Sift together flour, baking soda, salt and cinnamon. Add to zucchini mixture; mix well. Add nuts or raisins, if desired. Pour into 2 greased and floured 9 x 5-inch loaf pans. Bake for 1 hour or until done. Cool before slicing.

Yield: 2 loaves

NOTE: Breads like this will slice better if wrapped in foil or plastic and refrigerated overnight.

Enliven almost any menu with Judy Tucker's quickly-mixed corn bread. The use of all butter adds rich flavor. And, the creamy corn contributes to a dense, moist texture quite unlike the drier, crumbly style you may have tried before.

Green Chili Corn Bread

1 cup butter, softened
¾ cup sugar
4 eggs
½ cup canned green chilies, diced and drained
1½ cups cream-style corn
½ cup shredded Cheddar cheese
1 cup flour
1 cup yellow corn meal
2 tablespoons baking powder
1 teaspoon salt

Preheat oven to 325°. In mixer bowl, cream butter and sugar. Beat in eggs slowly, one at a time. Add remaining ingredients and mix well. Pour into well-greased 9-inch square pan. Bake for 1 hour or until done.

Serves 8 to 9

This is just one day brightener on the "hearty breakfast menu" served to guests at the Prairie Farm Bed and Breakfast, Lester Prairie, MN. Norma Dolliff, now of Excelsior, grew up in the area and decided in 1995 to restore the 1918 three-bedroom home and open it to visitors.

Almond-Rhubarb Coffeecake

2¼ cups buttermilk biscuit mix, such as Bisquick
1 cup packed brown sugar
1 egg
1 teaspoon vanilla
1¼ cups finely-chopped rhubarb
¾ cup (2¼ oz. package) sliced almonds, divided
½ cup granulated sugar
1 tablespoon firm butter or margarine

Preheat oven to 350°. Grease and flour a 10 x 15-inch jelly roll pan or use 2 pans, an 8 and a 9-inch square. Combine baking mix, brown sugar, egg, milk and vanilla. Beat vigorously 30 seconds. Stir in rhubarb and ½ cup of almonds. Spread batter in pan (it will be shallow). With a pastry cutter, mix the granulated sugar, butter and remaining ¼ cup almonds. Sprinkle mixture evenly over batter. Bake 25 to 30 minutes or until wooden toothpick inserted in center comes out clean.

Serves 18 to 24

Sue Schmidt of Edina treasures this heirloom recipe brought over from Finland by her grandfather's mother. "It's my most requested treat to bake," she says. Bread has always been an important part of Finnish meals, and sweet doughs like this one, flavored with cardamom, are staples for breakfast and morning coffee breaks. Once ground, cardamom quickly loses its intensity. So, the fresher the better, as with most spices.

Finnish Coffee Bread

Two ¼-ounce packages active dry yeast
½ cup warm water
1½ cups water
4 tablespoons margarine
1 cup sugar
1½ teaspoons salt
2 eggs
2 teaspoons ground cardamom
¾ cup non-fat dry milk powder
6 to 8 cups flour

TOPPING
1 teaspoon sugar
2 egg yolks

Dissolve yeast in the ½ cup warm water. Then, heat 1½ cups water with margarine until it melts. Add sugar and salt; cool. Beat eggs; add cardamom, milk powder and yeast/water mixture. Whisk until blended. Add water, margarine and sugar mixture and whisk until blended. Add flour, one cup at a time, beating well after each addition. Add enough flour so dough can easily be handled. Knead 5 to 8 minutes. Let rise until doubled, about 1½ hours. Punch down; cut into 4 pieces. Cut each quarter into 3 parts. Roll into smooth strands. Braid strands into a loaf. Place in greased and floured 9 x 5 x 3-inch bread pans. Let rise until doubled. Repeat for 3 more loaves. Preheat oven to 375°. Bake 25 to 30 minutes or until golden brown. Remove from oven. Mix sugar with egg yolks and use to glaze loaves while they are hot from the oven.

Yield: 4 loaves

A Christmas morning tradition passed down to Jenifer Harris from her mother. "We nibble as we're opening presents, and although it isn't terribly fancy, everyone loves it," says Jenifer of Edina. "I also make it to give as gifts to neighbors at holiday time."

Holiday Coffee Cake

1 cup sugar
¼ pound butter or margarine, softened
2 eggs
2 cups flour
1 teaspoon baking soda
1 teaspoon baking powder
½ teaspoon salt
1 cup sour cream
2 teaspoons vanilla

TOPPING
½ cup sugar
1 teaspoon cinnamon
¾ cup chopped walnuts

Preheat oven to 350°. Cream sugar and margarine. Add eggs. Combine dry ingredients. Add to bowl alternately with sour cream. Add vanilla. Grease and flour pan (1 tube or 2 loaf).

Put half of batter pan in first, then sprinkle with half of topping mixture. Then add remaining batter and finish with topping. Bake 50 to 55 minutes or until done.

Serves 16

ECC's Clubhouse Manager and Food & Beverage Director, Ken Galloway, volunteered to test Pat Meyers' recipe, and he obviously relished the task. "Preparation time was only 5 minutes plus baking time, and the results were excellent! Yes, I would certainly make them again," he said. Pat suggests serving them with soups, stews and main dish salads.

Velvet Cream Biscuits

4 cups all-purpose flour	2 tablespoons sugar
2 tablespoons baking powder	2½ cups whipping cream
1 teaspoon salt	¼ cup butter or margarine, melted

Preheat oven to 425°. Combine first 4 ingredients. Add whipping cream, stirring until dry ingredients are moistened. Turn dough out onto well-floured surface; knead 10 to 12 times. Roll dough to ½-inch thickness; cut with a 2-inch biscuit cutter. Place on lightly-greased baking sheets. Brush with melted butter. Bake for 12 to 14 minutes, or until golden brown.

Note: To make ahead, bake biscuits only 7 or 8 minutes. Cool on wire racks; wrap and freeze. To serve, thaw at room temperature and bake at 425° for 5 to 6 minutes.

Yield: 2½ dozen

"Blueberry or strawberry syrup makes the perfect topper for these pancakes," says contributor Jaye Vaaler of Golden Valley. Tester Terry Swanson commented on the "very light texture" which comes from stiffly-beaten egg whites folded into the batter.

Sour Cream Pancakes

3 large eggs, separated	1½ tablespoons sugar
¾ cup skim milk	1½ teaspoons baking powder
¾ cup sour cream	Dash of salt
1 cup plus 2 tablespoons flour	¾ cup butter, melted

Heat griddle while preparing batter. (Grease griddle unless it is non-stick variety.) Combine egg yolks, milk and sour cream in a large bowl. In a separate bowl, combine flour, sugar, baking powder and salt. Gradually add flour mixture to the sour cream mixture, stirring until smooth. Stir in melted butter. Beat egg whites at high speed with an electric mixer until stiff peaks form. Gently fold egg whites into the pancake batter. For each pancake, pour ¼ cup batter onto hot griddle. Turn pancakes when tops are covered with bubbles and edges appear cooked.

Yield: About 18 pancakes

"My son, Chris, always loved having these pancakes at Grandma's," says *Jenifer Harris. And now he can enjoy them at home because "Grandma" Phyllis Harris was generous in sharing the recipe with her daughter-in-law. No doubt Jenifer's husband, John, eats his share, too. Well known as a U.S. Amateur Golf Champion, John has been a member of two Walker Cup teams.*

Championship Buttermilk Pancakes

1 quart buttermilk
3 cups flour
2 tablespoons sugar
1 teaspoon baking soda
1 teaspoon baking powder
½ teaspoon salt
1 tablespoon oil
2 eggs

Heat griddle while mixing the batter. (Grease griddle unless it is the non-stick variety.) Using a large mixing bowl and rotary beater; beat eggs. Beat in buttermilk and soda. Mix the flour, sugar, oil, baking powder and salt. Combine the buttermilk and flour mixtures with the rotary beater until smooth. Test the griddle. If drops of water "skate" around the griddle it is ready to use. Drop the batter from a tablespoon onto hot griddle. When pancakes are full of bubbles, turn them over to brown the other side.

NOTE: For thinner pancakes, add a little more milk. For thicker pancakes, increase the flour.

Serves 4

Nothing ho-hum about these corn muffins. ECC chefs toss in some peppy chilies to add excitement. Jalapeño peppers, named for the Mexican town of Jalapa, range from mild to fiery hot. Try these muffins with a bowl of chili, salads and barbecued meats.

Jalapeño Corn Muffins

1 cup flour
1 teaspoon baking soda
1½ teaspoons baking powder
1 tablespoon sugar
1 teaspoon salt
¾ cup yellow corn meal
1½ cups buttermilk
2 eggs
4 tablespoons melted butter
2 medium jalapeño peppers

Preheat oven to 425°. Wearing gloves to protect hands, seed and dice peppers; set aside. Combine dry ingredients. In separate bowl, combine remaining ingredients. Blend wet and dry ingredients together just until mixed. Fold in chopped peppers. Pour into buttered muffin tins. Bake 12 to 15 minutes.

Yield: 12 to 13 muffins

Two festive fall ingredients — pumpkin and apple cider — combine in a spice-spangled harvest loaf. Tester Anita Anderson applauds the "full-bodied flavor and tasty addition of orange zest." Compliments once again to ECC chefs for sharing one more reason to be thankful!

Pumpkin Cider Bread

1 cup apple cider
16-ounce can pumpkin puree
2 large eggs
¼ cup vegetable oil
¾ cup light brown sugar, firmly packed
2 tablespoons grated orange zest
2 cups all-purpose flour
2 teaspoons baking powder
½ teaspoon salt
¼ teaspoon baking soda
¼ teaspoon ground mace
¼ teaspoon ground cinnamon
⅛ teaspoon ground cloves
¼ cup chopped walnuts

In small saucepan, simmer apple cider until reduced to about ¼ cup; cool. Preheat oven to 350°. In large mixer bowl, blend pumpkin puree, eggs, oil, sugar, orange zest and reduced cider. Sift together flour, baking powder, salt, baking soda and spices. Add dry ingredients to pumpkin mixture; blend well. Fold in walnuts. Spoon batter into a 9½ x 5½-inch loaf pan. Bake for 1 hour or until toothpick inserted in center comes out clean. Let cool in pan before removing.

Yield: 1 loaf

"This is our family's favorite bread," says Susan Flynn of Edina. "It always turns out beautifully and makes a wonderful gift." To produce a moist, tender loaf, take care not to overbake.

Chocolate Chip-Banana Bread

2 cups all purpose flour
1 teaspoon baking powder
½ teaspoon baking soda
½ teaspoon salt
½ cup butter or margarine, softened
1 cup sugar
2 large eggs
2 large ripe bananas, mashed (⅔ cup)
1 cup semi-sweet chocolate chips

Preheat oven to 350°. Coat 3 mini loaf pans (3 x 5½-inch) or one 9 x 5-inch loaf pan with non-stick cooking spray. Mix flour, baking powder, baking soda and salt. Beat butter and sugar with electric mixer until light and fluffy. Beat in eggs one at a time until blended. Beat in bananas. With mixer on low speed, gradually add flour mixture just until blended. Stir in chocolate chips. Pour into prepared pan(s) and bake 35 minutes for 3 mini pans or 60 minutes for loaf pan, or until toothpick inserted in center comes out clean. Do not over bake. Cool in pan 5 minutes before removing. Cool completely before slicing.

Yield: 1 loaf or 3 mini-loaves

All dressed up and plenty of places to go! Mary L. Miller of Edina tucks these muffins in green foil-lined baskets and garnishes with sprigs of holly for December hostess gifts. At home she serves the bite-sized beauties with turkey or ham entrées. Wonderful with main dish salads, as well.

Tomato-Rosemary Muffins

1¾ cups all-purpose flour
⅓ cup grated Parmesan cheese
2 tablespoons sugar
2 teaspoons baking powder
½ teaspoon dried rosemary, crushed
½ teaspoon parsley flakes
¼ teaspoon baking soda
⅛ teaspoon garlic powder
⅛ teaspoon black pepper
1 egg, beaten
½ cup milk
½ cup tomato sauce
⅓ cup olive oil or cooking oil
Grated Parmesan cheese

Preheat oven to 350°. In a 2-quart or medium-sized bowl, combine flour, Parmesan cheese, sugar, baking powder, rosemary, parsley flakes, baking soda, garlic powder and pepper. Make a well in the center. In separate bowl, combine egg, milk, tomato sauce and oil. Add all at once to flour mixture. Stir just until moistened (batter will be lumpy).

Lightly grease muffin cups. If desired, sprinkle cups with additional Parmesan cheese. Fill twelve 2½-inch muffin cups two-thirds full, or thirty-six 1¾-inch muffin cups two-thirds full. Bake 20 to 24 minutes. Do not overbake. Muffins freeze well in air-tight bag.

Yield: 12 regular-size or 36 mini muffins

"Light and delicious with just a touch of sweetness," is how Marde Olson describes her favorite corn muffins. Note that as a rule, the lighter the color of honey, the milder the flavor. It won't stick to the measuring cup if the cup is lightly coated with a non-stick spray.

Honey Corn Muffins

1¾ cups flour
¾ cup white corn meal
¼ cup sugar
1 tablespoon baking powder
1 teaspoon baking soda
1 teaspoon salt
½ cup milk
¼ cup orange juice
¼ cup butter, melted
¼ cup honey

Preheat oven to 350°. Grease or line 12 muffin cups. Combine dry ingredients in large mixing bowl. Blend liquid ingredients in small bowl. Add liquid to dry ingredients, stirring just until smooth. (Do not over-mix.) Batter will be thick. Divide batter among prepared muffin cups. Bake about 15 minutes or until golden. Serve warm.

Yield: 12 muffins

When slender, tender rhubarb stalks shoot up in the spring, be sure to try this delectable recipe from Liana Peterson, Edina business owner. The streusel topping makes it extra special. "This is such a hit with my family, I always make a double batch and freeze some," says Liana.

Crunch-Crowned Rhubarb Bread or Muffins

⅓ cup oil
¾ cup packed brown sugar
1 egg
½ cup buttermilk OR sour milk
1 teaspoon vanilla
1½ cups flour
½ teaspoon soda
½ teaspoon salt
1 cup diced fresh rhubarb
½ cup finely-chopped walnuts or pecans

TOPPING
¼ cup packed brown sugar
½ teaspoon cinnamon
¼ cup finely-chopped walnuts or pecans

Preheat oven to 325°. Combine oil, sugar, egg, milk and vanilla. Sift in flour, soda and salt; mix until combined. Fold in rhubarb and nuts. For bread, spoon batter evenly into a greased 9 x 5-inch loaf pan. Combine topping ingredients; sprinkle evenly over top of loaf. Bake 45 minutes or until bread tests done.

For muffins, spoon batter into 12 lined or greased muffin cups. Sprinkle each with some of the topping. Bake about 25 minutes or until done.

Yield: 1 loaf or 12 muffins

A golden gift from China, apricots are rich in potassium and a good source of dietary fiber. Here they add sunny flecks, flavor and appealing texture to a unique quick bread. Be sure to allow a little extra time for reconstituting the fruit and letting the batter set before baking.

Apricot Bread

1 cup chopped dried apricots
Warm water
2 cups flour
1 cup sugar
2 teaspoons baking powder
½ teaspoon salt
¼ teaspoon soda
2 tablespoons butter, softened
1 egg
½ cup orange juice
¼ cup water

Pour warm water over chopped apricots. Let stand 30 minutes; drain well. Combine flour, sugar, baking powder, salt and soda. Stir in butter, egg, orange juice and water. Fold in apricots. Line 9 x 5 x 3-inch bread pan with waxed paper. Preheat oven to 350°. Pour batter into prepared pan; let stand 20 minutes. Bake 50-60 minutes. Remove loaf from pan and paper from loaf while warm. Cool before slicing.

Yield: 1 loaf

Shirley Bard of Eden Prairie suggests topping piping hot French toast slices with fresh fruit — bananas, berries, kiwi or green grapes, and/or warmed maple syrup. "This is a Swedish recipe from Great Grandmother Bard, and over the years it's become a real family favorite," she adds. Tester Kathy Powers shares Shirley's affection for the recipe. "My children loved it, so I made extra and froze it. We microwaved the leftovers for another quick, delicious meal!"

Golden Crust French Toast

½ cup flour
1 teaspoon baking powder
⅓ cup milk
6 eggs
1¼ cups oil for frying
French bread cut in 1½-inch slices
Syrup of choice and/or fresh fruit

Combine flour and baking powder in medium bowl. Add milk; mix into a paste. Add eggs and mix well. Heat oil in frying pan. Dip French bread slices in egg batter, soaking slices thoroughly. Fry until egg is cooked, golden and crusty.

Serves 4 to 5

Chef Hallie Harron, Executive Chef of Premier Crew Restaurant Services in Walker, MN, took home the grand prize in a breakfast recipe competition with this fruit and jam-stuffed French toast. Tester Marde Olson found the syrup unnecessary, but suit your personal taste for sweetness.

Stuffed French Toast

Four ½-inch slices fresh egg twist bread or other slightly stale white bread of good quality
¾ cup egg product or 3 eggs
½ cup milk
½ cup non-fat vanilla yogurt
½ teaspoon vanilla
½ teaspoon cinnamon
¼ teaspoon cardamom
Strawberry all-fruit or other jam
1 medium banana, thinly sliced
Pure maple syrup, warmed
Additional fresh berries and bananas

Mix eggs or egg product, milk, yogurt, vanilla, cinnamon and cardamom. Set aside. Spread bread slices with all-fruit jam. Cover 2 slices with sliced bananas. Top each with another bread slice. Press down firmly on top slice to help enclose fruit. Dip sandwiches in egg mixture on both sides, letting liquid absorb into bread.

Cook on hot griddle or in sprayed frying pan until golden and firm on each side. (Turning toast smoothly takes concentration.) Slice each sandwich in thirds. Arrange on plate; garnish with fruit. Serve syrup on side.

Yield: 2 portions

A buttery batter is brightened with diced strawberries and bakes nicely in a springform tube pan preferred by contributor Peggy Dodge. "I like the attractive round shape with no worry about burned edges and a doughy center," she explains. Liana Peterson tested it using muffin tins, and found that to be a handy alternative.

Fresh Strawberry Bread or Muffins

1 cup fresh strawberries (ripe but firm)
6 tablespoons butter, softened
¼ cup salad oil
1 cup brown sugar
2 large eggs
2¼ cups flour
½ teaspoon baking soda
½ teaspoon salt
½ teaspoon nutmeg
½ cup chopped pecans

Preheat oven to 350°. Wash berries; remove stems. Cut into small pieces; set aside. Cream butter, oil and sugar. Beat in eggs until well mixed. Combine dry ingredients; blend into butter mixture. Fold in strawberries and nuts.

For round bread loaf, spread batter evenly in a greased 10-inch tube springform pan. Bake 40 to 45 minutes or until it tests done. Do not overbake.

For muffins, grease or line 14 to 16 muffin cups. Spoon batter into cups, dividing evenly. Bake at 375° about 25 minutes or until they test done.

Yield: 1 round loaf or 14 to 16 muffins

Dig out the old cast iron skillet and sample one of Pat and Jim Van Valkenburg's "at-the-cabin favorites." Only four ingredients and four preparation steps — what could be easier for a lazy day at the lake?

Dutch Baby

¼ cup butter or margarine

3 eggs

¾ cup flour

¾ cup milk

Powdered sugar, jam, and/or syrups

Preheat oven to 400°. Place butter in an 11-inch cast iron or other skillet with oven-proof handle. Place skillet in oven until butter is melted. While butter is melting, thoroughly combine eggs, flour and milk in mixing bowl. Pour this mixture over melted butter in hot-from-the-oven skillet. Return to oven and bake 15 to 20 minutes, or until top is puffed and golden. Cut into wedges. Serve with powdered sugar, jams, and/or syrups of choice. Fresh berries also make an attractive topping.

Serves 2 to 4

Rebecca Walser's "mini-loaves" feature popular Italian Parmesan in the freshly-grated version. If you don't want to tackle grating this very hard cheese, you will find it available in the dairy case of large supermarkets. The sweet nut-like flavor and straw color comes from proper aging in the Parma area of Italy. American versions are saltier in taste and softer in consistency.

Toasted Parmesan Loaves

1 loaf day-old sandwich bread, unsliced
½ pound butter, softened
⅛ teaspoon salt
Dash paprika
¼ pound freshly-grated Parmesan cheese

Preheat oven to 375°. Trim all crusts from bread. Cut loaf in half lengthwise and then into 16 loaf-shaped pieces. Combine butter, salt, paprika and cheese. Spread mixture on all sides of bread pieces except bottoms. Bake 10 to 12 munutes, until golden brown.

When guests at her Park Row Bed and Breakfast, St. Peter, MN, must depart at an early hour, home economist Ann Burckhardt bakes up one or more of these one-minute eggs. Ann, who served as recipe consultant for this book, was part of the Betty Crocker Kitchens' team for seven years, and was a food editor for the Taste section of the Minneapolis Star-Tribune *for 24 years.*

Microwaved Egg a la Suisse

Non-stick vegetable oil spray
2 teaspoons refrigerated crumbled bacon bits
1 large egg
1 tablespoon half-and-half
1 generous tablespoon shredded Swiss cheese

Spray a custard cup with non-stick spray. Cover bottom of cup with bacon bits. Break egg into cup being careful not to break yolk. Pour half-and-half evenly over egg. (This coating protects the egg white from becoming rubbery.) Sprinkle cheese evenly over all. Microwave at 80 percent power 1 minute or until egg is just set. Let stand a minute or two before serving.

Serves 1

Zena Kane, daughter-in-law of ECC members Dr. William and Elizabeth Kane, shares one of her favorite dishes for breakfast and brunch. "It's a quick, easy and tasty option when you are faced with houseguests rising at different times," she says. Zena and her family live in Reno, NV.

Reno Ranch Breakfast

24 ounces shredded hash brown potatoes, thawed
⅓ cup butter, melted
2 cups shredded Jack, Swiss and/or pepper cheese*
1 cup diced ham (may be omitted)
½ cup half-and-half
2 eggs
¼ teaspoon seasoned salt
*If at least half the amount of cheese is not pepper cheese, add ¼ cup salsa for extra "zip."

Preheat oven to 425°. Pat hash browns dry. Press potatoes into greased 10-inch pie plate. Brush potatoes evenly with melted butter. Bake for 25 minutes. Remove from oven and re-set oven to 350°. Top potatoes with cheese and ham. Mix half-and-half, eggs and seasoned salt. Pour over top. Continue baking for 25 to 30 minutes or until cooked.

Serves 6

"This recipe has great versatility," comments Evie Teegen who has had many opportunities to entertain in her long political career in Minnesota and while serving as a U. S. Ambassador to countries in the South Pacific. "Use slices as a base for poached eggs with Hollandaise Sauce, serve as a meal accompaniment or cut into smaller pieces for appetizers."

Sausage-Cheese Bread

18-ounce package hot roll mix
2 pounds spicy sausage
2 eggs, beaten
8 ounces shredded Mozzarella cheese
8 ounces shredded Cheddar cheese
½ cup minced parsley

Prepare hot roll mix according to package directions. Let rise. Brown and crumble sausage; drain well. Reserve a small amount of beaten egg to use later. Combine remaining egg with sausage, cheeses and parsley. Preheat oven to 350°. Divide dough into two parts. Roll each portion to a 4 x 12-inch rectangle. Place on jelly roll pan. Spoon sausage mixture evenly atop each rectangle. Fold over sides and ends of dough until filling is covered. Brush tops with reserve egg. Bake 35 to 40 minutes or until nicely browned.

Yield: 24 slices

One of the most attractive ways of presenting bacon and eggs comes from the Prairie Farm Bed and Breakfast in Lester Prairie, MN. Tester Pat Spring was particularly pleased that "they came out of the pan so easily and held their shape." She suggests careful monitoring during baking so eggs are done just the way you like them.

Bacon-Wrapped Eggs

Bacon
Eggs

Preheat oven to 400°. Partially fry bacon needed. Spray muffin tins with cooking spray. Put 2 strips bacon around edge of muffin tin. Place one egg in each bacon-lined muffin cup. Bake 10 to 12 minutes or until egg is done as desired.

The dream dish of every brunch host because most of the preparation is completed the night before serving. Contributor Mary Morton serves it with fresh fruits of the season and coffee cake. Tester Marie Lacy likes it made with spicy sausage and the addition of snipped chives or green onion. "Great for a group," she adds.

Make-Ahead Brunch Bake

3 cups seasoned croutons
1 to 2 pounds spicy sausage, browned and drained
2 cups sharp Cheddar cheese, grated
4 eggs
2½ cups milk
1 can condensed cream of mushroom soup
1 cup milk

In a 9 x 13-inch pan, layer croutons, sausage and cheese in that order. Beat eggs and milk together. Pour over the croutons, sausage and cheese. Cover and refrigerate overnight.

Preheat oven to 325°. Before baking, combine soup and milk; pour evenly over casserole. Bake, uncovered, about 1½ hours. Allow to set 5 to 10 minutes before serving.

Serves 8-10

Voila! A creamy quiche-like consistency in just a fraction of the time with Susan Passolt's unique muffin-based brunch recipe. Tester Gene Gaasedelen points out the importance of lowering the broiler rack so the topping has time to cook before browning too much. Sue is owner of Shoe Allée in Edina's 50th and France business district.

Kansas City Quiche

2 eggs, beaten
⅓ cup half-and-half
Dash pepper
Dash nutmeg
½ pound finely grated Swiss cheese
5 slices bacon fried crisp, crumbled
3 English muffins, sliced and toasted

Position broiling rack about 7 inches down from flame or heating element. Preheat oven to broil. Combine all ingredients except muffins. Top each toasted muffin half with a portion of the mixture. Broil until eggs are set and nicely browned, watching carefully to avoid over cooking.

Serves 3 to 4

"Practically foolproof and delicious with a spinach salad," says contributor Julie Waychoff of Edina. "Very reliable and universally liked," agrees tester Trish Ura. Versatility is part of the charm— serve for breakfast, brunch, luncheon or a light supper.

Creamy Quiche Lorraine

8 ounces Swiss cheese, grated
8 slices bacon, cooked until crisp and crumbled
4 or 5 fresh mushrooms, chopped
9-inch pastry crust, unbaked
1 cup heavy whipping cream
½ cup milk
½ teaspoon salt
¼ teaspoon pepper
Dash of cayenne
½ teaspoon garlic powder
½ teaspoon dry mustard
3 eggs

Preheat oven to 350°. Sprinkle cheese, bacon and mushrooms into pastry-lined pie or quiche pan. Beat remaining ingredients together; pour over cheese, bacon and mushrooms. Bake 55 minutes. Remove from oven and let stand 5 minutes. Cut into wedges and serve.

Serves 6 to 8

Another "eye-opener" from the Guadalupe Inn. A tortilla takes the place of toast and the choice of meat is up to the cook. Tester Shirley Bard recommends using cooked, crumbled sausage and beginning with only 2 cups of water for the green chili mixture. Add more, if necessary. for desired consistency. Cholesterol watchers may want to use just one fried egg in place of two.

Huevos Rancheros

1½ cups chopped fresh green chili
3 cloves garlic, finely diced
2 teaspoons salt or to taste
2 to 2½ cups water
½ cup meat of choice, finely diced
1 corn tortilla, softened in oil and patted dry to blot oil
Chopped onion to taste
Shredded Cheddar cheese to taste
2 eggs, fried over easy
Tomato and parsley for garnish

Make green chili sauce; combine green chili, garlic and water in saucepan. Add salt and simmer for 10 minutes. Sauté meat until done. Top tortilla with onion, Cheddar cheese and cooked eggs. Top with one ladle of green chili mixture. Garnish with slice of tomato and parsley.

Serves 1

Another morning meal special from Ann Burckhardt's Park Row Bed and Breakfast in St. Peter. "This is a good choice when guests do not eat meat," she finds. Serve with a selection of juices or fresh fruits of the season. Especially nice with melon.

Southwest Egg Puff

10 large eggs
½ cup all-purpose flour
1 teaspoon baking powder
Dash of salt
½ cup butter or margarine,
   melted

4-ounce can mild green chilies,
   chopped
12-ounce carton cottage cheese
1 pound Monterey Jack cheese,
   shredded
Sour cream and salsa for topping

Preheat oven to 350°. Grease a large casserole. In a large bowl, beat eggs until lemon colored and fluffy. Fold in the flour, baking powder, salt, melted margarine, chilies and both cheeses. Pour mixture into prepared casserole. Bake 35 minutes, or until set. Let stand about 10 minutes before serving. Make a pattern with small amounts of sour cream and salsa atop the casserole so that it will be attractive when served. Pass bowls of sour cream and salsa at the table.

Serves 6

Chef Jerry Cross of Santa Fe's Guadalupe Inn shares a pepper-flecked favorite for one. Of course, it's easily increased to serve more. Jerry presents it with sides of hash browns, bacon and toast. Great way to "fuel up" before horseback riding, hiking or sightseeing.

Western Omelette

1 tablespoon chopped green bell pepper
1 tablespoon chopped red bell pepper
2 mushrooms, sliced
1 tablespoon diced onions
1 teaspoon oil
2 eggs, beaten
Shredded Cheddar cheese, if desired

Combine first 5 ingredients and sauté. Add 2 beaten eggs, cook over medium heat. When done, top with Cheddar cheese, if desired.

Serves 1

Side Dishes and Vegetables

"Spring" this on dinner guests as a side dish or light entrée when asparagus makes a welcome appearance. Over the years, Terry Swanson has received enough compliments on it to say without reservation, "It tastes wonderful and offers an unusual option for entertaining." Why not team with baked ham for a special Easter gathering?

Asparagus Lasagna

4 pounds asparagus
3 tablespoons olive oil
6 sheets frozen lasagna sheets *
½ stick butter
¼ cup all purpose flour
1½ cups chicken broth
½ cup water
7 ounces goat cheese
1 teaspoon grated lemon zest
Salt to taste
1⅔ cups grated Parmesan cheese
½ cup cottage cheese
½ cup low fat sour cream

*Or, use ten 1-ounce lasagna strips cooked according to package directions

Preheat oven to 500°. Trim asparagus; cut off tips and save. Toss asparagus in olive oil to coat. Place in shallow roast pan. Bake 5 to 10 minutes until tender crisp. Lower oven to 400°. Cool, sprinkle with salt and cut into ½" lengths.

Soak lasagna sheets in cold water for 15 minutes; drain. In medium saucepan, melt butter. Add flour and cook roux for 3 minutes. Add chicken broth and water in a stream, whisking until smooth. Cook 5 minutes. Add goat cheese, lemon zest and salt. Whisk until cheese is melted and sauce is smooth.

Drain pasta well and arrange 1 layer of sheets in 8-inch or 16-inch baking dish. Spread with ¼ of sauce; top with ¼ asparagus. Top each layer with ⅓ cup Parmesan cheese. Continue layering, ending with a sheet of lasagna.

Whisk cottage cheese and sour cream until well blended and smooth. Spread on top sheet of lasagna. Arrange asparagus tips over top and sprinkle with remaining Parmesan cheese. Bake in 400° oven for 20-30 minutes until golden and bubbly. Let stand 10 minutes; serve.

Serves 8

No one will have to be coaxed to "eat your vegetables" with this side dish or meatless entrée from Betty Bajwa of Edina. A dietitian at Park-Nicollet Clinic, Betty suggests using low-fat cheeses and rounding out the menu with a green or fruit salad and crusty rolls. Tester Terry Swanson found that "leftovers reheat beautifully."

Vegetarian Lasagna

10-ounce package lasagna noodles
1 pound fresh spinach
1 tablespoon cooking oil
2 cups sliced fresh mushrooms
1 cup grated carrots
½ cup chopped onion
2 garlic cloves, diced
15-ounce can tomato sauce
6-ounce can tomato paste
½ cup chopped pitted ripe olives
1½ teaspoons oregano
¼ teaspoon crushed red pepper (optional)
16-ounce carton (2 cups) non-fat cream-style cottage cheese
16 ounces Monterey Jack cheese, sliced
Freshly-grated Parmesan

Preheat oven to 375°. Cook lasagna noodles in boiling water for 8 to 10 minutes or until tender; drain. Rinse spinach well. In covered saucepan, cook spinach without water except for drops that cling to leaves. Reduce heat until steam forms. Cook 3 to 5 minutes, turning occasionally. Remove from heat; drain spinach. Heat oil in saucepan. Cook mushrooms, carrots, onions and garlic in hot oil until tender, but not brown. Stir in tomato sauce, tomato paste, olives, oregano and red pepper. Add 2 to 3 tablespoons of water if mixture appears too thick.

Coat a 9 x 13-inch pan with vegetable oil spray. Layer half each of the noodles, cottage cheese, spinach, Monterey Jack cheese and sauce mixture. Repeat layers, reserving several cheese slices for top. Bake for 35 to 45 minutes. Let stand 10 minutes before cutting into serving pieces. Pass fresh Parmesan cheese to sprinkle over top.

Serves 8

Cooking for compliments? Try this red and green goodie from Sylvia Berg which received nothing but compliments from testers. "The colors are perfect for holiday parties and even my kids liked it," says Diane Lacy Harr. "The salad dressing mix gives it oomph," adds Pat Meyers. Sylvia and her husband, Wally, are realtors specializing in lake properties in the Bay Lake area of Minnesota.

Fresh Green Bean Casserole

2 pounds fresh green beans, trimmed
1 red pepper, cut julienne-style
7-ounce package dry Italian salad dressing
¼ cup butter, melted
¼ cup Parmesan cheese

Preheat oven to 350°. Cook green beans and pepper strips just until tender. Combine vegetables with dry dressing mix and melted butter. Spoon into oven-to-table casserole. Sprinkle with Parmesan. Bake just until heated through, about 15 to 20 minutes.

Serves 6

From Gretchen Pracht, a speedy stove-top combo with a creative mixture of ingredients. Tester Mary L. Miller suggests making ahead and warming in the oven as a preparation alternative if the burners are otherwise occupied. Whichever method you use, you're sure to enjoy!

Peppy Green Beans

Two 10-ounce packages frozen cut green beans
10½-ounce can golden corn soup
½ cup sour cream
¼ cup ketchup
½ teaspoon garlic salt

Cook beans according to package instructions; drain. Combine soup, sour cream, ketchup and garlic salt. Heat thoroughly, but do not boil. Pour over beans and serve immediately.

Serves 6 to 8

Storey Holland of Edina has no problem rounding up her three sons when they know this is on the menu. The hearty side or main dish simmers all day in the slow cooker while you're busy with other activities. "It's popular year around and tastes even better when made ahead," says Storey.

Round-Up Bean Bake

8-ounce can lima beans, undrained
8-ounce can kidney beans, undrained
15-ounce can pork and beans undrained
1 pound lean ground beef
¼ pound bacon, diced

Chopped onion to taste
⅓ cup brown sugar
¼ cup ketchup
1 tablespoon vinegar
¾ tablespoon prepared horseradish

Put beans, liquid and all, in electric slow cooker. Brown hamburger, bacon and onion; drain the fat. Add brown sugar, vinegar, ketchup and horseradish to meat. Stir into bean mixture. Cook 8 hours on low setting.

Serves 8

Get out the bean pot! Set the oven for some sloooooow baking and toss together the ingredients for Betty Weingartner's family reunion favorite. "It's just plain delicious!" she says. It's just plain easy too, according to tester Vicki Kattke.

Family Reunion Baked Beans

Two 1 pound 15-ounce cans baked beans
1 pound bacon, partially cooked and cut into pieces
2 bell peppers, cut into pieces
1 cup ketchup
1 cup brown sugar
1 tablespoon Worcestershire sauce

Preheat oven to 325°. Combine all ingredients in bean pot. Bake, covered, for 2½ to 3 hours.

Serves 12

From Marde Olson, a spicy little number which can be quickly prepared with on-hand ingredients. A self-described "recipe clipper and food magazine enthusiast," Marde teams this with crisp crackers or corn bread. Tester Diane Lacy Harr suggests tempering seasonings to suit personal tastes. "It's hot!" she says.

Black Bean Chili

14- to 18-ounce can peeled whole drained tomatoes
3 tablespoons corn oil
½ to 1 onion, chopped
4 cloves garlic, chopped
2 teaspoons cumin seed
½ teaspoon cayenne pepper
1 teaspoon ground coriander
½ teaspoon salt
2 tablespoons chili powder
One or two 16-ounce cans black beans
Rice wine vinegar, brown sugar and cilantro, if desired

Chop tomatoes in processor or blender. Heat oil in large skillet; saute onions until soft. Add garlic and seasonings. Cook for a few minutes. Add tomatoes and beans; simmer over low heat 20 to 30 minutes. If desired, sprinkle with vinegar, brown sugar and cilantro before serving.

Serves 4

When Elizabeth Eisenbrey of Edina journeyed back to Ohio for a class reunion, she had the good fortune to sample Chef Charlie Thomas' creation at the trendy Hammond Corners Grille in Bath. She didn't have to ask for the recipe because it was published by popular demand in The Cleveland Plain Dealer. Smaller cakes make a delightful appetizer or first course and made a bit larger, they become an intriguing entree.

Black Bean Cakes

3 cups cooked black beans
½ cup heavy cream
2 eggs, lightly beaten
1 cup bread crumbs
½ pound chorizo sausage
½ cup diced green pepper
½ cup diced onion
1 teaspoon minced garlic
1 jalapeño pepper, minced
½ pound diced shrimp
1 tablespoon Old Bay seasoning *
1 teaspoon cumin
1 teaspoon thyme
½ cup sherry
Salt and pepper to taste
Oil for frying

*Old Bay is a seafood seasoning mixture found in the spice department of large markets.

Purée half the black beans with the heavy cream. Fold in remaining beans, eggs and bread crumbs. Set aside.

Brown sausage in a heavy pan; add green pepper, onion, garlic and jalapeño pepper. Cook until vegetables are tender. Add shrimp, seasonings, and sherry and cook until shrimp is thoroughly done. Cool.

Add sausage mixture to bean mixture and salt and pepper to taste. Mold into cakes, about ¼ cup mixture per cake. Pan fry cakes in hot oil until crisp outside and heated through.

Serve over Tomato Mustard Sauce (recipe follows).

Makes about 18 cakes

Tomato-Mustard Sauce

1 or 2 tablespoons oil
1 teaspoon chopped shallots
1 teaspoon chopped garlic
1 cup chopped, peeled and seeded tomatoes
1 cup tomato-vegetable cocktail
½ cup dry sherry
½ cup heavy cream
½ teaspoon tarragon
1 tablespoon cornstarch
2 tablespoons Dijon mustard
Salt and pepper to taste

Brown shallots and garlic in oil. Add tomatoes, tomato-vegetable cocktail and sherry; cook out alcohol for about 3 to 5 minutes. Add cream and tarragon. Bring to a boil, stirring. Dissolve cornstarch in about 1 tablespoon of water and add to mixture, cooking and stirring for about 5 minutes. Add mustard and season with salt and pepper.

Yields about 2¾ cups

As ECC's secretary/receptionist, Glenna Hammond has the pleasure of greeting members and guests by phone and in person. "This dish, one of my son's favorites, is relished by everyone who samples it, even non-broccoli lovers," she says. Glenna contributed much more than this recipe to the cookbook. Her computer skills were invaluable to the preparation of the manuscript.

Broccoli, Rice and Cheese Casserole

½ onion, diced
2 tablespoons butter
8-ounce jar pasteurized process cheese sauce
  (such as Cheez Whiz)
10¾-ounce can condensed cream of mushroom soup
Two 10-ounce packages frozen chopped broccoli
1½ cups cooked rice
Salt and pepper to taste
Garlic to taste
Crumbled bacon for top, if desired

Preheat oven to 350°. Saute onion in butter. Melt cheese sauce and garlic in the undiluted mushroom soup. Cook broccoli; drain well. Cook rice according to package instructions. Combine all ingredients except bacon. Pour into lightly greased 3-quart casserole. Sprinkle crumbled bacon over top. Bake, uncovered, about 30 to 45 minutes or until bubbly hot.

Serves 8 to 10

"We love this so much, we've been known to eat cold leftovers for lunch," says Liz Krezowski of Minneapolis. "In fact, it's my children's favorite holiday dish. It freezes nicely and is easily multiplied for a crowd." Since cheese has an aversion to high heat, be sure to keep burner on low during melting step.

Broccoli and Cheese Dish

16 to 20 ounces frozen chopped broccoli, thawed and drained
1 medium onion, chopped
6 tablespoons butter
2 tablespoons flour
8 ounces American cheese, cut into cubes
3 eggs, beaten
½ cup corn flakes, crushed

Preheat oven to 325°. Place broccoli in large mixing bowl. Brown chopped onion in butter. Stir in flour. Add cheese cubes. Cook over low heat, stirring until cheese is melted. (This process can be done in a microwave.) Pour cheese mixture evenly over broccoli. Mix in 3 beaten eggs. Place in 2 to 2½-quart casserole. Top with corn flakes. Bake uncovered for 1 hour.

Serves 8

"Different and easy with year-around appeal," says Liz Krezowski about her fast and fresh entry. This would adapt nicely to microwave cooking, too. Count on the colorful appearance to brighten any dinner plate.

Sweet Carrots and Green Grapes

½ cup butter
4 cups baby carrots
1 cup green grapes
1 tablespoon honey
1 tablespoon lemon juice
Salt to taste
4 mint leaves, chopped
(optional)

Melt butter in large skillet. Add carrots and turn until coated. Cover and cook until almost tender. Add grapes, honey and lemon juice; heat through.

Serves 8

A fast-fix of vitamin A from Pat Clemmer. "Everyone seems to like this," she says. No need to scrape tender baby carrots — another bonus for busy cooks. Perfect to accompany an entree that requires a boost of color.

Microwaved Orange-Glazed Carrots

¼ cup orange juice	¼ teaspoon salt
3 tablespoons honey	Dash nutmeg
3 tablespoons butter	2 teaspoons cornstarch
or margarine, melted	1 pound baby carrots

In a 2-quart casserole, combine juice, honey, butter, salt and nutmeg. Stir in cornstarch and mix well. Add carrots. Cover and cook in microwave on High 7 to 8-½ minutes. Stir once during cooking time. Let stand, covered, for 3 minutes before serving.

Serves 4 to 6

When Dr. Robert and Mary Cooper put out the welcome mat for visitors to their winter home in Arizona, Mary relies on streamlined recipes like this one to minimize kitchen duty. To avoid overcooking the cauliflower, we suggest using a fork to check the underside for doneness at least once during microwaving. The size and density of the head may alter timing by a few important minutes. To speed cooking, cut a cross about 2 inches deep in the cauliflower stem.

Quick Company Cauliflower

1 medium head cauliflower	½ cup shredded Cheddar cheese
2 tablespoons water	1 teaspoon prepared mustard
½ cup mayonnaise	1 teaspoon chopped onion

Place cauliflower in a 1-½-quart casserole with 2 tablespoons water. Cover with plastic wrap and microwave on high for 8 or 9 minutes. Mix mayonnaise, cheese, mustard and onion. Spread cheese mixture over cauliflower and microwave 1-½ to 2 minutes. Let stand 1 minute before serving.

Serves 6

Joan Hoch of Edina couldn't leave Gulliver's Restaurant in Denver without this recipe. "Even though it's last-minute, it's worth the effort," says Joan. Gulliver's served it in individual ramekins, but Joan prefers using a casserole. Tester Donna Lundstrom used fat-free cream and found that didn't detract from either flavor or texture. "It's supreme," says Donna.

Gulliver's Corn

20-ounce package frozen corn
8 ounces heavy
   whipping cream (½ pint)
2 tablespoons sugar
1 teaspoon salt

Pinch cayenne pepper
2 tablespoons melted butter
2 tablespoons flour
6 to 8 ounces freshly-grated
   Parmesan cheese

Combine corn, whipping cream, sugar, salt and cayenne pepper in saucepan. Bring to boil; then simmer just 5 minutes, stirring constantly. Preheat broiler.

Make roux with butter and flour; add to corn mixture. Mix well and remove from heat. Put in shallow ceramic or glass casserole. Sprinkle with cheese. Place under broiler until brown and bubbly. Let sit 5 minutes before serving.

Serves 6

It's the topping which transforms ordinary onions into special-occasion fare to complement most entrées. Contributor Gretchen Pracht found it very tasty with Marian Hamilton's Chicken Florentine. For best results, select onions which are firm and dry with a mild aroma.

Onions Imperial

6 medium onions
¼ cup tomato juice
2 tablespoons brown sugar
2 tablespoons melted butter

1 teaspoon salt
¼ teaspoon paprika
Dill weed

Preheat oven to 350°. Peel onions; cut in half crosswise. Place cut-side-up in single layer in 8 to 10-inch buttered baking dish. In small bowl, combine tomato juice, brown sugar, melted butter, salt and paprika. Spoon evenly over onion halves. Sprinkle with dill weed. Bake, uncovered, about 1 hour or until tender.

Serves 4 to 6

Tester Marie Lacy admires the rich flavor of Pat Meyers' variation of a homespun favorite. "Perfect for entertaining," says Marie. Terrific teamed with ham, barbecued chicken or ribs.

Country Scalloped Corn

½ cup butter, melted
2 eggs, beaten
15-ounce can
  whole kernel corn, drained
15-ounce can
  cream-style corn

1 cup light sour cream
¼ to ½ cup chopped pimiento
9-ounce box corn muffin mix
Paprika

Preheat oven to 375°. Combine all ingredients except muffin mix and paprika. Then stir in mix. Pour into greased 7 x 11-inch or 9 x 9-inch baking dish. Sprinkle paprika over top. Bake for 35 to 40 minutes or until lightly browned.

Serves 6

Jean Giroulx's recipe enhances the mild, congenial flavor of this popular pear-shaped vegetable. Available year around, eggplant should be heavy and firm for peak flavor and freshness. Tester Karen Remund of Park Rapids rated the dish "excellent" and reports it can be ready for baking in only 20 minutes.

Eggplant Casserole

2 medium eggplants
6 slices bacon
¾ cup onion, chopped
⅔ cup seasoned bread crumbs
¼ teaspoon black pepper

2 tablespoons fresh parsley,
  minced
1 teaspoon salt, or to taste
¾ cup grated sharp
  Cheddar cheese

Preheat oven to 350°. Bake eggplant 45 minutes in regular oven or cook in microwave until they can be pierced easily with fork. Cool; peel and cut into 1-inch cubes. Fry bacon in large skillet. Drain and set aside, reserving 4 tablespoons drippings. Saute onion in drippings for 1 to 2 minutes. Stir in bread crumbs. Remove from heat and stir in eggplant, parsley, salt and pepper. Crumble bacon and add to mixture. Place in buttered 2-quart casserole. Top evenly with grated Cheddar. Bake 20 to 25 minutes.

Serves 6 to 8

"An Italian original, this recipe was passed on by my daughter's great grandfather who owned a liquor store across from Yankee Stadium. It has been modified for this decade of low-fat fanatics, and my family loves it," says Diana Hedges, Director of The Edina Art Center. "As a vegetarian, I frequently experiment with veggie creations, but I always come back to this recipe." Tester Heather King, who often orders this dish at Italian restaurants, loves this homemade version.

Eggplant Parmigiana

1 medium-large eggplant, peeled
Olive oil spray
1 egg plus 1 egg white, mixed
½ cup crushed garlic-flavored crackers
½ to ¾ cup whole wheat flour
3 cups homemade or high-quality purchased spaghetti sauce *
1 pound low-fat Mozzarella cheese, shredded or sliced
6 tablespoons grated Parmesan cheese
Olive oil

*If using commercial spaghetti sauce, Diana adds one or two chopped fresh tomatoes or a 15-ounce can stewed chopped tomatoes, minced garlic to taste, one teaspoon each basil and oregano and one small onion, chopped.

Preheat oven to 375°. Slice peeled eggplant into ¼ -inch slices. Spray large cookie sheet with olive oil spray. Combine cracker crumbs and flour. Dip slices of eggplant into egg mixture and then into flour mixture. Place in single layer on cookie sheet. Bake 8 to 10 minutes. Turn slices over; continue baking another 8 to 10 minutes until lightly browned. While eggplant is baking, heat sauce until hot. Butter a lasagna pan and layer sauce, Mozzarella cheese and eggplant slices. Repeat layers, saving a little sauce and Mozzarella for the top. Finally, sprinkle dish with Parmesan and drizzle evenly with a little olive oil.

Turn oven down to 350° and bake, uncovered, 30 to 40 minutes or until thoroughly heated and top is golden brown. If additional browning is desired, turn oven to broil for a very brief time, watching carefully.

Serves 4 to 6

Fresh mushrooms, the stars of Helen Schnobrich's savory side dish, should be selected with care and used at their very freshest. Choose only those which are firm and plump with no discoloration and clean them gently by rinsing with cold water. Soaking is unnecessarily damaging to both flavor and texture.

Mushrooms Supreme

1 pound whole mushrooms,
  cleaned
½ stick butter or margarine
2 tablespoons flour
2 beef bouillon cubes or
  2 teaspoons beef bouillon

½ cup hot water
½ cup cream
⅛ teaspoon salt
Dash pepper
¼ cup bread crumbs
¼ cup Parmesan cheese

Preheat oven to 350°. Melt butter in heavy saucepan. Add mushrooms and sauté 2 minutes. Add flour; cook and stir for 2 minutes. Add beef bouillon cubes, water, cream, salt and pepper. Heat to boiling, stirring occasionally. Pour into 1½ quart buttered casserole. Mix bread crumbs and Parmesan cheese; sprinkle over mushroom mixture. Bake uncovered for 30 minutes or until bubbly. Allow to stand 5 to 10 minutes. Serve in small sauce dishes or over beef or chicken.

Serves 4 to 6

To preserve their distinctive color and crunch, the pea pods are added near the end of baking in Judy Tucker's creative combo. Heartiness from the noodles and rice eliminate any need to serve potatoes. And, it's ready to pop in the oven in ten minutes or less!

Pea Pod Medley

½ pound fine egg noodles
½ cup instant rice
½ cup butter
1 envelope dry onion
  soup mix
1 cup water
8-ounce can sliced
  water chestnuts with liquid

14½-ounce can chicken broth
4-ounce can sliced mushrooms,
  with liquid
6-ounce package Chinese pea pods
  (snow), thawed and drained

Preheat oven to 350°. In a sauté pan, melt butter. Add noodles and cook 3 to 5 minutes. Combine browned noodles with all remaining ingredients except pea pods. Put mixture in buttered 1½-quart casserole. Bake, uncovered, for 30 minutes. Stir in pea pods and cook 5 minutes more.

Serves 6

Peppers have come into their own as colorful, stand-alone side dishes. This recipe from Ellena Prickett of Naples, FL, provides a bright accent for year-around menus. Peppers are surprisingly nutritious. In fact, the red variety contains three times as much Vitamin C as citrus fruit and an impressive amount of beta carotene.

Red Pepper "Boats"

2 red bell peppers, seeded and quartered lengthwise
⅓ cup Italian-flavored bread crumbs
1 or 2 tablespoons olive oil
2 tablespoons Parmesan cheese

Preheat oven to 375°. Mix bread crumbs, olive oil and Parmesan cheese in small bowl. Sprinkle crumbs on inside of each piece of pepper, 1 to 2 tablespoons, depending on size of pepper. Place peppers crumb-side-up on cookie sheet; cover with foil. Bake 30 to 40 minutes or until tender. Remove foil last 5 minutes.

Serves 4

Here's one you've been waiting for! When ECC Executive Chef Jerry Cegla toured Wisconsin's Silver Springs horseradish plant with the Club Chef's Club of Minnesota, he was inspired to develop this recipe. "The Germans still brew their schnapps and some beers with horseradish. But at ECC, we add it to mashed potatoes!" he says.

Pub Mashed Potatoes

8 russet potatoes, unpeeled and cooked
6 ounces sour cream
3 ounces buttermilk (⅜ cup)
1 tablespoon prepared horseradish
1 tablespoon butter
1 teaspoon fresh chives, chopped
Salt and pepper to taste

Place all ingredients in large mixer bowl. Beat or hand mash until creamy and well blended.

6 to 8 Servings

"A garlic lover's delight!" says contributor Mickie Borg of Edina. "These can be prepared ahead up to point of baking and refrigerated, if desired. Just bake a little longer so they are thoroughly heated." Tester Pat Clemmer dubs the creamy texture and flavor "Deluxe."

Whipped Garlic Potatoes

8 medium potatoes, peeled	1 teaspoon garlic powder
8 ounces cream cheese, softened	1 teaspoon garlic salt
	1 cup grated Cheddar cheese
8 ounces sour cream	1 teaspoon paprika

Preheat oven to 350°. Boil and mash potatoes. In large mixer bowl, combine potatoes with cream cheese and sour cream until light and fluffy. Beat in garlic powder and garlic salt. Place potatoes in greased 2-quart casserole; top with cheese and paprika. Bake, uncovered, for 1 hour or until thoroughly heated.

Serves 8

Comfort food never tasted so good! Terry Swanson's party-perfect potatoes can be prepared several hours ahead of baking, if desired. Calorie counters can use low-fat cream cheese and substitute low-fat evaporated milk for the light cream.

Marvelous Mashed Potatoes

5 pounds red potatoes, peeled and cubed
¼ pound margarine or butter
1 cup half-and-half, divided
8 ounces cream cheese, softened
1 teaspoon onion salt
1 teaspoon seasoned salt
1 teaspoon pepper
1 teaspoon celery salt

Preheat oven to 350°. Cook and rice or mash potatoes with margarine and ½ of half-and-half. Cream the cheese with remaining half-and-half. Add seasonings to cheese mixture. Add mashed potatoes; blend until free of lumps. Place in 2 quart casserole; dot with butter and sprinkle with paprika. Bake uncovered 30 minutes.

Serves 10

"This unusual method of preparing new potatoes is delicious with barbecued steak, fish or chicken," says contributor Cynthia Quinn. "Guests always love it!" Tester Jan Brower tried it out on guests and found that "everyone wanted the recipe!" Mint's refreshing flavor combined with tender, sweet new potatoes makes this a warm weather winner.

Potatoes Fontecchio

5½ pounds new red potatoes
6 to 8 cloves garlic,
   finely minced
1 to 1½ cups olive oil

1 large bunch of fresh mint
2 tablespoons coarse kosher salt
Freshly ground pepper

Preheat oven to 350°. Scrub potatoes; prick each about 6 times with a fork. Place in shallow roasting pan and bake for 2 hours.

Prepare mint by rinsing and removing stem. Chop leaves finely. Combine garlic, oil, chopped mint, salt and pepper in bowl. Cut each potato in half; toss lightly with oil and seasoning combination. Cover potatoes with foil and let stand at room temperature for 30 to 60 minutes before serving. Serve at warm temperature; do not reheat.

Serves 8

These "saucy" potatoes have the distinction of being served on the private boat used by Theo Foss Tug Company of "Tugboat Annie" fame. Pat Stark shares the recipe for all of us to enjoy — on land or sea.

Theo Foss Potatoes

3 pounds unpeeled, small,
   new red potatoes,
   cooked and drained
10¾-ounce can condensed
   cream of mushroom soup
8-ounce package cream cheese,
   softened

2 cups dairy sour cream
1 tablespoon instant minced onion
Freshly ground pepper to taste
1 cup chopped green onions,
   including tops
10-ounce package frozen peas,
   thawed

Preheat oven to 350°. Cut cooked potatoes into ½-inch cubes. Arrange in 2 or 3-quart shallow baking dish. Combine soup, cream cheese, sour cream, onion and pepper in saucepan. Cook and stir over medium heat until smooth and heated through. Stir into potatoes. Cover and bake about 30 minutes or until heated through. Just before serving, sprinkle with green onions and peas. Do not stir.

Serves 8 to 10

As Irish as the Blarney Stone, Sheran McNulty's old-world recipe brings welcome heartiness to wintertime menus. For variety, try substituting boiled turnips for potatoes as the Irish sometimes do. You will want to have the chopped onions and cabbage at the ready so potatoes can be served piping hot.

Colcannon

3 pounds potatoes
¼-½ cup butter
Milk
1 bunch green onions or chives, finely chopped
1 pound cabbage, cooked and finely chopped
Salt and pepper

Cook and mash potatoes. Add butter and milk and beat until well creamed. Add onions or chives and cooked cabbage. Season well with salt and pepper. Serve immediately.

Serves 6 to 8

No boiling required. These potatoes are popped in the oven with subtle seasonings for pleasant pairing with any entrée. Pat Stark peels the potatoes, but if you are using fresh, new potatoes you could omit that step, if desired.

Roasted Parmesan Potatoes

1½ pounds red potatoes, peeled
3 tablespoons olive oil
¼ teaspoon salt
¼ teaspoon black pepper
2 tablespoons grated Parmesan cheese

Preheat oven to 425°. Halve or quarter potatoes so they are in approximately 1½-inch pieces. Place potatoes on a 10 x 15-inch jelly roll pan. Drizzle with the oil and sprinkle with salt and pepper. Toss to coat completely. (Potatoes should be single layer.) Bake 20 minutes. Turn with spatula and sprinkle with cheese. Bake 20 minutes longer until golden brown and tender.

Serves 4

Sheran McNulty serves this for holiday dinners or for almost any meal featuring ham or turkey. After one bite, tester Richard King said, "This is better than dessert!" An appealing alternative to the usual marshmallow-topped rendition.

Sugar-Topped Sweet Potatoes

2 cups cooked
  mashed sweet potatoes
2 tablespoons cream
2 tablespoons melted butter
¼ teaspoon paprika
Pinch of salt

TOPPING
½ cup packed brown sugar
½ cup butter
1 cup pecan halves

Preheat oven to 375°. Combined mashed potatoes with remaining casserole ingredients; blend well. Spread in buttered baking dish (about 1½-quart size). For topping, heat brown sugar and butter just until melted and well combined. Pour evenly over potato mixture. Top with a layer of pecans. Bake, uncovered, about 30 minutes or until heated through and bubbly.

Serves 6

You're certain to find this dish served on festive occasions at the Edina home of Mary and Doug Olson. "This old family recipe is great with ham, fruit salad and a green vegetable," says Mary. Occasional basting during cooking promotes attractive glazing and careful timing avoids overbaking.

Sherried Sweet Potato Casserole

Three 23-ounce cans
  sweet potatoes, drained
1 cup brown sugar
2 tablespoons cornstarch
½ teaspoon salt
¼ teaspoon grated orange peel

2 cups orange juice
½ cup raisins
6 tablespoons butter
  or margarine
⅓ cup dry sherry
¼ cup chopped walnuts

Preheat oven to 325°. Arrange potatoes in 9 x 13 pan. In saucepan, combine sugar, cornstarch and salt. Blend in orange peel and juice. Add raisins, cook and stir until thick and bubbly. Cook one more minute. Add butter, sherry and walnuts, stirring until butter melts. Pour over potatoes and bake uncovered 30 minutes.

Serves 12

Spinach is all dressed up and ready for a party in Jean Giroulx's recipe. Described as "rich, flavorful and unusual" by tester Kathy Schmid, it takes only minutes to prepare and remains attractive on the buffet table until everyone is served.

Spinach Cabrini

9 ounces spaghetti,
  cooked and drained
Two 10-ounce packages
  frozen spinach,
  thawed and drained
¼ pound mushrooms, sliced
¼ cup onion, diced
½ cup margarine, melted

Dash of oregano
¼ teaspoon salt
¼ teaspoon pepper
4 cups shredded
  Monterey Jack cheese
¾ cup Parmesan cheese
2 cups light sour cream

Preheat oven to 350°. In large bowl, combine all ingredients. Spread into 9 x 13-inch pan. Bake uncovered for 1 hour.

Serves 8 to 10

Tester Lynda Oliver praises the "soufflé-like texture" of Judy Tucker's favorite holiday side dish. "To make ahead, combine all ingredients except eggs and flour," Judy advises. "Then, just before baking, mix in those two final ingredients and turn into casserole." Another tip? Be sure spinach is thoroughly thawed and drained.

Serbian Spinach

32-ounce carton
  small curd cheese
¼ cup butter or margarine
  cut in small pieces
4 ounces Cheddar cheese
  cut in small pieces
  or shredded

3 eggs, beaten
Two 10-ounce packages
  frozen chopped spinach,
  thawed and drained
¼ teaspoon salt
3 tablespoons flour

Preheat oven to 350°. Put cottage cheese, butter, Cheddar cheese, drained spinach, beaten eggs and salt into large bowl; mix well. Blend in flour. Turn into well-greased 3-quart baking dish. Bake, uncovered, 1 hour or until egg-cheese mixture is set.

Serves 8

Jan Nelson combines delicate summer squash with ingredients which enhance rather than overpower the flavor of this notably American vegetable. For peak flavor and texture, select small to medium-sized squash which are firm, brightly-colored and unblemished. They may be as close as your garden (or your neighbor's)!

Summer Squash Supreme

2 pounds small, tender
   summer squash
Salt
1 cup sour cream
2 egg yolks, beaten
   (reserve whites)
2 tablespoons flour

2 egg whites, stiffly beaten
1½ cups shredded
   Cheddar cheese
4 slices bacon,
   cooked and crumbled
½ cup bread crumbs
Butter

Preheat oven to 350°. Slice squash; boil in salted water until tender. Drain and mash with electric mixer. In a separate bowl, gently combine sour cream, egg yolks, flour, egg whites, cheese and bacon. Layer squash and egg mixture in a greased 1½ quart baking dish. Top with bread crumbs. Dot with butter. Bake, uncovered, for 30 minutes.

Serves 8

No matter how you spell it, this recipe from Sue Schmidt is indeed "excellent" according to tester Mary L. Miller. Its versatility makes it adaptable as a side dish, brunch feature or vegetarian entrée. Sue reports that leftovers reheat well in the microwave.

Eggsellent Zucchini

2 cups sliced zucchini
⅓ cup sour cream
8 eggs, beaten
1½ teaspoons seasoning salt
1½ teaspoons seasoned pepper

1 large tomato, sliced
5 pieces pre-sliced pasteurized
   process cheese food,
   such as Velveeta

Preheat oven to 350°. Place zucchini in bottom of a lightly greased 8 x 8-inch pan. Whisk sour cream into beaten eggs until thoroughly blended. Whisk in salt and pepper. Pour egg mixture over zucchini. Bake 20 to 25 minutes until set, but not dry. Remove from oven. Place a layer of tomato slices over baked mixture. Layer cheese on top. Return to oven approximately 5 minutes, or until cheese melts.

Serves 4 to 6

A gardener's delight from Sheran McNulty with the accent on fresh tomatoes and herbs. Judy Tucker tested it on friends and raved,"Everyone loved it!" Mozzarella and Fontina are mildly-flavored Italian cheeses, one creamy in color and the other golden yellow. Fontina's subtle sweetness makes it an excellent choice for fondues and to serve as a dessert cheese.

Fresh Tomato Pasta

2 to 3 pounds tomatoes, cored, seeded and diced
½ cup each fresh basil and parsley, shredded
1½ teaspoons salt
1 large clove garlic, chopped
1 cup Ricotta cheese, brought to room temperature

2 tablespoons whipping cream
Freshly ground pepper
2 ounces (½ cup) Fontina cheese, diced
2 ounces Mozzarella, diced
1 cup Parmesan cheese
2 tablespoons olive oil
1 pound penne pasta

Combine tomatoes, basil, parsley, salt and garlic. Mix and let stand at room temperature. In another bowl, fluff Ricotta cheese with a fork. Add cream and pepper. Mix in Fontina and Mozzarella. Let stand at room temperature. Cook pasta. Put pasta in heated bowl. Mix in oil. Add cheeses and mix. Serve with tomato mixture over pasta.

Serves 6

Jazz up those frozen vegetables with just a few enhancing ingredients. Thanks to Judy Tucker's mother, Verna Melius, for sharing one of her daughter's childhood favorites. It's easily doubled for buffet service.

Swiss Vegetable Medley

16-ounce bag frozen California vegetable mix, thawed (cauliflower, broccoli and carrots)
10¾-ounce can cream of mushroom soup
1 cup grated Swiss cheese, divided

⅓ cup sour cream
1 jar chopped pimiento
2.8-ounce can french fried onions
5-ounce can sliced water chestnuts
¼ teaspoon pepper

Preheat oven to 350°. Combine vegetables, soup, sour cream, ½ cup of the grated cheese, pepper, pimiento, and ½ can french fried onions. Pour into 1-quart greased casserole. Bake covered for 30 minutes. Top with remaining cheese and onions and bake uncovered 5 minutes longer.

Serves 4 to 6

A trio of vegetables bathed in a quickly-mixed sauce becomes a go-with-everything casserole. Terri Gulliford tried Virginia Krusell's recipe for Thanksgiving and even though she doubled the ingredients, "not a drop remained," she reports. "It was so well-liked, we plan to make it part of traditional holiday menus from now on."

Vegetable-Cheese Casserole

10-ounce package frozen cauliflower
10-ounce package frozen brussels sprouts
10-ounce package frozen chopped broccoli
10¾-ounce can condensed cream of mushroom soup
10-ounce jar pasteurized process cheese sauce
2.8-ounce can French fried onion rings

Preheat oven to 350°. Cook vegetables half the recommended time; drain. Place in buttered 2-quart casserole. Heat cream of mushroom soup and cheese sauce over low heat until well blended and cheese is melted. Pour evenly over vegetables; sprinkle with onion rings. Bake 30 to 45 minutes, or until bubbly.

Serves 8 to 10

Jean Giroulx turns to this recipe to serve as a sumptuous side for enchiladas and beans. Tester Mary Mulheran had it oven-ready in just 30 minutes, and suggests using canned, chopped jalapeño peppers when time is short. Low-fat sour cream and cheese can be successfully substituted if you're waist-watching.

Green Chili Rice

3 cups cooked rice (1 cup uncooked)
3 cups sour cream
1 or 2 jalepeño peppers, chopped
¼ cup chopped onions
½ teaspoon cumin
½ to 1 teaspoon salt
¾ pound Monterey Jack cheese, cut in strips

Preheat oven to 350°. Combine sour cream, peppers, onions, cumin and salt. Butter 1½ quart casserole dish; layer rice, sour cream mixture and cheese in 2 layers, ending with cheese. Bake, uncovered, 45 minutes or until heated through.

Serves 8

Before Mary Richardson moved to Williamsburg, Virginia, she was an active ECC member and served as President of the Women's 18-Hole Golf League. She was also the first woman elected to the ECC Board of Directors. She sends a satisfying side dish which reflects her Lebanese heritage and is compatible with a host of entrées.

Lebanese Rice

¼ stick butter or margarine
7-ounce package vermicelli
1 cup uncooked white rice
½ teaspoon salt
2¼ cups water

Melt butter over low heat. Break vermicelli into small pieces. Stir with butter until brown. Add rice, salt and water. Stir until boiling. Reduce heat to low. Cover and let cook (so it's still steaming) for 15 minutes. Do not lift lid during cooking.

Serves 4 to 5

Julian Plante, Ph.D., favors recipes like this one for entertaining so he can be with his guests as much as possible. "This is a wonderful Boeuf Bourguignon accompaniment and one serving contains only 8 grams of fat!" he says. Julian credits Cafe Carabella in the Airport Hilton for the basic recipe to which he has added more celery to suit his taste.

Wild Rice Chasseur

1⅛ cups uncooked wild rice
1 medium carrot, finely-diced
½ cup diced onion
½ cup diced celery
½ cup sliced mushrooms
1½ cups chicken stock

Preheat oven to 375°. Select 1-quart casserole dish with tightly-fitting lid. Coat pan with non-stick spray. Combine all ingredients except chicken stock in dish. Pour stock over rice mixture. Mix slightly. Cover. Bake for 45 minutes or until rice is tender and stock is absorbed.

Serves 4

A potpourri of potent spices turn up the heat in this snappy side dish. Transform into a main dish by adding additional ground pork and serve with a tossed green salad and plenty of iced tea or chilled Mexican beer. Tester Mary L. Miller commented on the "wonderful cooking aroma" and adds, "My husband had three helpings!"

Rio Grande Rice

¼ pound ground pork
2 tablespoons butter
½ cup each chopped onion,
   green pepper and celery
1 to 2 cloves garlic, chopped
2 bay leaves
1½ teaspoons salt
1½ teaspoons pepper
1½ teaspoons paprika
1 teaspoon cumin
½ to 1 teaspoon
   cayenne pepper
1 teaspoon dry mustard
½ teaspoon thyme
½ teaspoon oregano
¾ cup uncooked rice
14¾-ounce can chicken broth

Preheat oven to 350°. Brown pork in large saucepan; drain excess fat. Add butter and vegetables; sauté until tender. Add seasonings and rice. Stir in broth; bring to boil. Pour into 2 to 3-quart casserole. Cover and bake about 20 minutes or until heated through. Remove bay leaves before serving.

Serves 3 to 4

Terry Swanson uses a wok instead of a skillet for preparing this saffron-sparked dish. Arborio rice, found in most larger supermarkets, is a starchy white Italian native. The cooked consistency is pleasantly creamy because the round grains absorb up to five times their weight in liquid during cooking. Saffron, famous for its priciness as well as its flavor and bright yellow color, is derived from a particular species of crocus.

Risotto Classic

¼ teaspoon ground saffron
1 cup dry white wine
5 cups chicken broth,
   heated
¾ cup butter
1 small onion, chopped
2 cups arborio rice
1 cup grated Parmesan cheese
1 tablespoon chopped parsley
Salt and pepper to taste

In a small bowl, combine saffron and wine. Melt butter in large, deep skillet. Over moderate heat, sauté onion for 4 minutes. Add rice and sauté 2 minutes. Add wine and saffron; cook 2 minutes. Add chicken broth 1 cup at a time, stirring constantly until absorbed. Do not add more broth until each addition is absorbed. Stir in Parmesan and parsley. Season with salt and pepper as desired. Serve immediately.

Serves 6 to 8

ECC's fruit and nut-studded stuffing can be baked in a casserole or used as a stuffing for poultry, game, veal, pork or fish. Port, a blended sweet wine from Portugal, and rosemary, a piney-tasting herb, add character. Rosemary packs a punch if overdone, so use in moderation.

ECC Wild Rice Stuffing

½ cup golden raisins
5 tablespoons tawny port
½ pound pancetta or bacon
1 small onion, finely chopped
2 carrots, finely chopped
2 stalks celery, finely chopped
2 cups uncooked wild rice

1 teaspoon crumbled rosemary
1 bay leaf, crumbled
½ teaspoon crumbled thyme
3 cups chicken stock
½ unpeeled
    Granny Smith apple, diced
½ cup toasted almonds

Combine raisins and port in small bowl; let stand one hour. Meanwhile, sauté pancetta or bacon in heavy skillet until crisp; remove with slotted spoon. Cool slightly and crumble. Add onions, carrots, celery and rice to drippings in skillet. Cook just until vegetables are tender. Add herbs and chicken stock. Cook, covered, until rice has opened and all moisture is absorbed, 30 to 35 minutes. Stir in apple, toasted almonds and crumble pancetta or bacon. Use as a stuffing or bake in covered casserole at 350° for about 20 minutes or until piping hot.

Makes approximately 10 servings

Betty Palecek of Edina cherishes this recipe handed down by her German grandmother. "It's very popular in Bavaria and marries nicely with almost any entrée." says Betsy. German cuisine offers a variety of dumplings — some are used in soups and others, like spaetzle, are frequently gilded with rich gravies, sauces or meat drippings.

Bavarian Spaetzle

10½-ounce box spaetzle
½ pound Swiss cheese, diced

1 small onion, chopped
¼ pound butter or margarine

Cook spaetzle according to package directions. While the dumplings are cooking, melt butter or margarine in small frying pan. Add chopped onions; cook until almost blackened. Drain cooked spaetzle; put in a bowl. Sprinkle Swiss cheese on top and top with butter and onions. Let sit for about 2 minutes. Then toss until cheese is stringy and butter-onion mixture coats spaetzle evenly.

Yield: About 4 servings

Entrées

Company coming? Don't panic! Reach for this elegant ECC entrée that can be swiftly prepared while your guests are enjoying the final few minutes of the cocktail hour. Note that the butter can be clarified ahead of time. Ready your side dishes and have dinner plates warming so everything can be served piping hot when people are seated.

Pan-Seared Beef Filet with Spicy Tomato Marmalade

Eight 4 to 5-ounce beef filets
1½ tablespoons clarified butter, divided*
¾ cup chopped onions
1 teaspoon minced garlic
1 teaspoon minced fresh jalapeño pepper
2 cups diced fresh tomatoes
3 tablespoons honey
2 tablespoons cider vinegar
1 teaspoon cracked black pepper
Salt to taste

*To clarify butter, melt in small pan. When white solids float to surface, skim them off. Use only clear butter remaining. This can be done ahead of time.

Preheat oven to 325°. Heat skillet with ½ tablespoon butter to the smoking stage. Add filets and sear on both sides. Remove and place on a broiler rack prepared for the oven and bake for no more than 5 minutes.

While the filets are in the oven, add remaining butter to the already hot skillet. Add onions, garlic and jalapeños. Stir fry about 3 minutes. Add remaining ingredients; cook for an additional 2 minutes. Spoon over filets and serve.

Serves 8

Pour a full-bodied red wine, light the candles and set the scene for first-class presentation of an inviting ECC entrée. As tester Susan Fee remarked after trying the recipe, "It makes a very special dinner for two." The term "Chasseur" signals the fact that mushrooms and tarragon are key ingredients. Lovely with twice-baked potatoes and a colorful vegetable.

Sautéed Filet with Chasseur Sauce

Two 8-ounce center cut beef tenderloin filets
½ cup clarified butter*
Salt and pepper

SAUCE
½ cup butter, divided
1 teaspoon chopped shallots
1 cup fresh peeled and diced tomatoes
1 cup sliced fresh mushrooms
½ cup white wine
1 cup demi-glaze (bottled brown gravy)
1 teaspoon chopped fresh tarragon
Salt and pepper to taste

*To clarify butter, melt in small pan. When white solids float to surface, skim them off. Use only clear butter remaining. This can be done ahead.

Sauté beef in clarified butter to medium rare. Remove and keep warm. Drain excess fat from pan. For sauce, add ¼ cup of the fresh butter and the chopped shallots. Cook 1 minute. Add tomatoes and cook 1 minute. Add sliced mushrooms and white wine; cook until reduced to a syrup. Add gravy and cook until reduced. Remove from heat. Add tarragon, remaining ¼ cup fresh butter and salt and pepper to taste.

Serves 2

We thank Louise Saunders for evoking fond memories of Charlie's Café Exceptionale, a cornerstone of Minneapolis cuisine for many years. Fork-tender beef cubes mingle with seasonings and vegetables for a dish which tantalized thousands of loyal diners. After testing, Mary L. Miller said, "A must for inclusion in the cookbook — it's excellent!" "Serve with wild rice or rice pilaf," suggests Louise.

Charlie's Sliced Peppered Tenderloin Casserole

2 pounds sliced tenderloin tips
¼ pound butter, divided
2 tablespoons olive oil
1 teaspoon salt
1 teaspoon coarse crushed black peppercorns
Pinch sage
Pinch cumin powder
1 pound fresh mushrooms, quartered
2 garlic cloves, finely chopped
1 medium onion, cut into eighths
2 green peppers cut into 1-inch pieces
2 peeled tomatoes cut into eighths
2 tablespoons tomato paste
½ cup soy sauce
2 tablespoons vinegar

Heat half the butter and half the oil in large skillet. Sauté tenderloin tips. Season with salt, pepper, sage and cumin. Cook meat to medium rare. Transfer to large casserole. Reheat skillet with remaining butter and olive oil. Sauté mushrooms to golden brown. Add garlic, onions and green peppers; cook until about half done. Add tomatoes and remaining ingredients. Cook until tomatoes are heated through.

Preheat oven to 400°. Add vegetable mixture to meat in casserole. Mix lightly, cover and heat thoroughly in oven for approximately 15 minutes to marry the flavors. Be careful not to overcook. Vegetables should remain firm and colorful.

Serves 6 to 8

Mickie Borg begins marinating the meat for this tempting grilled entrée 8 hours before serving. To retain the beef's firm consistency, be sure to purchase a 2 to 3-inch steak so the marinade doesn't penetrate too deeply. Perfect with fresh sweet corn, sliced garden tomatoes and your favorite potato salad.

Grilled Pepper Steak

3 to 4 pounds sirloin steak, 2 to 3 inches thick

<u>MARINADE</u>
¾ cup red wine vinegar
½ cup corn oil
2 tablespoons instant minced onion
2 teaspoons leaf thyme
1 teaspoon marjoram
1 bay leaf
3 tablespoons cracked pepper
2 tablespoons unseasoned meat tenderizer
2 cloves garlic, minced
3 tablespoons lemon juice

Combine all marinade ingredients. Pour over sirloin in non-metallic pan. Cover and refrigerate 8 to 12 hours, turning occasionally.

Slash edges of steak every 2 inches to prevent curling. Grill to desired doneness (10 to 20 minutes per side, depending on thickness). Slice across the grain to serve.

Serves 6 to 8

Another day, another dinner? Well, it won't be boring when you serve this snappy beef-veggie duo. Contributor Dorothy Roskam adds a side of rice and passes additional soy sauce. If regular tomatoes aren't in their prime, substitute a pint of flavorful cherry tomatoes. Tester Peggy Dodge suggests additions of fresh ginger and minced garlic for variety.

Steak Oriental

4 teaspoons olive oil
1 large green pepper, cut into ¼ x 2-inch strips
1½ cups bias-cut celery pieces (about 3 large stalks)
1 to 2 pounds stir-fry beef (precut at the supermarket)
10½-ounce can beef broth
6 tablespoons soy sauce
½ can water
6 tablespoons cornstarch
2 teaspoons sugar
4 tablespoons cold water
2 medium tomatoes, skinned and cut into wedges
4 cups cooked rice

In hot oil, cook green pepper and celery until tender crisp. Remove from skillet. Brown beef in same skillet. Add beef broth, soy sauce and ½ can water. Cover and simmer for about 45 minutes or until tender. Combine cornstarch, sugar and 4 tablespoons cold water. Add to skillet. Cook and stir until thickened. Stir in reserved celery, green pepper and the tomato. Heat through. Serve over rice. Pass additional soy sauce, if desired.

Serves 4 to 6

"Berry tasty" trimmings of herbs, spices and cranberries give pot roast a whole new flavor boost. Thanks to David Kennedy of Thyme to Spare Personal Chef Service in Chanhassen, MN, for sharing a versatile entrée which can be prepared in the oven or stove-top. Make the most of the rich gravy by serving with noodles or mashed potatoes.

Cranberry-Beef Pot Roast

Nonstick cooking spray
½ cup flour
¼ teaspoon black pepper
2½ pounds top round
   beef roast
2 cups beef broth
1 cup red wine
1 tablespoon vinegar
Grated rind and juice of
   1 medium orange
16-ounce can whole berry
   cranberry sauce
1 medium carrot, sliced

2 medium onions,
   coarsely chopped
2 tablespoons molasses
1 bay leaf
2 teaspoons garlic powder
1 teaspoon freshly-ground
   black pepper
½ teaspoon powdered thyme
¼ teaspoon ground cinnamon
1 cup fresh cranberries
Gravy flour (such as Wondra) for
   thickening, as desired

Spray a deep braising pan with vegetable oil spray. Combine flour and pepper in a plastic bag. Add the beef and shake to coat with flour. Brown the coated meat on all sides in braising pan. Add the broth, wine, vinegar, orange rind and juice, cranberry sauce, carrots, onions, molasses, bay leaf, garlic powder, pepper, thyme and cinnamon to meat in pan. Cook on stove top 2 hours or until fork tender. If preferred, it can be covered and cooked in a 350° oven until tender. About halfway through cooking, add the fresh cranberries and continue cooking.

When cooking time is up, remove bay leaf and roast from pan. Stir in a tablespoon or two of flour. Place pan over medium heat; cook and stir until slightly thickened.

When roast has cooled about 15 minutes, cut into slices and serve with sauce spooned over. Or, layer into freezer container with sauce divided and spooned over each portion.

Serves 6 to 8

We all love recipes which are "tried and true" and this is just that. Julian Plante, Ph.D., has been making this French classic for two decades. He notes that white bacon or side pork may be used for regular bacon and it is unlikely you will need to thicken the sauce. Tester Pat Meyers had the meat cubed by the butcher and she served a side dish of wild rice. "The cooking aroma of the Bourguignon is almost as wonderful as the finished product," she comments.

Slow Cooker Boeuf Bourguignon

6 strips bacon cut in ½-inch pieces
3 pounds beef rump or chuck, cut into 1½-inch cubes
1 large carrot, peeled and sliced
1 medium onion, sliced
1½ teaspoons salt
¼ teaspoon pepper
3 tablespoons flour
10-ounce can condensed beef broth
1 tablespoon tomato paste
2 cloves garlic, minced
1 teaspoon whole thyme
1 whole bay leaf
½ pound white onions, peeled
1 pound fresh mushrooms, sliced
½ cup red or Burgundy wine
¼ cup flour
2 tablespoons butter, softened

Cook bacon in large skillet until crisp. Remove and drain. Add beef cubes and brown well. Place browned beef cubes in electric slow cooker. Brown carrot and onion. Season with salt and pepper. Stir in flour. Add broth, mix well and add to slow cooker. Add cooked bacon, thyme, tomato paste, garlic, bay leaf and onion. Cover and cook on low setting 8 to 10 hours. Sauté mushrooms in two tablespoons butter. About 1 hour before serving, add mushrooms and wine to slow cooker.

If you wish, to thicken sauce, turn slow cooker on high. Cream flour and butter. Roll into pea size balls and drop into slow cooker. Bring to boil and let thicken.

Serves 6 to 8

This practical slow cooker creation from Nancy Lindahl of Lake Minnetonka boasts a rich sweet-sour sauce to rival the flavor of any fine gourmet ragout. For variety, replace the hollowed-out bread option with ribbon noodles or rice. Nancy has brought her vigor and vision to many volunteer leadership positions in the Twin Cities.

Slow Cooker Sweet and Sour Stew

1 to 3 tablespoons vegetable oil
2 pounds round steak, cut into 1" chunks
2 cups chopped onions
2 cups carrots, cut in ½" slices
2 cups sliced celery, cut in ½" slices
15-ounce can tomato sauce
½ cup cider vinegar
½ cup light corn syrup
1 teaspoon prepared mustard
¼ cup firmly packed brown sugar
2 tablespoons quick-cooking tapioca
2 teaspoons chili powder
2 teaspoons paprika
½ to 1 teaspoon salt
½ to 1 teaspoon ground black pepper
6 small round loaves sourdough bread

In large skillet, heat oil and cook meat until browned, 4 to 5 minutes. Place meat in electric slow cooker. Stir in onions, carrots, celery, tomato sauce, vinegar, corn syrup, mustard, brown sugar, tapioca, chili powder, paprika, salt and pepper. Mix well. Cover and simmer on high for 4 to 6 hours or until meat is tender. To serve, cut off tops of bread with a thin, sharp knife. Tear out soft doughy insides of bread and set aside. (Serve along with the meal or freeze bread for stuffing.) Place bread on plate or in bowl and ladle stew into bread to overflowing.

Serves 6 to 8

The charm of this lusty dish from June Smith is preparation ease. Just combine ingredients and bake. Ample sauce makes reheating possible for evenings when everyone is on a different dinner schedule. June's husband, Glenn, is an Edina City Council member.

French Oven Stew

2½ pounds stew meat, cubed
12 small white onions, peeled
3 large ribs of celery,
   cut into 1-inch pieces
16-ounce package
   fresh peeled mini carrots
1½ cups tomato juice

½ cup dry red wine
¼ cup quick-cooking tapioca
1 tablespoon sugar
½ teaspoon dried basil
¼ teaspoon pepper
Salt to taste

Preheat oven to 300°. Put all ingredients in a Dutch oven and cover. Cook 3 hours, stirring once each hour.

Serves 10

Minnesota wild rice goes global in this Asian-inspired taste treat from Jan Collins. Conveniently, you can have most of the ingredients on hand. Just pair with a spinach-mandarin orange salad and ring the dinner bell.

Asian Beef-Rice Casserole

1½ pounds lean ground beef
1 cup uncooked wild rice
1 cup chopped onion
1 cup chopped celery
10 ¾-ounce can condensed
   cream of mushroom soup
8-ounce can sliced
   water chestnuts, drained

4-ounce can sliced
   mushrooms, drained
½ cup soy sauce
Salt and pepper to taste
1 can crunchy
   chow mein noodles

Preheat oven to 350°. Combine all ingredients thoroughly except chow mein noodles. Spoon mixture into oven-to-table casserole. Top evenly with chow mein noodles. Bake, uncovered, 1 hour.

Serves 6

Family and guests will simply inhale June Randall's economical skillet supper with the rich flavor of the pricier version. No pre-cooking of noodles which means just minutes until mealtime and one less pan to wash. A helpful suggestion from tester Annette Nelson to lower sodium content — add just one crumbled bouillon cube and omit salt addition entirely. And, using low-fat sour cream is always an option to reduce calories.

Beef-Noodle Stroganoff

¼ cup butter or margarine
¼ cup sliced green onions or chopped onion
1 minced clove garlic
1 pound sliced mushrooms
1 pound very lean ground beef
3 tablespoons Burgundy or other dry red wine
3 tablespoons lemon juice
10¾-ounce can condensed beef broth, undiluted
2 bouillon cubes, crumbled
½ teaspoon salt, or to taste
¼ teaspoon pepper
¼ pound (2 cups) medium noodles
1 cup sour cream
Snipped parsley

Melt butter in skillet. Sauté onions, garlic and mushrooms until lightly browned. Add meat, cooking and stirring, until red color disappears. Stir in Burgundy, lemon juice, beef broth, bouillon cubes, salt and pepper. Simmer, uncovered, 15 minutes. Stir in uncooked noodles. Cook, covered, 5 to 7 minutes or until noodles are tender. Mix in sour cream; heat quickly, but do not boil.

Serves 6

"I've adapted this heirloom recipe from one often made by my great-grandmother, Mary Lloyd," explains Mary Lloyd Miller. "My two grown children and six grandchildren can be counted on to request it when they come to visit," she adds. The long, slow simmering serves to thicken the mildly-flavored sauce and blends flavors beautifully for optimum enjoyment.

Great Grandmother's Spaghetti Sauce

2 tablespoons butter or margarine

1½ large onions, cubed

3 cloves garlic, minced

1½ to 2 pounds lean ground beef, crumbled

½ teaspoon salt

¼ teaspoon black pepper

1½ cups diced celery

1 large green pepper, diced

8-ounces fresh mushrooms, sliced
  (may substitute 4 ounces canned)

28-ounce can whole peeled tomatoes and juice, cut up

6-ounce can tomato paste

½ cup Burgundy or other dry red wine

¼ teaspoon hot pepper sauce

3 medium bay leaves, crumbled

Parmesan cheese, grated or shredded

Pasta of choice

Melt butter or margarine in a Dutch oven or large kettle. Brown onions and garlic. Add crumbled hamburger and brown; drain fat. Sprinkle meat with salt and pepper. Add all remaining ingredients and mix well. Bring to a low boil, stirring often. Reduce heat, cover kettle and simmer gently for 2½ to 3 hours, stirring every ½ hour or so. (Sauce will thicken, but not lose the "saucy" quality.) Serve over pasta.

Serves 10

This old-world entrée has endured for generations without wearing out its welcome. Virginia Krusell's version is excellent served with a side of rice so not a drop of the tomato-rich sauce is lost. Paring the center vein of the large cabbage leaves as instructed contributes to appealing overall tenderness. The leftover inner leaves will make a crisp slaw or savory soup for another meal.

Sweet and Sour Cabbage Rolls

One head green cabbage
1 pound lean ground beef
12 soda crackers, crushed
½ teaspoon lemon juice
1 medium onion, grated or minced
1 egg
1 teaspoon sugar

FOR SAUCE:
¾ cup sugar
3 tablespoons water
Juice of 1 lemon (2 to 3 tablespoons)
10½-ounce can condensed cream of tomato soup
About 2 cups stewed tomatoes, broken up with spoon,
    partially drained
2 medium onions, peeled and sliced
2 medium carrots, pared and sliced

Start heating large pot of salted water. Cut around core of cabbage to loosen leaves. Drop at least 8 large, outer leaves into boiling water. (Reserve rest for another use.) Parboil 3 to 4 minutes, until starting to soften. Drain. With peeler or small knife, pare thick center vein of leaf down to thickness of leaf. Stir together beef, crushed crackers, the ½ teaspoon lemon juice, egg and 1 teaspoon sugar. Place one-eighth of meat mixture (about ½ cup) in center of each leaf. Fold in sides, then roll into neat package. Place in single layer in greased baking dish.

Preheat oven to 350°. For sauce: Boil ¾ cup sugar and water together until soft crack or thread state, 270° to 288° on candy thermometer. Combine this syrup with tomato soup, stewed tomatoes, onions and carrots. Pour tomato mixture over rolls in pan. Cover and bake 30 to 35 minutes. Remove cover and bake another 30 minutes.

Serves 4 to 6

A midwestern accent exchanges beef for lamb and eliminates the layering step. But the featured eggplant and tomato will remind you of the traditional dish. Round out this nutritious, low-fat entrée with a Greek salad and seasoned flat bread, suggests contributor Heather King.

Minnesota-Style Moussaka

1½ pounds lean ground beef
1 medium onion, chopped
3 tablespoons olive oil
1 medium to large eggplant
14½-ounce can diced tomatoes, undrained
8-ounce can tomato sauce
⅓ cup dry red wine
1 cup shredded Parmesan cheese, divided
4 tablespoons snipped fresh parsley
1 teaspoon salt
¼ to ½ teaspoon seasoned pepper

Preheat oven to 350°. In large skillet, brown ground beef with chopped onion. Drain well. Peel eggplant; cut into 1-inch cubes. Heat olive oil. Add eggplant cubes. Cook briefly, stirring, until eggplant is softened. Add tomatoes, tomato sauce, wine and drained beef and onion. Simmer briefly, stirring to combine. Add ½ cup Parmesan, parsley, salt and pepper. Turn mixture into an ungreased 2-quart casserole. Top with remaining Parmesan. Bake, uncovered, 30 to 45 minutes or until bubbly and heated through.

Serves 6 to 8

Helen Schnobrich of Edina shares a favorite recipe of husband Don, who served as ECC president in 1985. "The sauce which bakes on the bottom of the loaf and the addition of ginger makes this a bit different," says Helen, who usually serves it with baked potatoes and a medley of carrots and peas. "It's great sliced cold for sandwiches, too," she adds.

Heartland Meat Loaf

½ cup brown sugar
½ to ¾ cup ketchup
1½ pounds lean ground beef
¾ cup milk
2 eggs, beaten

¾ cup crushed crackers
1 small onion, chopped
1 teaspoon salt
¼ teaspoon ground ginger
Pepper

Preheat oven to 350°. Grease loaf pan. Press brown sugar on bottom of pan. Spread ketchup over sugar. Combine remaining ingredients until well mixed. Place in pan over sugar and ketchup. Bake, uncovered, for one hour. Turn loaf out onto serving platter.

Serves 6 to 8

Mary Morton found that one of the perks of serving on the Cornelia Elementary School PTA Board was being privy to the monthly minutes in which Opal Posingies, secretary, always included a recipe. "This is one of her best!" notes Mary. Part of the sauce is blended with the meat mixture to produce a moist, flavorful loaf.

Opal's Meat Loaf

1 pound extra lean
  ground beef
2 eggs
1 cup crisp toasted rice cereal
Chopped onion to taste

SAUCE
¼ cup ketchup
3 tablespoons brown sugar
⅛ teaspoon mustard
⅛ teaspoon nutmeg

Preheat oven to 350°. In a large bowl, mix the ground beef, eggs, cereal and onion. Combine sauce ingredients; simmer a few minutes. Add ¼ of sauce to meat mixture; blend well. Pack into a 4 x 8-inch loaf pan. Top with remaining sauce. Bake for 1 hour.

Serves 4

Britton A. Goetze, Jr., harks back to the early 1900's for this adaptation of his Swedish grandmother's crowd-sized recipe. "The more you eat, the more you want," he confides. He emphasizes the importance of dusting the meat mixture with flour before rolling into meatballs. "It is impossible to shape them without this step." Britton adds accompaniments of white rice or wide noodles, green beans and a tossed salad.

Britt's Swedish Meatballs

3 pounds lean ground beef
1 pound regular ground beef
2 large eggs, well beaten
1 cup whole milk
1 cup fine dry bread crumbs
2½ to 3 tablespoons brown sugar
1 large onion, finely chopped
1 teaspoon salt
1 teaspoon nutmeg
¾ teaspoon cardamom
½ teaspoon each allspice, ginger and ground cloves
½ teaspoon pepper
½ teaspoon grated lemon peel
6 tablespoons butter
Flour for dusting meatballs
2 cups half-and-half

Preheat oven to 325°. In large bowl, combine ground beef, well beaten eggs, and all ingredients (except butter, flour and cream). Work together with fingers thoroughly. (It will be quite soft). Using two large spoons, drop mixture in mounds about 1½ to 2 inches in diameter onto waxed paper. Dust with flour; roll with palms of hands into balls. Melt butter in heavy skillet. Brown/sauté until evenly browned. Transfer meatballs to roaster or large casserole. Add cream and bake 35 to 40 minutes.

Serves 20 to 24
Yield: 60 to 64 meatballs

In a household with four sons and one or more friends frequently on hand for dinner, Maryanne Herman of Edina hit a home run with this dish. "The neighborhood moms requested the recipe and it became known as 'Johnny's Casserole'," she recalls. "It features easy one-skillet preparation and is great with a tossed salad or coleslaw."

Johnny's Hot Dish

1½ pounds lean ground beef
1 medium onion, diced
10¾-ounce can cream of tomato soup
1½ cans water
15-ounce can cream style corn
½ pound pasteurized process cheese food (such as Velveeta, shredded or diced)
8 ounces egg noodles

In large skillet, brown beef with onions. Drain off fat. Add tomato soup and water. Add egg noodles. When noodles are soft, add corn and half the shredded cheese. Preheat oven to 350°. Put meat mixture in 13 x 9-inch casserole; top with remaining cheese. Bake 45 minutes, or until cheese is melted.

Serves 6

This hot and hearty sandwich is sure to have everyone at the dinner table asking for seconds. When Mary Morton tested Pat Clemmer's recipe on the family, her son described these Sloppy Joes as "the best we've ever had!" And, don't kids always tell it like it is?

North Woods Sloppy Joes

1 pound lean ground beef
1 large onion, finely chopped
2 tablespoons sugar
2 tablespoons prepared mustard

1 tablespoon vinegar
1 teaspoon salt
¾ cup ketchup
Hamburger buns

Brown ground beef and onion in skillet. Drain fat. Add sugar, mustard, vinegar, salt and ketchup. Simmer for 30 minutes, stirring occasionally. Serve over buns.

Serves 4

Mary Schrock's family enjoys the Tex-Mex flavor and Mary appreciates the ease of preparation. Tester Terry Swanson suggests adding chopped onion and minced garlic to the meat mixture and using low or no-fat sour cream. We like it embellished with a lettuce and guacamole salad in keeping with the southwest theme.

Baked Taco Treat

1¼ pounds lean
  ground beef
1½-ounce package
  taco seasoning
½ cup water
8-ounce can
  refrigerated crescent rolls

2 cups crushed corn chips,
  divided
2 tomatoes, diced
1 cup sour cream
1 cup shredded Cheddar cheese

Preheat oven to 375°. Brown ground beef; drain well. Add taco seasoning and water; simmer for 5 minutes. Pat rolls into a greased 9-inch pie pan for the "crust." Sprinkle 1 cup of the corn chips over crust. Add meat. Top with diced tomatoes. Spoon sour cream evenly over top. Cover with cheese and top with remaining 1 cup chips. Bake 20 to 25 minutes, or until filling is bubbly and crust is brown.

Serves 4 to 6

Aprés skiing, skating, snowmobiling or for children's birthday parties, "these are just great," says contributor Dorothy Roskam of Edina. The chilling step builds in make-ahead convenience, leaving only simple assembly and baking before serving.

Pizza Burgers

1½ pounds lean
  ground beef
½ small onion,
  finely chopped
1 teaspoon sage
½ teaspoon salt

15-ounce can pizza sauce
8-ounce package
  shredded Mozzarella cheese
1 cup finely-diced
2 dozen hamburger buns

Brown ground beef, onion and spices. Drain off excess fat. Chill meat mixture. Mix in cheese and pizza sauce.

Preheat oven to 350°. Halve hamburger buns. Place cut-side-up on baking sheet. Spread meat mixture sparingly over each half. Bake for 15 to 20 minutes or until cheese melts and bun is crispy.

15 to 20 servings

Don't worry about wind chill. Turn up the heat with a piping hot bowl of ECC Pub Chili. Top with grated Cheddar if you wish and bake one of our corn bread recipes for a go-along. If you're serving a crowd, why not cool down with a make-your-own-sundae bar for dessert?

Club Pub Chili

1 pound lean ground beef
1 small onion, diced
1 small red pepper, diced
1 small green pepper, diced
16-ounce can tomatoes, diced
8-ounce can tomato sauce
½ cup tomato juice
16-ounce can chili beans
1 small clove garlic, chopped
1 teaspoon sugar

Pinch of oregano
¼ teaspoon chili powder
⅛ teaspoon paprika
⅛ teaspoon cumin powder
⅛ teaspoon chili pepper
¹⁄₁₆ teaspoon dry red
    pepper flakes
Pinch of cayenne pepper
Salt and pepper to taste

Brown beef to medium doneness; drain excess fat by half. Return to heat; add vegetables. Continue to cook until beef is evenly browned. Add remaining ingredients and simmer about 20 minutes or until flavors are blended.

Serves approximately 6 to 8

When you're hankering for hamburgers and it's parka weather outside, opt for Debbie Dimmock's indoor oven-baked variety. "The sauce is just delicious," claims tester Romona Tokheim. To avoid spattering or over-browning of burgers, you may want to cover pan with foil during last part of baking.

Barbecued Hamburgers

1 pound lean ground beef
1 cup cracker crumbs
½ cup milk
1 teaspoon salt
1 teaspoon pepper
2 tablespoons sugar

2 tablespoons vinegar
4 tablespoons
    Worcestershire sauce
1 cup ketchup
1 cup water
5 to 6 drops Tabasco sauce

Preheat oven to 350°. Combine ground beef, cracker crumbs, milk, salt and pepper. Form into 4 to 6 patties and brown well in frying pan. Place in baking dish.For sauce, combine sugar, vinegar, Worcestershire sauce, ketchup, water and Tabasco sauce. Cover meat patties evenly with sauce. Bake, uncovered, for 1 hour.

Serves 4 to 6

The rich cream (rather than tomato) base of this ECC pasta dish denotes its northern Italian origin. Since most of the Italians who settled in Minnesota and the U.S. as a whole emigrated from southern Italy, we are more accustomed to red sauces. Enjoy this sausage-sparked taste trip to the Val d' Aosta, Piedmont and Liguria provinces.

Fettuccine with Spinach, Sausage, and Roquefort Cream Sauce

1 pound fresh fettuccine
2 tablespoons olive oil
4 ounces spicy Italian sausage, freshly ground
2 cloves of garlic, chopped finely
8 ounces sliced mushrooms
4 ounces fresh spinach
2 cups heavy cream
4 ounces Roquefort or bleu cheese
2 teaspoons Dijon mustard
¼ cup coarsely chopped walnuts
Salt and pepper to taste

Cook pasta to al dente. Set aside and keep warm. Heat oil; add sausage and garlic. Cook until nearly done. Add mushrooms and spinach to pan; heat until limp. Add cream, cheese, mustard and walnuts. Cook, stirring, until cheese melts. Stir in pasta, salt and pepper. Serve immediately.

Serves 4 to 6

With a tip o' the hat to Edina's Irish settlers, here's a sweet-sour rendition of that popular St. Pat's Day favorite. You don't have to be from the Shamrock Isle to enjoy this recipe which originated with a <u>Los Angeles Times</u> food editor and is contributed by Heather King.

Peachy Corned Beef

3 to 4 pound corned beef brisket
Several bay leaves
1 medium onion, chopped
1 tablespoon prepared mustard
¼ cup brown sugar
Whole cloves
1 can spiced peaches, undrained (approximately 2-pound size)

Place brisket in large kettle; cover with water. Add bay leaves and onion. Cover pot and simmer 3 to 4 hours or until meat is very tender. Preheat oven to 325°. Remove meat from water and place in baking pan. Remove all fat. Make a paste of mustard and brown sugar. Spread mixture evenly over meat. Insert cloves at intervals. Drain peaches, reserving syrup. Pour syrup over and around meat. Bake for 1 hour, basting periodically with syrup. To serve, place brisket on platter and garnish with spiced peaches.

Serves 6 to 8

The traditional flavors you savor in the famous sandwich are neatly layered in a quickly-assembled casserole from Jan Collins. Small crescent-shaped caraway seeds are popular in European cooking in everything from breads to desserts, but most frequently are found in cabbage and sauerkraut dishes.

Reuben Casserole

1¾ cups sauerkraut, drained
½ pound cooked corned beef, thinly sliced
2 cups shredded Swiss cheese
3 tablespoons Thousand Island dressing
2 medium tomatoes, thinly sliced
2 tablespoons butter (optional)
½ cup butter
½ teaspoon caraway seed (optional)
1 cup seasoned Rye Krisp crumbs

Preheat oven to 425°. Butter a 1½ quart casserole. Thinly layer sauerkraut in bottom of casserole. Top with corned beef, then cheese. Dot salad dressing over top. Add tomatoes and dot with 2 tablespoons of butter. Melt ½ cup butter in small saucepan; sauté crumbs. Add caraway and spread over top of tomatoes. Bake 30 minutes or until thoroughly heated.

Serves 4

Mary Morton discovered this orange-kissed entrée while vacationing in Naples, FL. "The cooking aroma is tantalizing and seconds were in demand," recounts tester Julian Plante, Ph.D. He suggests using chops which are slightly thicker than usual (not the stuffing type) and very lean. In a mere 10 minutes, these are oven ready.

Nifty Naples Pork Chops

4 lean loin or rib pork chops,   ¼ cup brown sugar
   ¾-inch thick   1 teaspoon dry mustard
1 cup orange juice   ¼ teaspoon lemon pepper

Preheat oven to 350°. Place pork chops in 8-inch square baking dish. Mix remaining ingredients and pour over chops. Cover with foil. Bake for 30 minutes. Then, uncover and bake another 30 minutes.

Serves 4

"A wonderfully easy recipe with delicious flavor," says tester Jan Collins after sampling Pat Meyers' contribution. American consumers now enjoy pork that is considerably lower in fat, calories and cholesterol than it was a decade ago. And, it's a fine source of B vitamins and other important nutrients like iron, zinc and high-quality protein.

Pork Chops in Orange-Wine Sauce

4 thick pork chops,   1½ cups orange juice
   trimmed of fat   ½ cup white wine
Oil   ¼ cup brown sugar, packed
2 tablespoons butter   1 teaspoon salt, or to taste
1 tablespoon flour

Preheat oven to 350°. Brown chops in oil; drain. In saucepan over medium heat, cook and stir butter and flour until golden brown and thick paste forms. (Be careful not to scorch mixture.) Slowly stir in orange juice and wine. Cook and stir over low heat until thick. Add sugar and salt. Place chops in shallow casserole; pour sauce over. Cover and bake for 45 minutes or until chops are tender. Serve the chops with the remaining sauce.

Serves 4

Former Edina Country Club members, Helen and Sandy Couper, now enjoy sharing recipes with Jacksonville, FL, friends. Ever the gourmet cook, Helen transforms simple pork chops into a special entrée with a spicy wine glaze.

P.D.Q. Pork Chops

4 well-trimmed boneless pork loin chops
¾ to 1 cup dry white wine
2 teaspoons ground allspice
1 cup (or more) sliced mushrooms

Place chops in a skillet just large enough to hold them. Pour in just enough wine to reach the tops of the chops. Sprinkle each chop with ¼ teaspoon allspice. Cover skillet loosely and simmer chops 25 minutes. Turn chops over and again sprinkle each with ¼ teaspoon allspice. Simmer for another 25 minutes. Add sliced mushrooms to skillet. Remove cover from skillet and increase heat to cook down wine sauce. Continue cooking for about 10 minutes.

Serves 4

Sue Schmidt "curries" the favor of family and friends with this India-inspired entrée. "This same recipe works well with boneless, skinless chicken breasts and is tasty accompanied by white rice and a colorful vegetable," says Sue. Tester Karen Remund tried it using fat-free half-and-half and found that although her children were skeptical about the curry flavor, "they ended up enjoying it just as much as the adults." Using thick chops which require the full baking time will allow ample time for the sauce to thicken.

Pork Chops Indienne

1 tablespoon margarine
2 pounds center cut, boneless pork chops (6 to 8)
1 small onion, minced
1 green pepper, minced
6 medium apples, finely chopped
1½ teaspoons seasoned salt
1½ teaspoons seasoned pepper
4 cups half-and-half
3 tablespoons curry powder, or to taste
1 tablespoon paprika
2 chicken bouillon cubes
Cooked rice

Melt margarine in large pan or electric skillet. Brown chops on both sides. Cover with onion, green pepper, apples, salt and pepper. Pour half-and-half over all. Mix in curry powder and paprika. Break bouillon cubes into sauce. Cover and simmer for 2 hours or until chops are tender. (Timing will vary depending on thickness of chops.) Serve with rice.

Serves 6 to 8

Lean, tender cubed lamb is christened with traditional middle-eastern flavorings for a "favorite winter entrée" at the North Oaks home of Marjorie and John Kugler. Only simple accompaniments are needed — fluffy rice and a crisp green salad. "A special company dish where much of the work can be done ahead," comments tester Mary L. Miller.

Lamb-Eggplant Ragout

3 large eggplants
Salt
½ cup raisins
⅓ cup red wine vinegar or 2 tablespoons Balsamic vinegar
3 to 4 pounds lamb
½ cup olive oil
2 large onions, quartered or small frozen tiny onions
2 large cloves garlic, chopped
2½ pounds tomatoes, diced
1 tablespoon honey
1 large pepper diced
1 tablespoon cinnamon
1 cup parsley, chopped
1 tablespoon small capers

Heat oven to 350°. Peel and cut eggplant into 1½-inch squares. Sprinkle with salt and let set for 30 minutes. Drain off liquid. Combine raisins and vinegar. Set aside for 30 minutes. Cube lamb into 1½-inch cubes. Brown in olive oil. Transfer to large casserole.

Dry skillet and add 1 tablespoon olive oil. Cook eggplant about 12 minutes or until browned and softened. Add eggplant, onions, garlic, tomatoes, honey, pepper and cinnamon to casserole; mix gently. Bake, uncovered, for 1 hour. Use parsley and capers to garnish before serving.

Serves 10 to 12

Surprise dinner guests with an authentic east Indian blend of exotic and familiar flavors and an inviting aroma to greet them at the door. "This is a great dish to prepare a day in advance of serving," confides contributor Betty Bajwa. Tester Gretchen Pracht tried it out on friends from India and they all rated it "excellent!"

Punjabi Lamb (Spicy Indian Lamb)

4 cloves garlic, diced
1 medium-hot green chili, seeded (optional)
2-inch piece fresh ginger, peeled and chopped
4 tablespoons vegetable oil
2½ cups finely chopped onion
1 teaspoon turmeric
1¼ teaspoons chili powder
1 teaspoon ground cumin
1½ teaspoons ground coriander
Pinch of nutmeg

1-pound boneless lamb, cut into 1-inch cubes
3-inch cinnamon stick
2 bay leaves
½ teaspoon salt, or to taste
3 fresh medium tomatoes, diced
1 teaspoon garam masala*
1 tablespoon fresh lime juice
¼ cup fresh coriander leaves, chopped (cilantro)
Basmati rice

*Garam masala, which means "hot mixture," is a combination of ground spices. It may be found at Asian food stores or large supermarkets which carry specialty items.

In a blender, combine garlic, chili and fresh ginger. Process until smooth; set aside. In a large saucepan, heat the oil over medium-high heat. Add the onions and cook, stirring frequently, about 15 minutes or until dark golden brown. Stir in turmeric, chili powder, cumin, ground coriander and nutmeg; cook 30 seconds, stirring occasionally. Reduce heat to medium. Add the garlic mixture, and mix together for 30 seconds. Add the lamb, cinnamon, bay leaves and salt; cook 15 minutes, or until lamb is well browned. Add 1 to 3 tablespoons of water if necessary to prevent mixture from sticking to the pan. Reduce heat to low. Add tomatoes and cook, covered, for 1¼ to 1½ hours, or until lamb is tender. Add water if necessary to prevent mixture from sticking to pan. Stir in the garam masala and cook 5 minutes. Just before serving, stir in lime juice. Sprinkle with fresh coriander and serve with basmati rice.

Serves 4 to 6

ECC chefs skillfully combine complementary flavors of lamb and mint with fresh vegetables and other seasonings for a rewarding repast. Shank meat from the leg is the most popular cut to cube for stews such as this. This recipe offers the option of stove top or oven cooking for the final step.

Minted Lamb Stew

2 pounds 1-inch cubed lamb stew meat, well trimmed
⅛ cup butter
⅛ cup olive oil
½ cup diced onion
½ cup diced celery
½ cup diced carrot
½ cup sliced mushrooms
¼ cup diced bell pepper
1 clove garlic, minced
¼ cup mint apple jelly
1 tablespoon chopped fresh mint
¼ tablespoon EACH thyme and basil
Salt and pepper to taste
A roux made from ½ cup oil and 1 cup flour

In large kettle, heat butter and olive oil. Add cubed meat; cook to rare stage. Add onion, celery, carrots, mushrooms, green pepper and garlic. Cook until vegetables are barely tender. With a slotted spoon, remove meat and vegetables from pan; set aside. Bring liquid in pan to a simmer. Add jelly, mint, thyme, basil, salt and pepper. Prepare roux in separate pan by cooking oil and flour until slightly brown. Add a little roux at a time to liquid, stirring and heating until sauce is thickened to desired consistency. Return meat and vegetables to pan. Simmer for 45 minutes or until meat is cooked. Or, place combined meat, vegetables and sauce in large casserole. Bake at 350° for 1 hour or until done.

Serves 6 to 8

The ECC kitchen presents this lamb chop and mushroom entrée with rosemary and garlic-seasoned red potatoes and a seasonal vegetable. The presentation is first class and the flavor medley is a big hit with lamb aficionados. Thanks to modern breeding methods, lamb today is leaner and more tender than ever.

Lamb Chops Brossard

12 loin or rib lamb chops, 1½ inches thick	8 ounces fresh mushrooms, quartered
Salt and pepper	¼ cup heavy cream
4 beaten eggs	½ cup seasoned brown sauce
1 cup bread crumbs	Mint jelly
8 ounces butter	

Trim chops of any fat. Season with salt and pepper. Dip in beaten eggs and then in bread crumbs. Melt butter in skillet. Sauté chops until nicely browned on both sides, about 4 minutes. Meanwhile, simmer mushrooms and cream briefly in saucepan until slightly thickened. Heat seasoned brown sauce. To serve, arrange chops in a crown or other decorative manner on serving dish. Fill crown center with mushrooms and cream. Border chops with brown sauce and add a small spoonful of mint jelly on the side for garnish.

Serves 4 to 6, depending on size of chops

When you're stressed and the family is starving, stir up this ECC chili, toss a salad and heat up some sourdough rolls. Presto! Dinner is ready in no time. Ground lamb, like ground beef, should be stored in the coldest part of the refrigerator and used within two days after purchasing.

Spicy Lamb and Black Bean Chili

1 pound lean ground lamb	Three 8-ounce cans black beans, drained
½ cup diced onion	
½ cup diced green pepper	14-ounce can diced or whole tomatoes, undrained
¼ cup diced celery	
2 teaspoons chili powder	13-ounce can chicken broth
2 teaspoons ground cumin	Two 4-ounce cans chopped green chilies, undrained
½ teaspoon cayenne	

Brown and crumble meat with onions, peppers and celery. Drain well; add all remaining ingredients. Bring to a simmer and continue cooking for about 30 minutes.

Serves 6 to 8

Adelaide Callan and her family "enjoy this change of pace from the usual turkey for holiday menus." Meat should be ordered ahead with a request to have the two pork loin strips shaped into a "crown." Note that there are two baking steps for roast — one before stuffing is added and one after. Very impressive results with minimal effort!

Crown Roast of Pork with Savory Stuffing

6 to 7 pounds pork loin; two strips containing 16 ribs
Salt, pepper and thyme to taste.

SAVORY STUFFING
1 pound pork sausage
4 cups fresh bread crumbs
⅔ cup milk
2 to 4 tablespoons butter
1 cup minced onion
1½ cups chopped celery
½ cup chopped raisins
½ cup chopped raw cranberries
3 to 4 medium tart apples, peeled and chopped
Salt, pepper, sage and thyme to taste

For stuffing, crumble and cook pork sausage. Drain well and set aside. Moisten bread crumbs with milk; squeeze crumbs dry. In large skillet, melt butter. Sauté onion until soft but not browned. Add remaining stuffing ingredients including sausage and bread crumbs to skillet. Cook gently 5 minutes. (Stuffing can be made ahead and refrigerated. Or, it can be made during first phase of cooking the pork.)

Preheat oven to 400°. Place crown roast in large baking pan. Sprinkle chops with salt, pepper and thyme to taste. Place an empty can, top and bottom lids removed, into cavity to keep crown in shape. Cover chop ends with foil. Bake for 20 minutes. Reduce heat to 325° and continue baking for 40 minutes. Remove meat from oven. Remove can from center. Lightly mound stuffing into cavity. Put remaining stuffing in buttered casserole dish. Return meat to oven along with extra stuffing. (Casserole of stuffing should be covered to avoid excess browning.) Bake 1 hour and 10 to 20 minutes or until pork reaches desired degree of doneness. Slice by running knife close to bone of each rib.

Serves 10 to 12, depending on serving sizes

Marde Olson describes her recipe as "easy, yet elegant" and suggests side dishes of rice or poppy seed noodles. Carol Cronk, tester, extolled the "family appeal" but added, "It is certainly special enough for guests!" When it's -30°, you might prefer using the oven preparation method kindly supplied by Carol, a home economist.

Grilled Pork Tenderloin Oriental

1½ pound pork tenderloin

MARINADE
½ cup lemon juice
¼ cup soy sauce
3 tablespoons honey
1 teaspoon chopped garlic
1 bay leaf
1 teaspoon salt
1 teaspoon pepper
½ teaspoon dry mustard
¼ teaspoon ground ginger
¼ teaspoon onion powder

Combine marinade ingredients in non-metallic container. Add pork tenderloin. Marinate in refrigerator at least 4 hours or overnight. Grill pork over medium-hot coals for 20 to 25 minutes. While pork is cooking, simmer remaining marinade until thickened, 5 to 10 minutes. Serve pork with sauce.

NOTE: To prepare in conventional oven, bake at 425° for 20 to 30 minutes per pound or until meat thermometer registers 160°.

Serves 4

Michelle Lass' brother-in-law, Rick Kettelhohn of Saginaw, MI, perks up mild pork tenderloins with a piquant bouquet of seasonings. Allow several hours for the marinating step before baking and take the guesswork out of timing by using an indispensable meat thermometer.

Curried Pork Tenderloin

Two 1-pound pork tenderloins
2 tablespoons honey
1 to 2 tablespoons curry powder, or to taste
3 teaspoons red wine vinegar, divided
2 strips bacon
¼ cup olive oil
¼ cup soy sauce
1 tablespoon grated onion
1 clove garlic, minced
½ teaspoon sugar

Place tenderloins in baking dish. Slice lengthwise about ¾ down. Combine honey, curry powder, and 2 teaspoons red wine vinegar; spoon between slices. Wrap each tenderloin with bacon strip, securing with toothpicks, using extra toothpicks along seam. Combine olive oil, 1 teaspoon red wine vinegar, soy sauce, onion, garlic and sugar; pour over meat. Wrap dish tightly with plastic wrap and marinate meat in refrigerator for 3 or 4 hours, turning meat once.

Preheat oven to 425°. Bake uncovered, seam side up, for 1 hour or until meat thermometer registers 160°. Baste frequently with marinade and pan juices. Slice into ½-inch medallions, remove toothpicks and serve.

Serves 6

Diane Lacy Harr found Gretchen Pracht's recipe "easy, inexpensive and great for entertaining." Assemble ahead, if desired, and bake starting an hour or so before serving. Country-style ribs are meatier and leaner than regular spareribs since they are cut from the shoulder end of the loin. Calorie count per serving is considerably less, as well.

Cranberry Country Spareribs

6 meaty country-style spareribs (boned or boneless)
¼ cup butter
16-ounce can whole berry cranberry sauce
¾ cup heavy cream
¾ cup apple juice
½ cup brown sugar
½ cup red wine

Preheat oven to 350°. In large frying pan, brown ribs in the butter. Remove ribs to baking dish. Stir remaining ingredients into the frying pan. Heat thoroughly about five minutes. Then, pour mixture over ribs. Cover casserole and bake for an hour or until ribs are tender. Baste frequently while baking. Serve the ribs with the sauce poured over, if desired.

Serves 4 to 6

These "extremely tender and tasty ribs" come from the kitchen of Mary L. Miller. She notes that leftovers may be topped with any remaining sauce and reheated, covered, for another meal. Ribs and sauce also may be frozen in an airtight container. Tester Annette Nelson can't wait to make them again — "this time for company."

Chinese Barbecued Ribs

3 to 4 pounds country-style pork ribs (with bone or boneless)
2 ounces butter or margarine
1 medium onion, finely chopped
2 cloves garlic, minced
¾ cup cider or red wine vinegar
¾ cup granulated sugar
¾ cup ketchup
¼ cup soy sauce
½ teaspoon ginger, ground
½ teaspoon hot pepper sauce
1 tablespoon cornstarch

In a medium-sized saucepan, sauté onion and garlic in butter until soft. Add vinegar, sugar, ketchup, soy sauce, ginger and pepper sauce. Stir to blend. Add cornstarch and stir until thickened, approximately 3 minutes. Remove from heat and let stand 5 minutes. Preheat oven to 350°. Line 11 x 15-inch pan with foil and coat with oil spray. Place ribs in single layer on foil. Baste with warm sauce. Bake, uncovered, 1½ to 2 hours, or until fork tender, turning and basting with sauce every 20 or 25 minutes. Remove to warm platter and serve with remaining sauce. Sauce may be prepared in the morning or the previous day and heated just before use.

Serves 4 to 6

"This recipe from my mother is one of Marty Lass' favorite meals," confides Lynne Kilmer, Marty's mother. "He always requests it for his birthday and other special occasions." Tester Pauline Anderson found it "one of the easiest recipes I've made and so tender, the meat just falls off the bones!"

Barbecued Ribs Par Excellence

4 to 5 pounds country-style pork ribs
Salt and pepper to taste
Garlic powder to taste
3 large onions, sliced

SAUCE
3 tablespoons vinegar
2 tablespoons Worcestershire sauce
¼ cup brown sugar
¾ teaspoon paprika
¾ teaspoon chili powder
3 to 4 drops hot pepper sauce, such as Tabasco
1 cup ketchup
¼ cup water

Preheat oven to 350°. Place ribs in roaster pan; sprinkle with salt, pepper and garlic powder. Place sliced onions on top of ribs. In medium sized bowl, combine sauce ingredients. Pour over ribs; cover and roast slowly 1½ hours until almost tender. Remove cover and cook an additional one-half to 1 hour until fork tender. Baste frequently while cooking.

Serves: 8

Count on making a grand entrance when you serve this special occasion entrée. "Elegant," comments tester Sabra Otteson. "This provides beautiful presentation as well as a very good meal," adds Chef Jerry Cegla, who suggests accompaniments of pasta or rice and fresh root vegetables. Rely on a meat thermometer for no-fail timing.

Veal Edina

6 to 9 pound veal loin, boned and trimmed
2 tablespoons kosher salt
2 tablespoons cracked pepper
2 tablespoons olive oil
¼ cup shallots, chopped
¼ cup cognac
¼ cup Balsamic vinegar
½ teaspoon 5-spice powder
2 tablespoons honey
½ cup heavy cream
1 pound fresh Morel mushrooms, sliced
   (reserve some for garnish)
1 pound drawn butter

Preheat oven to 350°. Rub the roast with kosher salt and cracked pepper. Sear in hot skillet with olive oil. Reserve drippings. Remove veal to roasting pan. Bake uncovered to 140° internal temperature, about 1 hour. Remove roast and let stand. In same pan, sauté shallots in pan drippings. Add cognac, Balsamic vinegar, 5-spice powder, honey and cream. Reduce by half. Add Morels. Cook 2 minutes and add butter. Slice veal roast into ½-inch slices, dress with sauce and garnish with reserved mushrooms.

Serves 10 to 12

A Minnesota favorite festively presented to ECC diners. The savory butter can be prepared the day before so flavors blend. "Try both stuffing and butter with bass as well as walleye," urges Jerry Cegla, Executive Chef.

Stuffed Walleye with Herb Butter

Four 8-ounce walleye fillets

STUFFING

1 tablespoon canola oil
1 teaspoon garlic, finely diced
1 jalapeño pepper, seeded and diced
2 tablespoons diced onions
8 dinner rolls, diced
2 tablespoons toasted pine nuts

SAGE BUTTER

½ cup butter, softened
3 scallions, finely minced
3 tablespoons fresh sage leaves, chopped
2 tablespoons lemon juice
½ teaspoon paprika
½ teaspoon salt
½ teaspoon black pepper

Gently rinse fillets; pat dry with paper toweling. Place fillets in single layer in buttered baking dish. Preheat oven to 350°. For stuffing, heat oil. Add garlic, jalapeño and onion; cook until transparent. Add diced rolls and toasted pine nuts. Cook until heated through. Top each fillet with a portion of stuffing. Bake fillets for 10 to 12 minutes.

For sage butter, combine all ingredients thoroughly. Form into a long roll surrounded by plastic wrap. Refrigerate. Cut off portions just before serving; place one slice atop each baked fillet.

Serves 4

An epicurean delight! This ECC recipe tops fresh salmon with a forcemeat, a well-seasoned finely-chopped or minced mixture used in a variety of ways — as a stuffing, in patés and for garnishes. A creamy sauce is spooned over the elegant but easy entrée.

Salmon Olympia

3-pound side of fresh salmon
Thinly-sliced onions
Fresh tarragon sprigs
White wine
¼ cup heavy cream

FORCEMEAT

11 ounces well-trimmed halibut
½ cup heavy cream
1 egg white
½ teaspoon salt
½ teaspoon chopped dill weed
½ teaspoon tarragon leaves, blanched

Preheat oven to 375°. In a food processor combine forcemeat ingredients just until thickened. Do not overprocess. Place salmon in a buttered baking dish. Spread forcemeat evenly over the top. Cover with a layer of sliced onions and tarragon leaves. Add a small amount of white wine. Cover dish with foil and bake approximately 20 to 30 minutes or until fish is firm and flakes easily with a fork. Remove salmon to heated platter; keep warm. Combine pan juices and ¼ cup cream in saucepan. Cook over low heat, stirring, until slightly reduced. Cut salmon into 10 to 12 portions; top with cream sauce.

Serves 10 to 12

Julian Plante, Ph.D., offers a delicately-flavored company casserole for shrimp lovers. Plus, he tosses in two important cooking tips. A splash of olive oil added to boiling water keeps vermicelli strands from sticking. And, watch boiling time very carefully so pasta is not fully cooked before baking step.

Shrimp Elegante

1 thinly sliced green onion
½ cup butter, divided
5 tablespoons flour
2½ cups chicken broth
½ cup clam juice
½ cup dry white wine
½ cup heavy cream
½ teaspoon oregano
½ cup freshly-grated Parmesan cheese, divided
4 whole cloves garlic
½ pound fresh mushrooms, sliced
8 ounces vermicelli
4 cups extra-large shrimp, cooked and shelled

Preheat oven to 375°. Sauté green onions in ¼ cup butter. Mix in flour. Blend in chicken broth, clam juice, white wine, cream and oregano. Simmer 3 minutes. Stir in ¼ cup Parmesan cheese. Set aside. Melt remaining ¼ cup butter. Add garlic and mushrooms; sauté quickly.

Cook vermicelli in boiling salted water until just barely done. Rinse and drain pasta; combine with sauce and shrimp. Pour mixture into a 9 x 13-inch oven-to-table casserole. Top evenly with remaining Parmesan. Bake uncovered until bubbly, about 30 minutes.

Serves 6 to 8

The firm, relatively dry texture of swordfish makes it ideal for marinating and grilling. In this ECC rendition, it is complemented with bacon and colorful cherry tomatoes. A very tasteful departure from the usual barbecued fare and rated "excellent" by tester Peggy Bishop.

ECC Swordfish Kebobs for Two

¾ pound swordfish, cut into 1-inch cubes
1 large garlic clove, finely chopped
2 teaspoons lemon juice
½ teaspoon grated lemon zest
2 teaspoons virgin olive oil
8 to 10 large extra-thick bacon strips
1 dozen firm, ripe cherry tomatoes

In non-metallic container, combine swordfish with chopped garlic, lemon juice, zest and olive oil. Refrigerate up to 30 minutes. Cook bacon slices until soft, pliable and beginning to brown. Alternate swordfish, bacon and cherry tomatoes on skewers. Cook over hot coals for approximately 3 to 4 minutes on each side.

Serves 2

Beverly Soshea, a Florida transplant, remembers the "fun of driving my two daughters down to John's Pass on St. Pete's beach to buy fresh shrimp from the fleet of fishermen." A registered dietitian now in marketing with 3M, Beverly favors festive and fast skillet entrées like this one, fashioned for a busy lifestyle.

St. Pete's Shrimp Creole

1 clove garlic, diced
½ teaspoon salt
3 tablespoons butter
1 tablespoon flour
1 pound raw shelled shrimp
2 ounces tomato paste
1 small onion, diced
1 small green pepper, diced
¹⁄₁₆ teaspoon cayenne pepper
¼ teaspoon thyme
Bay leaf
¼ cup hot water
Dry white wine
Cooked rice

In skillet, crush garlic with salt to a paste consistency. Add butter and melt. Add flour gradually, stirring to a smooth paste. Cook slowly about 5 minutes or until mixture browns, stirring constantly. Add shrimp and stir until coated with flour mixture. Stir in tomato paste. Add onion, green pepper, cayenne, thyme, bay leaf and water. Cover pan and cook gently, about 10 minutes. Thin sauce with additional water or wine. Serve with cooked long grain rice.

Serves 2 to 3

Colorful company fare with partial make-ahead possibilities from Heather King. She serves a simple rice side dish so as not to detract from the mild but distinctive entrée flavors. If there is too much sauce for your taste, use a slotted serving spoon. Or, drizzle the extra sauce over the rice.

Greek Shrimp Bake

2 medium onions, chopped or thinly sliced
3 tablespoons olive oil
14½-ounce can diced or quartered tomatoes, undrained
½ cup chopped fresh parsley
2 cloves garlic, chopped (or to taste)
½ teaspoon salt
¼ teaspoon pepper
1 pound medium uncooked shrimp, shelled and deveined
10-ounce package frozen peas, thawed and drained
8 ounces Feta cheese, crumbled

Over medium heat, sauté onion in olive oil until tender. Stir in tomatoes, parsley, garlic, salt and pepper. Reduce heat to low, cover pan and gently simmer mixture for 20 minutes, stirring periodically. Preheat oven to 375°. Remove sauce from stove; stir in shrimp and peas. Transfer mixture to shallow oven-to-table 8 x 8-inch baking dish; sprinkle evenly with crumbled Feta cheese. Bake, uncovered, for 20 to 30 minutes. (Overcooking will toughen shrimp, so test for doneness when bubbly and thoroughly heated.)

Serves 4

Charlotte Tudor can count on guests requesting "seconds" when she offers this baked seafood salad. "I serve it in medium-sized shells for luncheons. It's as attractive as it is delicious," she remarks. Tester De Evenson, ECC's Banquet Pantry Supervisor, used the seafood mixture to fill puff pastry-lined muffin tins and transformed the versatile recipe into appetizers.

Shrimply Divine

1 cup cooked,
   deveined shrimp
1 cup cooked, flaked
   crab meat, rinsed
   and drained
1 cup celery, chopped
1 cup mayonnaise
¾ cup onion, minced

½ cup chopped green pepper
1 teaspoon
   Worcestershire sauce
½ teaspoon salt
Bread crumbs
Dots of butter
Paprika
Lemon slices

Preheat oven to 300°. If shrimp are large, cut into smaller pieces. Combine first 8 ingredients; mix well. Place mixture in individual baking shells or other individual baking dishes. (Fills about 9 to 11 medium shells.) Top evenly with bread crumbs, dot with butter and sprinkle with paprika. Bake, uncovered, for about 30 minutes. Serve with slices of lemon.

Serves 4

Tuna salad for grown-ups! Shirley Bard enlivens the "same old" with a few uncommon companions and ends up with an appealing blend of flavors and textures. Just ask tester Margy Schaller of Bloomington who proclaimed it "a very satisfying lunch with only ten minutes of effort." Try it on bagels topped with sprouts — yum!

Tuna Croissants

6-ounce can
   water-packed tuna
¼ cup apples, chopped and
   unpeeled, mixed with
   few drops lemon juice
   to prevent browning
¼ cup mayonnaise
¼ cup chopped pecans or walnuts

¼ cup golden raisins, chopped
1 tablespoon honey
½ teaspoon prepared
   horseradish
Alfalfa sprouts, if desired
4 small to medium croissants

Drain tuna; flake with a fork. Combine with remaining ingredients. Use as filler for croissants or other sandwich buns.

Serves 4

You are bound to stir up mouth-watering memories when you combine the familiar ingredients for Kay Bach's homey recipe. Bake potatoes along with the salmon loaf and add a green vegetable. Then, sit down and savor a nutritious, satisfying family supper.

Old-Fashioned Salmon Loaf

14½-ounce can salmon,   1 tablespoon melted butter
   drained and flaked   1 tablespoon chopped parsley
2 eggs, slightly beaten   Dash of salt and pepper
1 cup milk   Lemon wedges for garnish
1 cup seasoned bread crumbs

Preheat oven to 350°. Combine all ingredients and mix thoroughly. Shape into loaf and bake in buttered 9 x 4½-inch loaf pan. Set in pan of water to bake. Bake for 35 to 40 minutes. May serve with white sauce if desired.

Serves 4

Three generations of cooks have been making this for Christmas dinners in Marlys Wahlberg's family. Tester Bonnie Damkroger "found it delicious for a special treat when fresh oysters are available." Delicately-flavored gifts from the sea, oysters are complemented by mild seasonings which don't overpower.

Scalloped Oysters

3 cups coarse cracker crumbs   ½ teaspoon salt
½ pound melted butter   ⅛ teaspoon pepper
1 pint fresh,   ¼ teaspoon nutmeg
   small-sized oysters,   ¼ cup oyster liquid
   drained (reserve liquid)   2 tablespoons milk

Preheat oven to 450°.Combine cracker crumbs and butter. Place in thin layer over bottom of an ungreased 9-inch square baking dish. Alternate layers of oysters and crumb mixture, sprinkling each layer evenly with seasonings. (Use only 2 layers of oysters.) Combine oyster liquid and milk; pour evenly over oysters. Top with remaining cracker crumbs. Bake, uncovered, for 30 minutes.

Serves 6

Trendy, contemporary seasonings highlight Karen Gaasedelen Herman's southwestern-style roasted chicken. Carry out the theme with a green chile and rice bake, your favorite fruit and jicama salad and warm tortillas or corn bread. Even Lena and Ole will say olé!

Tex-Mex Roast Chicken

¼ cup nonfat yogurt
1 tablespoon chili powder
2 teaspoons cider vinegar
1½ teaspoons minced garlic
1 teaspoon each ground cumin, dried oregano and salt
1 whole broiler-fryer chicken (3 to 3-1/2 pounds)
   skin and wings removed

Preheat oven to 350°. Line a jelly roll pan with foil for easy cleanup. Lightly grease a rack to fit in pan. Blend all ingredients except chicken in a small bowl. Rub evenly over chicken. Tie legs together with string. Place chicken, breast-side-up, on rack in roasting pan. Roast 1 hour, or until drumsticks move easily and juices run clear when thigh is pierced. Let stand at least 5 minutes before carving.

Serves 4

If you love garlic you're bound to relish this ECC gem. And, the cooking aroma will sweep you off your feet! Marinating begins up to six hours before baking, and fresh herbs work their magic right through the roasting process.

Roast Chicken with Rosemary and Garlic

2½ pound broiler-fryer chicken, halved or quartered
1⅕ cups olive oil
8 to 10 large cloves of garlic, chopped
3 tablespoons chopped fresh rosemary
2½ tablespoons chopped fresh thyme
Salt and pepper to taste

Combine oil, garlic and seasonings in large glass dish. Add chicken and marinate 4 to 6 hours. Preheat oven to 450°. Remove chicken; place skin-side down in a roasting pan. Strain oil; sprinkle garlic and herbs evenly over chicken pieces. Bake, uncovered, approximately 50 minutes or until done.

Serves 4

Cynthia Quinn finds this subtly-flavored entrée "wonderful for holiday serving because of the colorful additions of red and green." "Beautiful presentation," remarks tester Gene Gaasedelen. "It took only 30 minutes to ready for baking and one could prepare it ahead up to baking step."

Supremes of Volaille

¾ cup flour
3 cloves garlic, minced
¾ teaspoon salt
¾ teaspoon pepper
1 tablespoon paprika
8 boned, skinless chicken breast halves
5 tablespoons butter
5 tablespoons olive oil
2 tablespoons chopped shallots
Pinch of sage
1 cup chicken broth
½ cup port wine
24 thin slices of avocado
1/4 cup lemon juice
24 thin wedges of tomato
Grated Parmesan cheese

Combine flour and seasonings in a large plastic bag. Add the chicken breasts one by one, lightly pounding in the closed bag. Heat the oil and butter in a skillet over medium heat. Add the floured breasts, sautéeing until golden. (It may be necessary to do this in several batches.) Place chicken in a shallow baking dish.

Add shallots and sage to skillet and sauté until lightly colored. Add broth and port wine; mix with shallots. Cook sauce gently until liquid is reduced by half. Preheat oven to 275°.

Dip cut avocados in lemon juice. Alternate with slices of tomato for a garnish. Sprinkle with Parmesan cheese. Spoon 2 tablespoons sauce over each breast; pour remaining sauce around chicken. Sprinkle again with cheese and place dish in oven for 25 to 30 minutes or until chicken is cooked.

Serves 8

Shirley and Roy Erickson, formerly of Edina and now living in Rio Verde, AZ, serve this frequently when entertaining houseguests. "We use oranges from our own tree and serve Minnesota wild rice as the side dish," says Shirley. Expert tester Ken Galloway, ECC's Clubhouse Manager and Food & Beverage Director gave the recipe high marks for overall quality. He suggests the option of thickening ¾ cup of the pan juices with cornstarch for an accompanying sauce.

Chicken a la Orange

3 chicken breasts, skinned, boned and halved
2 oranges, peeled and cartwheel sliced
2 tablespoons orange liqueur, such as Triple Sec
2 teaspoons curry
½ teaspoon salt
Dash white pepper
1½ cups fresh orange juice
2 teaspoons Dijon mustard
2 tablespoons grated orange peel
1 tablespoon honey

Preheat oven to 350°. Sprinkle orange slices with liqueur; let stand at room temperature. Rub chicken with curry, salt and pepper. Arrange in 9 x 12-inch pan. Combine the remaining ingredients; pour over chicken. Bake covered 30 minutes. Uncover and bake 15 minutes more. Top with the flavored orange slices and serve with wild rice.

Serves 4 to 6

A dandy dinner for four when fresh raspberries debut. The ECC kitchen serves this with pasta or rice to capture the choice sauce. Tester Norine Ahmann loved the "tenderness of the chicken, flavor of the sauce and attractive appearance." If desired, sauce may be thickened.

Broiled Chicken Breasts with Raspberry-Thyme Sauce

1 cup fresh raspberries
3 tablespoons Chablis, or other dry white wine
2½ tablespoons minced fresh thyme
1½ teaspoons sugar
Four 6 to 7-ounce boneless, skinless chicken breasts
Light soy sauce
Pepper to taste

In small saucepan, crush raspberries slightly. Add wine, thyme and sugar. Simmer over medium heat until slightly thickened. Remove from heat, strain and set aside.

Rub chicken breasts with a small amount of light soy sauce. Sprinkle breasts with pepper. Broil over open flame until just done, approximately 5 minutes per side. Top with sauce.

Serves 4

"Dinner guests can't seem to get enough of this," confides Shirley Bard about her recipe. "Overnight marinating is the key to zesty flavor." Tester Jaye Vaaler halved the chicken breasts before baking to simplify serving. "Very rich and tasty," she reports.

Chicken Breasts Extraordinaire

3 whole chicken breasts
1 cup sour cream
2 teaspoons celery salt
1 teaspoon paprika
1 teaspoon salt
¼ teaspoon black pepper
1½ tablespoons lemon juice
2 teaspoons Worcestershire sauce
2 cloves garlic, minced
⅞ cup fine bread crumbs
¼ cup butter, softened
¼ cup shortening, softened

Rinse chicken, pat dry. Combine sour cream, celery salt, paprika, salt, pepper, lemon juice, Worcestershire sauce and garlic. Place chicken in non-metallic pan. Spread evenly with sour cream mixture. Cover and refrigerate overnight.

Preheat oven to 350°. Dredge marinated chicken in bread crumbs. Place in 9 x 13-inch pan. Combine butter and shortening. Spoon ½ of this mixture over chicken. Bake uncovered for 30 minutes. Spoon remaining butter-shortening mixture over chicken. Bake 15 to 20 minutes longer, or until golden brown.

Serves 4 to 6

This ECC recipe offers imaginative options. Chef Jerry Cegla suggests using favorite dried fruits, vegetables or other nuts in place of the pecans. Try raisins, cranberries, chopped spinach, mushrooms, broccoli or whatever you fancy or have on hand. Also, a creamy tarragon sauce can be served on the side, if desired.

Chicken Breasts with Celery-Pecan Stuffing

6 tablespoons butter or margarine, divided
1 medium onion, chopped
1 cup diced celery
½ cup chopped pecans
¾ cup hot water
2 cups herb stuffing mix
6 boneless breasts of chicken
Salt and pepper

Preheat oven to 400°. Melt 4 tablespoons of the butter. Sauté onion and celery until transparent; mix in pecans. Combine sautéed vegetables, nuts, hot water and stuffing mix. Form mixture into 6 oval-shaped patties. Shape chicken breasts around patties to form little "packages." Place breasts, rounded-side-up, on jelly roll pan. Brush tops of chicken with remaining butter. Sprinkle with salt and pepper. Bake 30 to 35 minutes or until juices run clear.

Serves 6

If you're tiring of usual chicken preparations, try a perked-up version with creative ECC touches — dried sweet cherries and Boursin cheese spread in the stuffing. Once chicken breasts are flattened, assembly is speedy and results succulent. Fine company fare!

Stuffed Chicken Breasts with Chardonnay Cream Sauce

Six 6 to 7-ounce boneless, skinless chicken breast halves
3 ounces Boursin cheese spread
3 ounces cream cheese, softened
Lemon juice, if needed
8 teaspoons dried sweet cherries
¾ cup flour seasoned with ¾ teaspoon salt and ¼ teaspoon pepper
Egg wash (1 egg beaten with 1 cup milk)
About 2 cups dry bread crumbs or crushed corn flakes
Chardonnay Cream Sauce (see recipe for Chicken Chardonnay)

For each stuffed breast: Pound chicken out thin and flat. Mix Boursin and cream cheese until well blended. If too thick, add a little lemon juice. Top flattened chicken with 2 tablespoons cheese mixture. Sprinkle 1 teaspoon cherries (about 8) over cheese. Fold breast over, enclosing cheese and cherries.

Set up three flat bowls of the seasoned flour, egg wash and crumbs. Dip each breast first in flour, then wash, then crumbs. Arrange in shallow pan. Bake at 350° about 30 minutes, or until juices run clear. Serve with Chardonnay Cream Sauce.

Serves 6

ECC Sous Chef Scott Rochat developed this recipe at home for his family. He reports that "they love it." So did tester Mary L. Miller who adds, "It's delicious and very rich so needs only a simply-prepared vegetable on the side." Be sure to stir constantly after adding the flour and broth for a creamy smooth consistency.

Chicken Fettuccine

2 cups water
1 tablespoon chicken bouillon granules (or 2 cubes)
2 large bone-in skinless chicken breasts
¼ cup butter
3 small shallots, minced finely
1 bulb garlic, minced finely
¼ cup flour
Reserved chicken stock
1 quart heavy whipping cream
1 cup grated Parmesan
Two 8-ounce packages fettuccine or other pastas

In medium saucepan, bring water and bouillon to a boil. Add chicken breasts. Cover and simmer until cooked thoroughly, 30 to 45 minutes. Remove chicken and cool. Reserve strained chicken stock. Separate meat and slice or dice. Melt butter in heavy pan. Add shallots and garlic and sauté until transparent. Stir in flour and cook, stirring constantly, until the paste bubbles, about 2 minutes. Add reserved chicken broth; cook and stir until sauce thickens. Whisk in cream; simmer 10 minutes, stirring frequently. Add Parmesan and simmer an additional 5 minutes. Add chicken to sauce. Serve over pasta.

Serves 4 generously

This contemporary Club combo makes cooking for one or two a treat rather than a task. And, it leaves no pesky leftovers to clutter the refrigerator. In fact, you can use up dibs and dabs of vegetables and poultry if you wish. A side of fresh fruit and one or two crusty rolls round out the supper or lunch.

Capellini Primavera

1 teaspoon olive oil
¾ cup broccoli flowerettes, steamed
½ small tomato, diced
2 ounces sliced mushrooms
1 ounce black olives, sliced
1 ounce artichoke hearts, halved
1 teaspoon minced garlic
3 ounces pesto sauce
2 ounces Parmesan cheese
4 ounces fresh angel hair pasta, cooked al dente
8 ounces cooked chicken breast

Sauté vegetables and garlic in olive oil until tender. Add pesto, Parmesan and hot pasta. Toss to combine. Top with chicken breast.

Serves 1 for dinner, 2 for lunch

When the theme was "Desert Classic" at an annual ECC Guest Day, this southwestern entrée won raves. Each serving is only 236 calories, another reason for an appreciative audience. Pass additional picante sauce and serve with rice and a fresh fruit salad. A simple sorbet and sugar cookie dessert tops off the menu.

Country Club Chicken Roll-Ups

4 whole chicken breasts, skinned, halved and boned
  (about 2 pounds)
4 canned whole green chili peppers, halved and seeded
3 ounces Monterey Jack cheese, cut into 8 strips
¾ cup fine dry bread crumbs
1 tablespoon chili powder
1 to 1½ teaspoons ground cumin
¼ teaspoon salt
¼ teaspoon garlic powder
¼ cup skim milk
4 cups shredded lettuce
½ cup bottle picante sauce
¼ cup plain low-fat yogurt or dairy sour cream

Preheat oven to 400°. Trim excess fat from chicken. Place each chicken breast half between 2 sheets of plastic wrap. With flat side of meat mallet or rolling pin, flatten to ¼- inch thickness. Place 1 green chili pepper half and 1 cheese strip in center of each; roll up lengthwise, tucking edges under. Secure with toothpicks. Combine bread crumbs, chili powder, cumin, salt and garlic powder. Dip chicken rolls in milk, then in bread crumb mixture, coating well. Place chicken in well-greased 12 x 8 x 2-inch baking dish. Bake about 30 minutes or until chicken is done. Place each chicken roll on ½ cup shredded lettuce; top with 1 tablespoon picante sauce and 1½ teaspoons yogurt. Serve immediately.

Serves 6

They will crow over this down-home dish which originated with Terri Gulliford's mother, Beatrice Carlson. Ideal for luncheon or supper served with a crisp green salad and crunchy bread sticks to add complementary textures.

Creamy Chicken-Noodle Casserole

8 boneless, skinless chicken breast halves
¼ cup butter
½ cup chopped onions
¼ cup flour
2 tablespoons paprika
Salt to taste
½ teaspoon pepper
10½-ounce can chicken broth
2 cups sour cream
1 tablespoon Worcestershire sauce
8-ounce package medium noodles, cooked

Preheat oven to 325°. Melt butter in large skillet. Brown chicken breasts. Remove chicken from pan. Add onion; blend in flour, paprika, salt and pepper. Add broth; stir and cook until smooth. Stir in sour cream and Worcestershire sauce. Mix one-half sauce with noodles and place in 3 quart casserole. Arrange chicken over noodles. Pour remaining sauce over chicken. Bake, covered, for 45 minutes; uncovered for additional 15 minutes (1 hour total).

Serves 6 to 8

What could be easier? No need to pre-cook the rice or brown the chicken. ECC chefs conjured up this creation tailor-made for cool days when you welcome an oven-baked entrée. Add a little greenery in the form of broccoli spears, peas, zucchini rounds or Italian green beans and you've got yourself a pretty plateful of great eating.

Italian Chicken and Rice

14 ounces whole tomatoes, undrained and coarsely chopped
⅕ cup water or chicken stock
1 cup white rice (mixed rice can be an option)
½ cup chopped onions
2 ounces shredded skim Mozzarella cheese
1½ teaspoons dried Italian seasoning
¼ teaspoon granulated garlic
¼ teaspoon black pepper
¼ teaspoon salt
Four 5-ounce skinless and boneless chicken breasts
1 teaspoon dried Italian seasoning
½ teaspoon garlic powder
½ cup grated Parmesan cheese

Coat a 2 to 3-quart baking dish with vegetable non-stick spray. Preheat oven to 375°. Combine chopped tomatoes, water or stock, onion, Mozzarella cheese, Italian seasoning, garlic, pepper and salt in baking dish. Arrange chicken breasts evenly over mixture. Top with final three seasoning ingredients. Cover dish and bake for 45 minutes. Uncover and bake an additional 15 minutes or until most of liquid is absorbed.

Serves 4

Fast food with French flair from the ECC kitchen! Tester Peggy Dodge appreciated the "flavorful sauce and the brief preparation time." Delicious over pasta or rice accompanied by a simple steamed vegetable for added color and nutrition.

ECC Chicken Chardonnay

Four 8-ounce boneless skinless chicken breasts
Flour and seasoned salt (enough to dust breasts)
2 tablespoons olive oil
2 tablespoons drawn butter
1½ tablespoons chopped shallots
1½ tablespoons chopped garlic
¾ cup Chardonnay
¼ cup heavy cream
2 tablespoons flour-butter paste
10½-ounce can chicken broth, undiluted
Salt and pepper to taste

Dust chicken lightly in seasoned flour. Preheat a skillet. Add oil and butter. When hot, add chicken and brown lightly on both sides (about 3 minutes per side or until desired doneness). Remove chicken and keep warm in oven or cover with aluminum foil. Sauté shallots and garlic in remaining oil in the skillet until translucent. Add wine and reduce by half. Add broth and reduce by one-third. Add flour-butter paste and thicken. Finish by adding cream and returning chicken breasts to pan. Adjust flavor with salt and pepper.

Serves 4

Count on Dr. Robert and Mary Cooper of Edina and Sun City West to entertain in style. This can be readied before dinner guests arrive and refrigerated until baking time. Rice or pasta and a citrus-avocado salad make appealing additions. Artichokes, by the way, are iron-rich and low in calories when fresh or canned without a marinade as called for here.

Chicken-Artichoke Bake

4 chicken breasts, 5 if small, cooked and cut up
14-ounce artichoke hearts, drained and quartered
8-ounce jar mushroom pieces
⅔ cup mayonnaise

10¾-ounce can condensed cream of chicken soup
2 tablespoons lemon juice
1 cup packaged stuffing mix, finely crushed
¼ cup Parmesan cheese
Melted butter

Preheat oven to 350°. Place chicken, artichoke hearts and mushroom pieces in 8 x 11 pan. Combine mayonnaise, cream of chicken soup and lemon juice. Spread evenly over chicken. Cover with crushed stuffing; top with Parmesan cheese. Drizzle with a little melted butter. Bake, uncovered, 45 minutes.

Serves 4 to 6

Linda Maetzold's contribution is a favorite because it can be partially prepared ahead, no precooking of the rice is necessary and it requires nary a nod while baking. "I use lower-fat soups with very good results," says Linda. Her husband Dennis serves on the Edina City Council.

Minnesota Chicken-Rice Medley

1 cup uncooked wild rice
1 medium green pepper
1 small jar pimiento, cut up
10¾-ounce can cream of mushroom soup
10¾-ounce can cream of celery soup

1 soup can skim milk
4 to 6 skinless chicken breast halves, approximately 2½ pounds
1 envelope dry onion soup mix (from a 1.8-ounce package)

Preheat oven to 350°. Wash rice and spread on bottom of buttered 8 x 12-inch pan. Slice green pepper into ¼-inch rings. Arrange pimiento over rice. Heat soups and milk until blended; pour evenly over rice. Place chicken pieces on top and sprinkle with dry onion soup. Cover pan with foil. Bake for 1½ to 2 hours, removing foil during last half hour.

Serves 4 to 6

This could be called "Mystery Chicken Breasts" because we received the recipe with no contributor name attached. What we do know is that tester Kathy Hanson rated it excellent, commenting "I would definitely serve it to guests!" Keep filo dough covered until ready to use so it remains pliable and easy to fold around chicken and sauce.

Filo-Wrapped Chicken Breasts

4 whole chicken breasts, halved and boned	6 sprigs parsley, minced
4 cups chicken stock	Salt and freshly-ground pepper to taste
1 cup dry white wine	6 tablespoons butter, divided
2 celery stalks, chopped	4 tablespoons flour
2 carrots, chopped	8 sheets filo dough
1 onion, chopped	

In 3½ quart pan place chicken breasts, stock, wine, vegetables, salt and pepper. Cover and cook over medium heat until chicken is tender, about 20 minutes. Remove chicken breasts and set aside to cool. Reduce stock to about half. Place vegetables and stock in blender and purée. Pour purée into saucepan and keep warm, but do not let boil. In small saucepan, melt 3 tablespoons butter. Blend in flour and cook over medium heat 2 minutes, stirring constantly, to make a flour-butter paste. Add this paste to warm purée, whisk until smooth. Place over medium heat. Bring to a slow boil, stirring until sauce thickens, about 2 minutes. Set sauce aside, keeping it warm.

Preheat oven to 350°. Place each half chicken breast at one end of filo sheet; top with 1 tablespoon sauce. Fold sides of filo inward to partially cover chicken. Roll chicken in filo the entire length of the sheet. Brush top with 1 tablespoon of butter and place in a buttered 9 x 13-inch pan. Bake until nicely browned, about 15 minutes. Brush with melted butter and bake 15 more minutes. Serve with warm sauce.

Note: After wrapping chicken in filo, brush generously with butter and freeze, if desired. Freeze sauce separately in airtight container. Bake directly from freezer an additional 15 minutes (45 minutes in all); brush with butter twice every 15 minutes.

Serves 8

ECC golf champion Marian Hamilton hits a culinary hole-in-one with spinach and cheese-stuffed chicken breasts. Tester Gene Gaasedelen wanted to show off the stuffing, so she cut the breasts diagonally into 1/2-inch slices after a 5-minute stand time following baking. Her family enjoyed a Yogurt-Tomato Sauce on the side, and we include that recipe with Salads, Dressings and Condiments.

Chicken Florentine

8 large boneless, skinless chicken breast halves
Salt, pepper and other seasonings as desired
10-ounce package chopped spinach, cooked and drained
1 tablespoon butter, melted
3 ounces cream cheese, softened
½ cup shredded Swiss cheese
½ teaspoon lemon juice
6 tablespoons butter
½ cup grated Parmesan cheese

Preheat oven to 350°. Pound chicken until thin; season as desired. Combine spinach with butter, cream cheese, Swiss cheese and lemon juice. In center of each breast, place ½ cup spinach mixture. Fold chicken to cover stuffing completely. Place in large shallow baking dish seam-side down. Spread butter over top of each piece. Sprinkle with Parmesan. Bake, uncovered, for 25 minutes or until just brown or until juices run clear.

Serves 6 to 8

Marian Clay, who teaches flute and piano lessons, finds this unique fruited chicken ideal for her schedule. "I assemble it ahead and it bakes in a cooking bag while I'm teaching. When we're ready for dinner, it's ready too," she says. Rice and a green vegetable or salad are perfect complements. Marian's husband is Pastor of Edina Morningside Church.

Jubilee Chicken

2 to 3 pounds your favorite chicken parts
1 cup flour, seasoned with 1 teaspoon salt and ¼ teaspoon pepper
Cooking oil
Instant minced onion, if desired
12 to 16-ounce can or jar of pitted white cherries
2 to 4 navel oranges, peeled and sliced
10-ounce jar currant jelly
1 tablespoon Beau Monde seasoning

Place seasoned flour with salt and pepper in a brown paper bag. Shake chicken pieces until evenly coated. In large skillet, brown chicken in hot oil. If desired, sprinkle chicken with instant minced onion as it is browning.

Preheat oven to 300°. Prepare large oven bag as directed by shaking 1 tablespoon of flour inside bag. Place bag in a 9 x 13-inch baking pan (bag should not hang over pan sides). Place chicken pieces in single layer in bag. In medium bowl, combine cherries, orange slices, jelly and Beau Monde. Pour over chicken pieces. Close bag with nylon tie which comes with bag. Cut six ½-inch slits in top of bag. Bake for 2 to 3 hours until chicken is fork tender.

Serves 6 to 8

Betty Hemstad refers to her contribution as "an old friend appreciated by all ages. It's impossible to ruin and is simply prepared," she adds. An active civic and church volunteer, Betty carries out the Italian theme by serving the chicken with rosamarina pasta. Marie Lacy tested the recipe using chicken thighs first and then chicken breasts. "Delicious with either," she reports. Cooking time will vary, of course, depending on size of chicken pieces used.

Cabin Cacciatore

12 large chicken thighs
Flour
¼ cup olive oil
1 cup chopped onion
1 red pepper, chopped
8 to 12 ounces fresh mushrooms, sliced
3 cloves garlic, minced
6-ounce can tomato paste
1 cup chicken stock
¾ cup dry white wine
¼ cup brandy
2 tablespoons flour
1 tablespoon sugar
1 teaspoon salt
1 teaspoon thyme
1 teaspoon basil
1 teaspoon marjoram
¼ teaspoon white pepper

Flour chicken; sauté in olive oil until golden. Place chicken in a deep 9 x 13-inch baking dish. Preheat oven to 350°. Combine remaining ingredients in saucepan. Simmer for 10 minutes; pour over chicken. Bake, covered, 45 to 60 minutes or until juices run clear. If desired, serve with rosamarina pasta cooked in ½ water and ½ chicken broth. Toss pasta to taste with butter (or olive oil) and freshly-grated Parmesan cheese.

Serves 9 to 12

Pat Stark's mellow cheese and chicken combo can be assembled ahead and refrigerated until baking time — ideal for busy days. Just add a little extra oven time if dish is coming right from the frig. Round out the menu with your favorite rice pilaf and a crisp vegetable salad.

Swiss Chicken Bake

4 whole chicken breasts, boned and skinned

8 slices of Swiss cheese

½ can French onion soup

10¾-ounce can cream of chicken soup, undiluted

4 tablespoons butter or margarine

2 cups herb stuffing mix

Preheat oven to 325°. Place chicken in 9 x 13-inch pyrex casserole. Cover with cheese, then soups. Melt butter and mix with stuffing. Place on top of chicken. Bake, uncovered, for 1½ hours. Can be made ahead, but do not bake ahead of time.

Serves 8

"Delicious, easy to make and always receives rave reviews," says contributor Diane Aves. Forget stove-top splattering because the "frying" is done in the oven. Serve with what else — mashed potatoes and a favorite vegetable. You will think you're back at Grandma's house for Sunday dinner!

Oven-Fried Chicken and Gravy

1 chicken, cut up

1 cup biscuit mix

⅓ cup crushed corn flakes or other cereal flakes (not sugar coated)

1 tablespoon chicken bouillon granules

⅛ teaspoon thyme

⅛ teaspoon poultry seasoning

⅓ cup butter, melted

Ground pepper

Pan drippings)

2 tablespoons flour

1 cup cold milk

Preheat oven to 375°. Remove skin from chicken pieces. Combine biscuit mix, cereal flakes, bouillon granules, thyme and poultry seasoning in plastic or paper bag. Shake chicken pieces in bag to coat. Spray jelly roll or shallow baking pan wih non-stick vegetable oil spray. Place chicken in single layer in pan. Spoon remaining biscuit mix mixture over chicken. Spoon melted butter over chicken. Season with pepper. Bake for 1 hour or until nicely browned. Remove chicken from pan and keep warm on serving platter while gravy is prepared. Combine pan drippings with 2 tablespoons flour in small saucepan. When bubbly, stir in milk. Heat and stir until gravy thickens. Pass with chicken.

Serves 4 to 6

Tester Dianne Safley loved the fresh papaya pieces which perk up an easy oven-baked chicken entrée. Contributor Laura Carlson of Edina doesn't add the fruit until the final ten minutes of baking so it retains flavor, color and perfect consistency. Use boneless chicken breasts, if desired, instead of fryers.

Polynesian Chicken

2 chicken fryers, cut up
1 cup flour
1 teaspoon seasoned salt
½ pound butter or margarine
1 cup diluted frozen orange juice
2 tablespoons lemon juice
½ cup brown sugar
1 tablespoon soy sauce
½ teaspoon salt
1 tablespoon cornstarch
2 cups cubed fresh papaya
Green pepper, finely chopped (optional)
Sesame seed (optional)

Preheat oven to 350°. Shake chicken parts in paper bag with flour and seasoned salt. Melt butter; use 2 tablespoons to grease a large baking dish. Place chicken in dish, brushing remaining butter over each piece. Bake in oven 50 minutes or until juices run clear when pierced with fork.

Combine orange and lemon juices, brown sugar, soy sauce, salt and cornstarch in a saucepan; bring to a boil, stirring constantly. Remove from heat when clear and thickened. Add papaya. Pour mixture evenly over browned chicken. Bake 10 minutes longer. Garnish with chopped parsley or a mixture of finely-chopped green pepper and sesame seed, if desired.

Serves 8

Wake up those tired taste buds with Mary L. Miller's "zingy" wine-barbecue sauce. Opt for easy oven method or grill if you will, remembering to baste as directed with the special sauce. Tester Angela Fox found the recipe easy to prepare for a large group. "I served this at a family gathering (grandchildren included) and everyone like it. The aroma is as wonderful as the taste," she reports.

Oven-Barbecued Chicken

1 cup red port wine
¾ cup cider vinegar
½ cup corn oil
¼ cup water
3 tablespoons flour
2 tablespoons ketchup
2 tablespoons Worcestershire sauce
Salt and pepper
1½ tablespoons garlic salt
1½ tablespoons hot pepper sauce, such as Tabasco
Two 2-pound chickens, quartered — or 4 breasts split in half

Combine all ingredients except chicken in medium saucepan. Heat to boiling. Stir and cook 2 minutes. Keep warm for basting. (Sauce may be made ahead and reheated.)

Preheat oven to 350°. Place chicken in single layer in lightly-greased, foil-lined pan, cavity side up. Baste generously with sauce. Bake 20 minutes or more for breasts, 30 minutes more for quarters. Turn chicken, baste with sauce and bake 20 minutes more, basting every 20 minutes.

Chicken can be barbecued on the grill using medium to low setting and frequent basting.

Serves 6 to 8

Ken Galloway, ECC's Food & Beverage Director and Clubhouse Manager, won high honors for his originality in developing this far-from-ordinary pizza. It was chosen by the American Dairy Association as one of the eight best recipes in the U.S. using cheese. And, it was published in the ADA book entitled "Great Chefs of America." Tester Carol Cronk praised the "wonderful flavor and excellent blend of cheeses. Very fresh tasting," she adds

Mediterranean Grilled Chicken Pizza

Six 15-inch Lahvosh crackers
6-ounce chicken breast,
  halved, boned and skinned

MARINARA SAUCE
1½ cups canned tomato sauce
1½ cups canned tomatoes,
  undrained
1 cup diced onion
2 cloves garlic, minced
2 teaspoons sugar
2 teaspoons dried basil
1 teaspoon dried oregano
1 teaspoon pepper

MARINADE
4 tablespoons white wine
1 tablespoon olive oil
1 teaspoon fresh rosemary
¼ teaspoon salt

TOPPINGS
6 ripe tomatoes, thinly sliced
  (or equivalent of sun-dried
  tomatoes)
2 green peppers, sliced
2 red peppers, sliced
1 medium onion, sliced
6 cups shredded Fontina cheese
3 cups shredded Mozzarella
  cheese
2½ cups freshly-grated Parmesan
  cheese

Combine ingredients for marinara sauce in saucepan. Bring to boil; reduce heat and simmer, stirring occasionally 20 to 30 minutes. Set aside. (Only ½ cup of sauce is needed for each pizza. Remainder can be frozen, if desired.)

Combine marinade ingredients. Arrange chicken in 9 x 13-inch pan. Pour marinade evenly over top. Marinate chicken 30 minutes or longer, covered and refrigerated. Broil chicken; cool. Cut into thin strips.

Preheat oven to 400°. Prepare toppings and have close at hand for assembling process. For each pizza, spread ½ cup sauce over one cracker. Arrange over sauce: chicken strips, tomato, pepper and onion slices, shredded cheeses and grated Parmesan. Bake 10 to 12 minutes or until cheeses are melted and crust is golden brown. Cut into wedges and serve immediately.

Serves 12

Whether you cook chicken especially for this dish or utilize leftover poultry, you will appreciate this one-dish meal from Maxine Thorkelson of Minneapolis. A palate pleaser for luncheons and buffet suppers accompanied by a colorful cranberry salad and crunchy bread sticks.

Chicken-Broccoli Bake

1 bunch broccoli
3 cups cooked chicken, cut up
10-ounce can cream of chicken soup
½ cup sour cream
½ cup mayonnaise
⅓ cup chicken broth
1 tablespoon lemon juice
1 cup mild Cheddar cheese, grated
2 tablespoons butter, melted
2 slices white bread, crusts removed
Paprika

Cut broccoli into bite-sized pieces. Cook until tender-crisp. Preheat oven to 350°. Grease a 9 x 13-inch baking dish. Cover the bottom with the broccoli. Arrange chicken over the broccoli. Combine the soup, sour cream, mayonnaise, broth and lemon juice. Pour evenly over the chicken. Sprinkle Cheddar cheese over the mixture. Break bread into small pieces; toss with the melted butter. Use to top casserole mixture. Sprinkle with paprika. Cover and bake for 30 minutes or until heated through.

Serves 6

Hurrah for high-style and hearty! Contributor Jaye Vaaler complements this "simple company or family dish" with a mixed green salad and crusty rolls. Although wild rice soup isn't readily available in every state, you know for certain you can find it in Minnesota!

Chicken-Wild Rice Casserole

1 cup wild rice
4 cups water
1 teaspoon salt
1 quart wild rice soup (canned, homemade or frozen)
8-ounce carton mushrooms, cleaned and sliced
2 tablespoons dry sherry (optional)
8 boneless chicken breasts
½ cup grated Parmesan cheese
Paprika

Preheat oven to 375°. Place rice, salt and water in a saucepan; bring to a boil. Reduce heat to low and cook, covered, 30 to 40 minutes until rice has puffed and most water is absorbed. Let stand covered 5 minutes. Heat soup with the mushrooms and sherry. Butter a 9 x 13-inch pan. Put rice on the bottom; cover with half the soup. Put the chicken on top and cover with remaining soup. Sprinkle with rice and paprika. Cover dish with foil and bake for 30 minutes. Uncover and bake for an additional 20 minutes or until done.

Serves 8

When you try this trendy dish from ECC, let your palate guide you in determining the amount of pesto you add. Executive Chef Jerry Cegla suggests beginning with half the amount and taste-testing before adding more. Leftover pesto refrigerates well up to a week.

Basil Pesto Chicken Pasta

8 ounces fresh basil leaves
2 cloves garlic
¼ cup pine nuts
½ to ¾ cup olive oil
Salt and pepper to taste
Two 4-ounce chicken breasts
Chicken broth
3 tablespoons olive oil
½ cup diced tomatoes
½ cup ripe olives, halved
12 to 16 ounces pasta, cooked al dente
½ cup shredded Parmesan cheese

For pesto, grind basil, garlic and pine nuts in food processor. Slowly add ½ to ¾ cup olive oil, salt and pepper. Set aside. Cut chicken into strips. Poach in chicken broth. Drain and let cool. Heat 3 tablespoons olive oil in large skillet. Sauté poached chicken strips slightly. Add diced tomato, olives and cooked pasta. Toss in amount of pesto desired and heat through. Sprinkle each serving with Parmesan cheese.

Serves 4

Joyce Franzen of Golden Valley serves up a moist, flavorful turkey breast that can be made a day ahead of serving and reheated. Or, it can be served the day it is baked. "We think this is fantastic with pasta, rice or potatoes," says Joyce, "and the turkey looks fabulous! Even though the sauce contains horseradish, it's mild enough to appeal to children."

Turkey Breast in Horseradish Sauce

1 large turkey breast, fresh or thawed
½ cup brandy
1 cup chicken stock
1 small onion, chopped
1 garlic clove, chopped
Salt & pepper
2 cups whipping cream (do not substitute)
5-ounce jar horseradish

Preheat oven to 325°. Brown evenly in butter; place in baking dish. Pour brandy over turkey and carefully light with match. When flame burns out, add chicken stock, onion, garlic, salt and pepper. Cover with a foil tent and bake for 1 hour. Uncover and continue baking for 30 minutes.

Combine whipping cream and horseradish; pour over turkey. Continue baking, basting every 15 minutes for an hour. Remove from oven. Separate and strain drippings and put in separate bowl. Refrigerate turkey overnight for easier slicing. Put in oven-proof serving dish; pour sauce over sliced turkey and warm in low oven until heated through.

Serves 8 to 10

Peggy Kelly, who has served several terms as an Edina City Council member, offers a recipe her family "loves made with leftover turkey from holiday dinners." Tester Terry Swanson prepared it with chicken and since she wasn't serving it to children, added chopped green onion for a little "bite." Peggy's husband Mike is a member of the Edina Foundation Board of Directors.

Hot Turkey Salad

2 cups crushed potato chips, divided
3 cups cooked turkey or chicken, cubed (1½ pounds)
2 cups celery, diced
1 cup mayonnaise*
2 tablespoons lemon juice
2 teaspoons grated onion
¼ teaspoon celery seed
½ teaspoon salt, or to taste
½ cup grated Cheddar cheese
½ cup toasted almonds
*½ cup low or non-fat sour cream can be substituted for ½ cup of the mayonnaise.

Preheat oven to 375°. Cover bottom of ungreased casserole with 1 cup of the crushed chips. Combine cubed poultry with celery, mayonnaise, lemon juice, grated onion, celery seed and salt. Spoon mixture over chips in casserole. Top with grated cheese, remaining 1 cup chips and almonds. Bake, uncovered, 30 minutes or until heated through. (Do not overbake.)

Serves 6

Kathleen Danford of Edina, a firm believer in healthful meals and daily exercise, contributes a speedy skillet supper chock full of nutritious ingredients. Serve with a side of your favorite tomato salsa and offer warm corn tortillas. Tester Gene Gaasedelen used a "generous amount of red, yellow and green pepper for color and crunch" and suggests a garnish of fresh cilantro.

Turkey-Black Bean Skillet Supper

¾ pound ground turkey
1 medium chopped onion
2 cloves garlic
1 red, yellow and/or green pepper, chopped
1½ cups cooked rice
14½-ounce can black beans with cumin (Southwest-style)
4.5-ounce can chopped green chilies
½ teaspoon lemon pepper
Chili powder and salt to taste

In large skillet, brown turkey, breaking into small pieces as it cooks. Stir in chopped onion, pepper and garlic. When onion becomes translucent, add rice, beans, chilies, lemon pepper, chili powder and salt. Heat until serving temperature, stirring gently to combine ingredients.

Serves 4

This meatless luncheon or supper dish from Judy Tucker involves several simple preparation steps, but as tester Mary L. Miller reports, "It's well worth the effort and the dish freezes well." Ricotta, a mild, slightly sweet Italian cheese, should be used within a day or two after purchasing.

Spinach-Stuffed Shells with Tomato Sauce

12-ounce package jumbo shell pasta (30-36 shells),
   cooked al dente and drained

FILLING:

10-ounce package frozen chopped spinach, defrosted

1 cup Ricotta cheese

10 ounces diced Mozzarella cheese

½ cup grated Parmesan cheese

3 eggs, beaten with fork

2 teaspoons margarine, melted

¼ teaspoon nutmeg, grated

¼ cup dried parsley flakes

SAUCE:

30-ounce jar chunky spaghetti sauce with mushrooms
   and diced tomatoes

8-ounce can tomato sauce

4 teaspoons sugar

1 tablespoon margarine

¼ cup dried parsley flakes

Squeeze of fresh lemon

Additional Parmesan cheese for topping

Drain spinach thoroughly. Combine spinach with Ricotta, Mozzarella and Parmesan cheeses, eggs, margarine, nutmeg and parsley flakes. Place about 1 heaping teaspoon of filling in each shell. Arrange stuffed shells in 9 x 13-inch buttered casserole.

Preheat oven to 350°. In large saucepan, heat spaghetti sauce, tomato sauce, sugar, margarine, parsley and lemon. Pour evenly over shells. Top with additional grated Parmesan cheese. Bake, uncovered, for 30 minutes or until heated through.

Serves 12

When he says "no-fail" that's exactly what Scott Rochat, ECC chef, means. "This is absolutely the easiest lasagna you will ever make — you don't even need to cook the noodles! It's a favorite recipe of Catie Caron, my mother-in-law." Our testers agreed that in addition to being easy to prepare, it is delicious with just the right amount of sauce.

No-Fail Lasagna

1 medium onion, diced
1½ pounds lean ground beef
32 ounces of your
   favorite spaghetti sauce

3½ cups water
1 pound uncooked lasagna noodles
4 cups shredded Cheddar cheese
4 cups shredded Mozzarella cheese

First, make sauce. In large skillet, brown beef with onion, breaking up meat chunks with spoon. Drain excess fat. Transfer to large saucepan. Add spaghetti sauce and water. Simmer 30 minutes. Preheat oven to 350°. Make a single layer of 6 uncooked lasagna noodles in bottom of 9 x 13-inch oblong pan. Ladle ⅓ of meat sauce evenly over noodles. Toss together Cheddar and Mozzarella cheeses. Sprinkle ⅓ of cheese over sauce. Repeat these layers two more times, ending with cheese. (May not need all the noodles.) Cover and bake 1 hour. Remove cover and bake another 10 to 15 minutes. Let stand out of oven 15 minutes before cutting.

Serves 8 to 10

Thanks to Richard Hoyt, Executive Director of the Youth Hunting Club of Minnesota in Excelsior, MN, for one of his favorite game recipes. "This originated with writer/chef Bob Schranck and it works well with game hens and doves as well as quail," says Richard. Great with what else but Minnesota wild rice!

No-Fail Quail

4 quail	1 can chicken consommé
Salt and pepper	¼ teaspoon thyme
4 tablespoons butter, melted	1½ bay leaves
2 tablespoons flour	1 cup dry white wine

Split the quail down the back and flatten. Salt and pepper lightly. Brown slowly in melted butter in a large skillet. Sprinkle flour over the birds; add consommé, thyme, bay leaves and wine. Bring to a bubble, cover and simmer until tender, about 30 to 40 minutes. Remove bay leaves. Put pan juices into serving dish to be spooned over the birds.

Serves 4

Jim Keeler, Editor of the ECC newsletter, the UPDATE, promises that slow cooking in wine will result in "a game dinner that's tops in flavor and tenderness. It will fall off the bones and your reputation as a chef will be cinched!" Pheasants and geese may be used interchangeably with ducks.

Lucky Duck Dinner

2 ducks OR pheasants, cleaned	Salt
1 cup chopped onion	½ cup Rhine wine
1 cup chopped celery	½ cup water

Place chopped celery and onions in electric slow cooker. Lightly salt inside of game. Place over vegetables in even layer. Combine wine and water; pour over the game. Set slow cooker on low setting and cover. Cook 5 to 6 hours or until tender.

Serves 4

This rich bird with the moist, dark meat has been the centerpiece of Scandinavian and European celebrations since the 16th century. Popular side dishes include red cabbage, braised onions, slaws with sweet-sour dressing, applesauce, sauerkraut and baked fruit compotes. A fresh goose should be roasted within two or three days after purchasing, and a frozen bird should be used within six months.

ECC's Christmas Goose

1 goose (allowing 1 pound per serving)
Favorite stuffing

Clean bird thoroughly, trimming extra pieces of fat and removing neck, giblets, etc. ECC's Executive Chef prefers a "simple stuffing mixture of bread, celery, onion, apple, fresh sage, rosemary, salt, pepper and a small amount of garlic." This is moistened with egg and chicken stock. Bird should be stuffed lightly leaving ample room for stuffing to expand.

Bake goose breast-side-up at 350° for 20 to 25 minutes per pound or until meat thermometer reaches 180° and juices run clear. During cooking, baste frequently to retain moisture and obtain a beautiful color. For easy carving, allow goose to stand about 15 minutes after removing from the oven.

Britton A. Goetze, Jr., of Edina describes his recipe as "the very best non-rich preparation for pheasant. You can substitute 1/2 cup olive oil for butter, if you wish," he adds. The sherry-infused sauce with dressy dark sweet cherries spells special occasion fare.

Pheasant Fantastic

4 pheasants, quartered
½ cup flour, seasoned (5 teaspoons salt, ½ teaspoon pepper,
　¼ teaspoon cardamom)
¾ cup butter (1½ sticks)
1 large onion, finely chopped
¾ cup seedless golden raisins
1 cup chili sauce
½ cup water
½ cup brown sugar, packed
2 tablespoons Worcestershire sauce
¼ to ½ teaspoon garlic powder
1 cup dry sherry wine
16-ounce can pitted dark cherries, drained

Wash pheasants and pat dry. Dust evenly with seasoned flour. Preheat oven to 325°. Melt butter in heavy skillet. Brown birds thoroughly. Place pheasants in deep casserole. In same skillet, combine onion, raisins, chili sauce, sugar, water, Worcestershire sauce and garlic. Simmer briefly, 1 to 2 minutes. Scrape skillet bottom and sides clean; then pour mixture evenly over birds, covering thoroughly.

Bake, covered, for 2 to 2½ hours. Remove cover and add sherry and cherries. Continue baking 20 minutes longer (test for tenderness) and transfer to a deep chafing or warming dish.

8 Servings

Eleanor Ostman, popular St. Paul food writer, shares one of her favorite methods of preparing pheasant. Although the long-tailed bird with the bright markings is considered gourmet fare, there is no need to serve it "under glass" for elegant presentation. This recipe, served with rice pilaf, very tastefully proves that point.

Sun-Kissed Pheasant

1 dressed pheasant (1½ to 2¼ pounds), cut up with skin removed
⅔ cup all-purpose flour
3 tablespoons margarine or butter
3 tablespoons olive oil
Juice from 3 large oranges, or 1½ cups prepared orange juice
1 cup dry white wine
½ cup golden raisins
1 tablespoon snipped fresh oregano leaves
1 tablespoon snipped fresh parsley
1 tablespoon snipped fresh rosemary leaves

In large plastic food-storage bag, combine pheasant pieces and flour. Shake to coat. In 12-inch nonstick skillet, heat margarine and oil over medium-high heat. Add pheasant pieces. Cook for 10 to 12 minutes, or until meat is browned, turning occasionally. Transfer pheasant pieces to warm platter. Drain and discard fat from skillet. In same skillet, combine remaining ingredients. Bring to a boil. Reduce heat to low. Return pheasant pieces to skillet. Cover and simmer for 40 to 50 minutes, or until meat is tender and juices run clear.

Serves 3 to 4

Instead of "bringing home the bacon," bring home some buffalo and give this unique ECC recipe a shot. Buffalo is readily available in most larger supermarkets, but call ahead just to be sure they have a supply on hand. Since some of the steps can be done ahead, like cooking and shredding the meat and making the sauce, we suggest reading through the entire recipe before beginning preparation. Then, plan the timetable that works best for your schedule.

Shredded Buffalo and Green Chili Enchiladas

FILLING
5-pound buffalo roast
   (inside round)
27-ounce can
   whole green chili peppers,
   cut in julienne strips
4 each yellow,
   green and red bell peppers,
   cut in julienne strips
1 red onion, thinly sliced
1 tablespoon chopped cilantro
1 pound shredded
   Cheddar cheese
1 pound shredded
   Mozzarella cheese
Chili powder, cumin, minced
   garlic, paprika and cayenne
   to taste
SAUCE
¼ cup olive oil
¼ cup vegetable oil

4 pounds onions, chopped
2 cups finely-diced celery
2 tablespoons minced garlic
12 to 13 cups tomato sauce
⅛ cup sugar
5 tablespoons cumin
3 tablespoons chili powder
1 tablespoon paprika
¼ teaspoon cayenne

OTHER
24 corn tortillas (6-inch size)
1 cup heavy cream

GARNISHES
Additional shredded Cheddar
   and Mozzarella cheeses
Sliced black olives
Sliced scallions
Pickled baby corn
Pepperoncini peppers

For filling, cook buffalo to medium doneness. While still warm, shred meat using two forks. Combine meat with remaining filling ingredients. French fry corn tortillas; roll into cylinders. Stuff with filling mixture. Arrange seam-side-down in one or more greased baking dishes. **For sauce,** combine olive and vegetable oils in large saucepan or skillet. Add onions and cook, stirring, until onions are heavily caramelized. Add garlic and celery; simmer to soften. Add tomato sauce and continue simmering. Add remaining sauce ingredients. Simmer, stirring occasionally, for an hour. Preheat oven to 350°. Pour sauce evenly over stuffed tortillas. Bake about 20 minutes. Meanwhile, reduce 1 cup cream. Pour over enchiladas. Top with additional cheeses and continue baking until heated through. (Do not brown cheese.) For a finishing touch, garnish with olives, scallions, baby corn and/or peppers.

Serves 12 or more

Desserts and Sweet Snacks

With help from her ten-year-old, Jacqui Jarnes tested Jaye Vaaler's Apple Crisp with great success. "The topping tastes like a pastry crust, but is much easier to make. We ate it all as soon as it was out of the oven!" she reports. Be sure to use cooking apples so slices keep their attractive shape and tender but firm texture. Jaye suggests topping each serving with slightly-sweetened whipped cream or vanilla or cinnamon ice cream.

All-American Apple Crisp

1 cup all-purpose flour
¾ cup sugar
1 teaspoon baking powder
¾ teaspoon salt
1 egg
5 cups peeled and sliced tart pie apples
  (such as Granny Smith or Haralson)
2 tablespoons brown sugar
⅓ cup butter, melted (do not use margarine)
1 teaspoon cinnamon/sugar mixture
Sweetened whipped cream or ice cream, if desired.

Preheat oven to 375°. With a fork or pastry blender, mix flour, sugar, baking powder, salt and egg until crumbly. (Mixture should be crumbly, not lumpy.) Place apples in a buttered 2-quart baking dish; sprinkle with brown sugar. Sprinkle flour mixture evenly over apples. Drizzle melted butter over the topping and sprinkle with the cinnamon/sugar mixture. Bake, uncovered, for 30 minutes or until apples are tender. Leftovers reheat well in microwave.

Serves 6 to 8

Several make-ahead steps in Sylvia Berg's red and white confection lead to a fabulous contrast in textures and flavors. Tester Peggy Dodge suggests the alternative of "spooning the meringue into individual mounds (clouds) and baking for 30 to 40 minutes before turning off the oven." What a divine dessert for the Christmas holidays, Valentine's Day and 4th of July! And it's perfect to take to another home when co-hostessing a meeting.

Cherry Berries on a Cloud

6 egg whites
¼ teaspoon salt
½ teaspoon cream of tartar
1½ cups sugar

FILLING
Two 3-ounce packages cream cheese, softened
¾ cup sugar
1 teaspoon vanilla
2 cups whipping cream, whipped
2 cups miniature marshmallows

SAUCE
1 teaspoon lemon juice
21-ounce can cherry pie filling
10-ounce package frozen strawberries, thawed or equal amount
        of fresh berries), sliced and sweetened to taste.

Preheat oven to 275°. Beat egg whites until foamy. Add salt and cream of tartar. Then, add sugar slowly, beating on low speed, about 15 minutes until stiff. Place in greased 9 x 13-inch pan. Bake for 1 hour. Then turn off oven and leave in for 12 hours.

For filling, combine cream cheese with sugar and vanilla. Mix in whipped cream and marshmallows. Spoon evenly over meringue. Refrigerate 12 hours.

For sauce, combine all ingredients. Just before serving dessert, top each portion with a generous tablespoon (or more) of sauce.

Serves 12

"A wonderfully light dessert and pretty, too," says tester Patty Simmons. "It takes a little while to prepare because of the necessary cooling step, but I just did other things in the meantime." ECC Pastry Chef Joe Frieler advises that it can be made a day or so ahead of serving, but does not adapt to freezing.

ECC Lemon Mousse

¼-ounce envelope
   unflavored gelatin
3 tablespoons water
½ cup fresh lemon juice
Zest of one lemon
1 cup sugar, divided

4 pasteurized eggs,
   separated
1 teaspoon vanilla
¼ teaspoon cream of tartar
1 cup heavy cream

Soften gelatin in the water. Bring juice, zest and ½ cup sugar to a simmer. Place egg yolks in a bowl. Slowly pour lemon mixture over yolks, whisking constantly. Return to heat, stirring constantly until just barely simmering. Whisk in gelatin and vanilla. Cool to room temperature. Beat egg whites to a soft peak. Gradually add remaining ½ cup sugar. Beat on high speed until stiff but not dry. Fold ¼ of whites into lemon mixture; place remaining on top. Whip cream in same bowl to a soft peak. Fold whites and cream into lemon mixture. Pour into cups or mold and chill at least 2 hours or overnight.   **Serves 12**

This favorite light dessert (only 200 calories) from Jaye Vaaler is refrigerated several hours or overnight before serving. "We like it with an Oriental menu served with small ginger cookies," says Jaye. Star anise, often used in Chinese dishes, has a spicy licorice flavor, a bit different than that of regular anise.

Ginger-Spiced Pears

1 cup water
1 cup orange juice
½ cup sugar
1 tablespoon grated fresh ginger

1 cinnamon stick
1 star anise
4 medium pears with stems
1 lemon, halved

Combine all ingredients excepting pears and lemon. Bring to a boil; reduce heat and simmer 5 minutes. Remove from heat. Cut a thin slice from the bottom of each pear so it stands upright. Remove peel and core. Rub with lemon to prevent discoloring. Place pear in the juice mixture and repeat with remaining pears. Squeeze remaining lemon juice over the pears; add lemon halves to the pan. Cover and cook pears until just tender, 15 to 20 minutes. Be sure to check often, and cook only until pears are tender when pierced with a paring knife. Discard lemons. Put pears in a bowl big enough to hold them upright. Return juice to heat and boil 5 minutes until slightly syrupy. Pour the juice over pears and refrigerate until cold, preferably overnight.   **Serves 4**

When it's your turn to host the family Thanksgiving feast or any other autumnal gathering, try Jan Nelson's creative change of pace from the usual pumpkin pie. You will appreciate the foolproof crust, traditional filling and crunchy topping for this crowd-sized hit. Jan tops each square with whipped cream.

Caramel-Crowned Pumpkin Squares

CRUST
1 cup sifted flour
½ cup quick cooking rolled oats
½ cup brown sugar, firmly packed
½ cup butter, melted

FILLING
2 cups canned pumpkin
13-ounce can evaporated milk
2 eggs
¾ cup sugar
½ teaspoon salt
1 teaspoon cinnamon
½ teaspoon ginger
½ teaspoon cloves

TOPPING
½ cup chopped pecans
2 tablespoons butter
½ cup brown sugar, firmly packed
Whipped cream, as desired.

Preheat oven to 350°. Mix crust ingredients in food processor. Crust can also be mixed with pastry blender or on low in electric mixer. Press into bottom of 9 x 13-inch pan. Bake 15 minutes. Combine filling ingredients in large mixer bowl. Beat thoroughly. Pour over crust. Bake for 20 minutes. Combine topping ingredients. Sprinkle over pumpkin filling. Return to oven and bake 15 to 20 minutes or until filling is set. Cool and cut into 2 inch squares. Serve with whipped cream.

Yield: 2 dozen

Club member Theresa Waldman of Edina, who won the "Name the Cookbook Contest," shares a recipe given to her by her husband's 90-year-old grandmother. "She is from England and traditionally serves this for Thanksgiving, Christmas and family birthdays," says Theresa. "It's been in her family for years."

Pineapple Cheesecake

1½ cups crushed graham crackers (about 12)
2 tablespoons sugar
¼ cup melted butter
12 ounces cream cheese, softened
½ cup sugar
½ teaspoon vanilla
20-ounce can crushed pineapple, well drained

TOPPING
1 pint sour cream
3 tablespoons sugar
1 teaspoon vanilla

Preheat oven to 375°. For crust, combine graham crackers, sugar and melted butter. Press over the bottom and sides of a 9-inch springform pan. Mix cream cheese, sugar and vanilla in a bowl until blended. Fold in well-drained pineapple. Pour over crust and bake for 20 minutes. Remove from oven and cool 1 hour.

For topping, combine sour cream, sugar and vanilla. Spread over cooled cheesecake. Bake for 5 minutes. Remove from oven and cool 1 hour.

Serves 10 to 12

A honey of a dessert from Lynne Kilmer (Marty Lass' mother). Working with filo dough is not difficult. However, we suggest covering unused sheets of dough with a dish towel so they don't dry out before layering process is completed. And, as Lynne suggests, "Have all ingredients assembled and ready before you open the package of dough."

Baklava

3 cups ground walnuts
1 cup sugar
1 tablespoon cinnamon
3 tablespoons water

½ pound unsalted butter, melted
1-pound box filo dough, thawed
¾ cup honey

Preheat oven to 300°. Mix walnuts, sugar, cinnamon and water; set aside. Melt butter. Unroll dough; cut to fit 19¼ x 11½-inch baking sheet. Put half of filo sheets in pan. Top with filling. Cover with remaining filo except last three sheets. Brush butter between last three sheets. Cut through top sheets (down to filling) with a sharp knife into diamonds (diagonally). Pour remaining melted butter over pan of baklava. Bake 45 minutes to 1 hour or until golden brown. Remove from oven and immediately pour honey evenly over top. With sharp knife, continue cutting through all sheets of baklava. Cool completely. Store in airtight container with waxed paper between layers up to 2 weeks. Or wrap and freeze.

Serves 18 to 20

"Unbelievably good!" says contributor Debbie Dimmock of Edina. "After baking, you have a brownie-like topping over a softer pudding layer." Tester Karen Remund suggests spooning it into shallow dessert dishes and topping with dollops of whipped cream or vanilla ice cream. "It's just delicious," she adds.

Fudge Fantasy Dessert

½ cup sifted flour
½ cup cocoa
2 cups sugar

4 eggs
1 cup butter, melted
2 teaspoons vanilla

Preheat oven to 350°. Combine flour, cocoa and sugar. Beat eggs, butter and vanilla together. Blend egg mixture into flour mixture. Spread evenly in a 9-inch square pan. Set pan in larger pan with 1 inch hot water. Bake for 1 hour or slightly longer. Let set for 30 minutes before serving

Serves 6 to 8

Just a hint of brandy sparks the mousse-like texture and flavor of Allison Gaasedelen's heavenly dessert. Chocolate can also be melted in the microwave with scorch-free results. Choose your prettiest serving dishes for this dinner party dazzler.

Creamy Chocolate Celeste

8 ounces semi-sweet chocolate
1 ounce unsweetened chocolate
2 tablespoons butter or
 margarine
2 cups whipping cream
2 tablespoons strong coffee
Dash salt
2 pasteurized eggs, separated
1 tablespoon brandy

Melt chocolate with butter over hot, not boiling, water, stirring to blend until smooth. Remove from heat. Stir in coffee, salt, egg yolks and brandy. Cool slightly. Beat egg whites until stiff. Slowly fold whites into chocolate mixture until thoroughly combined. Whip cream until it mounds softly but is not stiff. Fold into chocolate mixture to obtain marbled effect. Spoon into dessert dishes, mounding high. Chill several hours. If desired, garnish with cherries, whipped cream, shaved chocolate and/or chopped nuts

Serves 8

"This has been a special favorite in my family for several generations," says contributor Nathalie Person of Edina. And, now it's a favorite of tester Marlys Wahlberg as well. "It took only 15 minutes to prepare and both flavor and appearance are excellent!" she reports. On the Swedish table, rice puddings can be found as a side dish to the entrée or as a dessert.

Swedish Rice Pudding

½ cup long grain rice
4 eggs
¾ cup sugar
2 cups milk
1 teaspoon vanilla
½ teaspoon salt
½ cup raisins
Nutmeg

Boil rice according to package directions until fluffy; drain. Beat eggs well; add sugar. Warm the milk and add rice. Combine with egg and sugar mixture. Add vanilla, salt and raisins. Preheat oven to 350°. Pour into 2-quart baking dish. Place in pan of warm water. Sprinkle nutmeg over pudding. Bake until set, about 1 hour. Test doneness by placing a knife in the center. Knife should come out clean.

Serves 8

What's for dessert? Jean Lein of Naples, FL, suggests a creamy molded mixture contrasted with colorful fresh fruits to spoon over each serving. "It's as delicious as it is attractive," she comments. Sharon Hundt, who tested this make-ahead recipe, trimmed calories using non-fat sour cream.

Russian Cream Dessert

¾ cup sugar
¼-ounce envelope unflavored gelatin
½ cup water
1 cup heavy whipping cream
1½ cups sour cream (12 ounces)
1 teaspoon vanilla
Berries or other fresh fruit, or mix of peaches and blueberries

Blend sugar and gelatin in small saucepan. Add water and mix well. Let stand 5 minutes, then bring to a full boil. Remove from heat and add unwhipped whipping cream. In bowl, mix sour cream and vanilla. Gradually beat in hot gelatin mixture, using wire whisk. Pour in 4 to 5-cup ring mold and chill at least 4 hours. Serve with fruit in center.

Serves 6 to 8

Marie Lacy treats us to a specialty of The Commander's Palace in New Orleans.
This upscale version of an old-timer will be a big hit at your next dinner party.
The pudding may be served warm from the oven or made ahead and chilled.
Serve the sauce warm to bring out the brisk brandy flavor.

Fruited Bread Pudding with Tipsy Sauce

PUDDING

3 cups cubed bread
½ cup raisins
½ cup canned mixed fruit cocktail, drained
1¼ cups milk
4 eggs
1½ cups sugar
2 tablespoons vanilla
1 tablespoon butter

SAUCE

2 cups hot milk
2 eggs
¾ cup sugar
4 tablespoons cornstarch
2 teaspoons butter
2 teaspoons vanilla
½ cup brandy or whiskey

Preheat oven to 300° For pudding, place bread cubes, raisins and fruit cocktail in an 11 x 13-inch or equivalent casserole. Bring milk to a boil. Combine eggs, sugar and vanilla in separate dish. Pour milk over that mixture and beat thoroughly. Pour over bread, raisins and fruit. Dot with butter and bake until firm, about 70 minutes. Serve hot or cold.

For sauce, bring milk to a boil. Combine eggs, sugar, cornstarch and butter in a double boiler. Add milk and cook over low heat until thickened. Remove from heat. Add vanilla and brandy just before serving.

Serves 6

From the files of Louise Saunders' family recipes comes one of her husband's favorite desserts. The old-fashioned flavor is enhanced by soaking the raisins in the rum-lemon mixture overnight or several hours before proceeding.

Charlie's Favorite Rum Rice Pudding

1 teaspoon lemon juice	Dash of salt
Zest of 1 lemon	2 tablespoons butter
2 tablespoons rum	2 eggs, separated
½ cup seedless raisins	⅓ cup sugar
2 cups milk	¼ teaspoon nutmeg
¼ cup rice	

Combine lemon juice, zest, rum and raisins in non-metallic container. Let stand overnight or at least several hours. In double boiler or heavy saucepan, combine milk, rice and salt. Cook gently just until rice is softened. Mix in butter. Beat egg yolks slightly. Pour a little of rice into yolks. Add sugar, remaining rice, nutmeg and raisins. Cool. Preheat oven to 325°. Beat two egg whites; fold into cooled rice mixture. Pour into buttered 1-quart soufflé baking dish. Set dish in pan of water. Bake for 30 to 40 minutes or until pudding is cooked.

Serves 6

A fast and fabulous finale from Marde Olson. Tester Judy Tucker advises keeping consistency thick and rich by not letting ice cream soften too much before blending. Have serving dishes or glasses ice cold for an extra frosty touch.

Brandy Bliss

½ cup brandy
¼ cup cold strong coffee
¼ cup chocolate syrup
1 quart coffee ice cream, slightly softened
Chocolate curls or dollop of whipped cream for garnish, if desired.

Combine all ingredients in blender or with electric mixer until smooth. Pour into serving dishes or glasses and garnish, if desired. Serve immediately.

Serves 4

Marianne Jasper, retired dental hygienist and wife of endodontist Dr. Eugene Jasper, provides us with a recipe which is very close in flavor to a frozen treat most of us have enjoyed at a popular soft-serve chain. A former chair of ECC's Women's 18-hole golf group, Marianne likes this best when made with coffee ice cream.

Fudge-Topped Freeze Royale

FUDGE SAUCE:

2 cups powdered sugar
1½ cups evaporated milk
⅔ cup chocolate chips
½ cup butter
1 teaspoon vanilla

TO COMPLETE RECIPE:

1 pound creme-filled chocolate sandwich cookies
½ cup butter, melted
1 cup Spanish peanuts, divided
½ gallon vanilla or coffee ice cream, slightly softened
Maraschino cherries, if desired

Combine powdered sugar, evaporated milk, chocolate chips, butter and vanilla in a medium pan. Boil 8 minutes, stirring constantly. Cool while stirring occasionally.

Crush cookies for crumb crust. Combine with melted butter. Press into 9 x 13-inch pan. Sprinkle evenly with 1/2 cup Spanish peanuts. Spread ice cream over top. Sprinkle with remaining nuts. Spread fudge sauce over top. Cover and freeze. Move to refrigerator to allow to soften for cutting.

For parfaits instead of squares, layer ingredients in parfait glasses, alternating fudge sauce, nuts, ice cream and crushed cookies. Top each with stemmed maraschino cherry, if desired.

Serves 16 to 20

Aloha and bon appetit! This island medley from Pat Borth of Phoenix, AZ, appears lengthy but is uncomplicated. And, in a pinch, canned pineapple can be substituted for fresh as tester Terry Swanson discovered. For variety, Terry suggests adding firm banana slices.

Seared Pineapple Sundae with Rum Sauce

½ cup granulated white sugar, divided
½ cup light brown sugar, divided
¼ cup cider vinegar
¼ cup unsweetened pineapple juice
½ cup whipping cream, unwhipped
½ cup dark rum, or to taste
1 vanilla bean, cut in half lengthwise
1 ripe medium pineapple
4 large scoops vanilla ice cream or frozen yogurt
4 sprigs fresh mint, washed

Prepare pineapple by trimming, paring and coring. Then cut into twelve ½-inch thick slices. In medium saucepan, combine ¼ cup of the white sugar, ¼ cup of the brown sugar, vinegar and pineapple juice. Bring to a simmer over medium-high heat. Cook until golden and thick enough to coat the back of a spoon, about 10 minutes. Add the whipping cream, rum and vanilla bean, cooking until thick enough to coat the spoon again, about 10 minutes. Remove from heat and keep warm. Remove the vanilla bean to a cutting board. With a paring knife, scrape inside of the vanilla bean to collect the tiny black seeds. Return seeds to the sauce. Discard the vanilla bean.

Preheat broiler to 550°. In a small bowl, combine remaining ¼ cup granulated sugar and ¼ cup brown sugar. Place 12 pineapple slices on broiler pan. Sprinkle pineapple with sugar mixture. Broil pineapple until sugar turns bubbly and golden, about 5 to 10 minutes, depending on your broiler. (Keep a close eye on this because the sugar can smoke quickly under some broilers.)

To serve: Place 3 pineapple rings slightly overlapping in a triangle shape in the center of warm serving plates. Position a large scoop of ice cream or frozen yogurt in the center of each pineapple triangle. Spoon warm sauce over the ice cream and pineapple. Garnish with a sprig of mint; serve immediately.

Serves 4

The development of this recipe was a team effort by former office colleagues, June Randall and June Swedberg. Tester Shirley Bard was most appreciative of their collaboration. "This is tastier than a dish of your favorite ice cream," she remarks. "Excellent on all counts!"

Frozen Pistachio Pleasure

CRUST
45 buttery round crushed crackers, such as Ritz
¼ pound butter or margarine, melted

FILLING
Two 3-ounce packages pistachio-flavored instant pudding
1½ cups milk
1 quart vanilla ice cream
8-ounce container whipped topping
3 milk chocolate English toffee candy bars, crushed

For crust, combine crackers and butter or margarine. Place in bottom of 9 x 13-inch cake pan; freeze about 15 minutes.

For filling, beat pudding, milk and ice cream together. Pour mixture over cracker crust. Cover with whipped topping. Sprinkle top with crushed candy. Refrigerate or freeze until serving.

This dessert can be made a day ahead and should be kept in freezer until 2 hours before serving. Refrigerate for the 2 hours before cutting into serving pieces.

Serves 8 to 12

Romona Tokheim's frozen lemon dessert is as cool and refreshing as a summer breeze. We suggest using fresh lemon juice for peak flavor and pasteurized eggs to conform to food safety guidelines. Garnish each yummy slice with a perfect strawberry or a lemon cartwheel.

Frosty Lemon Freeze

¾ cup fine graham cracker crumbs   ¼ cup lemon juice
   (about 6 crackers), divided   2 teaspoons lemon peel, grated
3 pasteurized eggs, separated   1 cup whipping cream
½ cup sugar

Sprinkle half of crumbs over bottom and sides of well greased 9-inch pie plate. Beat egg whites until frothy. Gradually add sugar, beating until stiff and glossy. In separate bowl, beat egg yolks until thick and lemon-colored. Fold in egg white mixture. Whip cream. Fold lemon juice and grated peel into whipped cream. Fold into egg mixture. Pour over crumbs. Sprinkle remaining crumbs on top and freeze. Remove from freezer 5 to 10 minutes before serving, or serve while still frozen.

Serves 6 to 8

"Very easy to make — rich but light and wonderful after a hearty meal," says tester Annette Nelson, who chose to try the cherry version. Contributor Ruth Hauskins of Edina keeps this on hand in the freezer for dinner parties or to delight drop-in guests. She makes it using raspberry pie filling. A taster who sampled the strawberry version likened it to old-fashioned strawberry ice cream.

Easiest-Ever Homemade Fruit Ice Cream

14-ounce can sweetened condensed milk
¼ cup lemon juice
21-ounce can raspberry, strawberry or cherry pie filling
8-ounce can regular crushed pineapple with juice
8-ounce carton whipped topping (regular or light)

Cherries or berries, whipped cream and chopped nuts for garnish
Combine all ingredients. Pour into 9 x 13-inch pan. Cover and freeze. Remove from freezer; cut into dessert-size pieces. Garnish with a dollop of whipped topping, whole berries or cherries and chopped nuts.

Serves 16 to 20

Dale Miller, ECC's General Manager, calls this "Texas Style" homemade ice cream because that's where he first enjoyed it some years ago at his soon-to-be inlaws. Nothing will cool you off better than a refreshing bowl (or two).

Texas-Style Homemade Vanilla Ice Cream

4 large or 6 medium eggs
14-ounce can sweetened
  condensed milk
2 cups sugar

1 gallon whole milk
  (entire gallon not needed)
1½ teaspoons vanilla

In large bowl, mix eggs with a fork. Add sweetened condensed milk and sugar; stir to combine well. Mix in 1 quart milk and vanilla. Pour mixture into ice cream freezer container. Add enough remaining milk to fill to 4-quart line. Follow manufacturer's directions for freezing step. If using a hand-cranked freezer, wipe ice and salt from can lid before removing. Remove dasher and smooth down ice cream with large spoon. Cover can opening with waxed paper and clean lid. Cover lid with additional ice and salt as needed. Let stand several hours for ice cream to thoroughly harden.

NOTE: Mashed bananas or peaches can be stirred into liquid in freezer can before freezing step. Use about a dozen ripe peaches or 6 to 8 bananas. Over-ripe bananas should not be used for fear of spoiling flavor and color quality. **Yield: One gallon**

Eat your cereal and help yourself to a cookie at the same time. Judy Tucker has successfully combined the two in these quickly-mixed, sugar-dusted morsels. Tester Mary L. Miller found that for a deliciously tender texture, baking time should not exceed 12 minutes. She also reports that the cookies freeze beautifully.

Round-the-Clock Cereal Cookies

1 cup butter, softened
1 cup sugar
1½ cups flour
1 teaspoon soda
½ teaspoon salt

½ teaspoon cream of tartar
½ teaspoon vanilla
½ cup chopped pecans
2 cups corn flakes
Powdered sugar

Preheat oven to 350°. Cream butter and sugar. Add remaining ingredients. Mix well. Drop by rounded teaspoonsful onto ungreased cookie sheet (15 per sheet works well). Bake 10 to 12 minutes or until lightly brown. Allow to set on cookie sheet 2 to 3 minutes before removing. Sprinkle with powdered sugar when cooled.

Yield: 5 dozen cookies

Terry Swanson's cookies are just the thing to munch on for a morning coffee break or any other time of day. Allow time to chill the dough so it rolls easily into balls. For added orange flavor, mix a little grated zest to the batter.

Coffee Break Cookies

1 cup shortening	2 cups flour
1 cup white sugar	1 teaspoon baking soda
1 cup brown sugar	1 teaspoon salt
2 eggs	1 teaspoon baking powder
3 tablespoons orange juice	1 cup coconut
½ teaspoon vanilla	2 cups oatmeal

Preheat oven to 350°. In mixer bowl, cream shortening and sugars. Add eggs one at a time; beat 2 minutes. Add orange juice and vanilla. Add dry ingredients divided in 3 stages for thorough mixing. Chill dough until easily handled. Form balls and flatten with a glass which has been dipped in water, then in sugar. Place on greased cookie sheet. Bake 8 minutes.

Yield: 36 cookies

Another gem from Judy Tucker's cookie jar! Crisp and delicate, these are as easy to eat as they are to make. The name comes from the fact that the batter separates into a lacy texture as cookies bake.

Oatmeal Lace Cookies

1 cup quick oatmeal	1 egg, beaten
1 cup sugar	½ teaspoon vanilla
2 tablespoons flour	¼ teaspoon salt
½ cup melted butter	

Preheat oven to 350°. In mixer bowl, combine oatmeal, sugar and flour. Beat in butter, egg, vanilla and salt. Cover cookie sheets with aluminum foil. Drop batter by teaspoonsful 3 inches apart. Bake 5 to 8 minutes or until light to medium brown. (Do not over-bake.) Cool; remove cookies from foil.

Yield: 6 dozen cookies

Not too sweet and egg-free for the allergy-prone. Jan Collins advises chilling dough for easy handling. If desired, use ½ cup margarine and ½ cup butter to retain rich flavor with a little less cholesterol.

Oatmeal-Walnut Cookies

1 cup butter, softened
½ cup granulated sugar
½ cup brown sugar,
   firmly packed
1 teaspoon soda
1 tablespoon hot water

3 cups quick oats
1 cup flour
½ teaspoon vanilla
1 cup walnuts, chopped

Preheat oven to 375°. Cream butter and sugars. Add soda, water, oats, flour and vanilla. Beat until well combined. Fold in chopped nuts. Chill dough 30 minutes. Roll dough into balls. Place on greased cookie sheet. Flatten with a glass which has been dipped in water. Bake 10 minutes.

Yield: 36 cookies

Crushed potato chips are a surprise ingredient in Pat Meyers' drop cookies and they eliminate the need for salt. Tester Mary L. Miller skipped the chocolate-dipping step and enjoyed them as is. So, suit yourself and your timetable.

Chipper Butter Cookies

1 cup unsalted butter, softened
¾ cup sugar
1½ cups flour
1 teaspoon vanilla
¾ cup finely-crushed potato chips
Melted chocolate, if desired

Preheat oven to 325°. Cream butter and sugar. Add flour gradually. Stir in vanilla and chips. Drop dough by teaspoonsful onto ungreased cookie sheet. Bake about 15 minutes or until lightly browned. Remove to wire rack. Try dipping cooled cookie into melted chocolate for a variation.

Yield: About 50 cookies

From June Randall, a dressy chocolate-drizzled cookie with an Italian heritage. Candied orange peel can be found in specialty stores or in the baking products area of many large supermarkets. Transfer delicate cookies from cookie sheet to cooling rack with care to avoid breaking.

Florentines

½ cup heavy whipping cream
3 tablespoons butter
½ cup sugar
1¼ cups finely-chopped
   almonds

⅓ cup flour, sifted
¾ cup finely-chopped
   candied orange peel
Melted chocolate

Preheat oven to 350°. Combine cream, butter and sugar in saucepan; bring to a boil. Remove from heat and stir in almonds, flour and candied orange peel. Drop by tablespoonsful 3 inches apart onto greased, floured cookie sheet. Bake about 10 minutes; cool 5 minutes. Remove carefully with spatula to cooling rack. Cool. Spiral melted chocolate over cookie tops.

Yield: About 2 dozen 3-inch cookies

"A frequently-requested recipe of our children and grandchildren," says Mary Gregory Rischmiller of Edina. An hour of chilling makes the batter easy to roll before baking. Tester Pat Meyers tried these out over the holidays and used colored sugars. "Great old-fashioned flavor," she found.

Ginger-Molasses Cookies

¾ cup shortening or butter
1 cup sugar
¼ cup molasses
1 egg
2½ cups flour

2 teaspoons baking soda
½ teaspoon ground cloves
½ teaspoon ginger
1 teaspoon cinnamon
½ teaspoon salt

Melt shortening. Add sugar, molasses and egg. Beat until mixed well. Combine flour, soda, cloves, ginger, cinnamon and salt. Add to shortening mixture. Beat thoroughly until mixed. Cover and chill for at least 1 hour in refrigerator. Preheat oven to 375°. Form dough into balls the size of a walnut and roll in sugar. Bake on greased cookie sheet for 10 minutes.

Yield: 4 dozen

Freshly-grated ginger root offers a mild rather than robust flavor for these golden, crisp make-ahead cookies. The thin tan "skin" of fresh ginger is removed before grating. The leftover portion can be stored for months in the freezer if wrapped tightly.

Fresh Gingersnaps

⅓ cup butter, softened
⅓ cup solid vegetable shortening
1¼ cups sugar (divided)
1 egg
2 tablespoons dark corn syrup
1 heaping tablespoon freshly-grated ginger root
2 cups flour
1 teaspoon ground cloves
1½ teaspoons baking soda
½ teaspoon salt
1 teaspoon cinnamon

Cream together butter, shortening and 1 cup sugar. Add egg and mix well. Stir in syrup and ginger root. Sift together flour, cloves, baking soda and salt; add to butter mixture. Continue to mix until well blended. Cover and chill dough for one hour or overnight. Preheat oven to 350°. Combine cinnamon and remaining ¼ cup sugar. Form dough into 1-inch balls and roll in cinnamon-sugar mixture until evenly coated. Place balls 2 inches apart on greased cookie sheets. Bake for 10 to 12 minutes, or until lightly browned and beginning to crackle on top. Cool slightly, then remove to wire racks to cool.

Yield: 60 cookies

This recipe is aptly named for Leanne Plessel, who was ECC's Pastry Chef when the Club reopened in 1989. She was a member of the culinary staff for over three years before leaving to open her own bakery and deli. We thank her for leaving behind this delicious reminder of her cookie-making skills

Leanne's Sugar Cookies

1 cup butter, softened
1½ cups sugar
3 egg yolks
1 teaspoon vanilla
1½ to 2 cups sifted cake flour
    (depending on size of yolks)

1 teaspoon soda
½ teaspoon cream of tartar
Additional sugar

Preheat oven to 350°. Cream butter and sugar. Add egg yolks and mix well. Add vanilla. Combine dry ingredients and fold into above mixture until blended. Form into balls and roll in sugar. Place on lightly greased cookie sheet about 3 inches apart. Flatten with water glass dipped in sugar. Bake 8 to 10 minutes or until bottoms of cookies are light brown.

Yield: 4 dozen 2½ inch cookies

"A nice white sugar cookie that's easy to make," says tester Vicki Kattke about June Randall's butter-rich recipe. Use of brown as well as white sugar makes this a little different than most sugar cookies.

Crisp Sugar Cookies

1 cup butter or margarine
¾ cup brown sugar
¾ cup white sugar
1 egg
1 teaspoon baking soda,
    dissolved in teaspoon of warm water

1 teaspoon vanilla
2¼ cups flour
1 teaspoon baking powder
1 teaspoon salt

Preheat oven to 400°. Cream butter or margarine and sugars. Add egg and mix well. Add soda and vanilla. Combine dry ingredients and add to creamed mixture. Roll dough into walnut sized pieces. Place on greased cookie sheet; press with a fork crisscross style. Bake 10 to 12 minutes or until light brown.

Yield: 4 dozen

"This makes a big enough batch so you can share with friends," says Terri Gulliford about her rolled sugar cookies. The chilling step of several hours is very important and will ease preparation. Why not plan a cookie decorating party for little ones? Have cookies baked and cooled, frosting ready to spread and a variety of sprinkles and candies available to top each creation.

Friendship Sugar Cookies

1½ cups powdered sugar
1 cup butter or margarine, softened
1 egg
1 teaspoon vanilla
½ teaspoon almond extract
2½ cups flour
1 teaspoon soda
1 teaspoon cream of tartar

FROSTING
1 pound powdered sugar (3½ cups)
¼ cup butter or margarine, softened
¼ cup milk
1 teaspoon vanilla
¼ teaspoon salt, optional

For cookies, cream sugar and butter. Add egg and flavorings; mix thoroughly. Sift dry ingredients together. Blend with butter mixture in cusinart or mixer. Refrigerate 2 to 3 hours. Preheat oven to 375°. Divide dough and roll ³⁄₁₆-inch thick on lightly-floured pastry sheet. Use cookie cutters of choice. Place on lightly-greased cookie sheets. Bake 6 to 8 minutes. Cookies will not brown. Cool and frost.

For frosting, beat all ingredients until smooth. (Add more milk, if necessary, for easy spreading consistency.) Frosting can be tinted red, pink or green for holidays.

Yield: 5 dozen (give a dozen to a friend)

A trio of favorite ingredients — oatmeal, coconut and chocolate chips, with the interesting crunch of rice cereal, gives Judy Tucker's stir-and-drop cookies mouth watering appeal. A lunch box and after-school treat that can't be beat! Tester Heather King used 12 ounces of chocolate chips and froze some of the cookies for a later date.

Triple Treat Drop Cookies

1 cup butter or margarine
1 cup brown sugar
1 cup white sugar
1 cup oil
1 egg
2 teaspoons vanilla
3½ cups flour
1 teaspoon salt
½ to 1 teaspoon soda
1 teaspoon cream of tartar
1 cup quick oats
1 cup flaked coconut, toasted
1 cup crispy rice cereal
6 or 12-ounce package chocolate chips

Preheat oven to 350°. In large mixing bowl, cream butter and sugars. Mix in oil, egg and vanilla. Combine dry ingredients; add to creamed mixture and blend well. Stir in oats, coconut, rice cereal and chocolate chips. Drop by teaspoonsful onto ungreased cookie sheets about 2 inches apart, shaping into mounds with fingers. Bake about 12 minutes or until lightly browned. Cool just briefly on sheets before transferring to racks.

Yield: About 5 dozen

Rebecca Walser has just the formula for a kid-pleasing dessert. And, it provides plenty for the whole team! Make the cake portion ahead, if desired, and add filling and frosting later. Note that the frosting is spread as soon as chips are melted.

Homemade Ho-Hos

LAYER 1

¼ pound butter or margarine

1 cup water

½ cup oil

3 tablespoons cocoa

2 cups flour

1 cup sugar

1 teaspoon soda

1 teaspoon salt

1 teaspoon vanilla

2 eggs

½ cup buttermilk

FILLING

2 cups powdered sugar, divided

¼ teaspoon salt

1 teaspoon vanilla

1 tablespoon water

1 cup butter or margarine

½ cup milk

FROSTING

2 cups sugar

¾ cup butter or margarine (1½ sticks)

¾ cup milk

1 cup chocolate chips

Preheat oven to 350°. In saucepan, combine butter, water, oil and cocoa until butter is melted. In bowl, combine flour, sugar, soda, salt and vanilla. Add butter mixture to bowl; beat until well mixed. Beat in eggs and buttermilk. Pour batter into 10 x 15-inch greased jelly roll pan. Bake 20 to 30 minutes; let cool. For filling, cream 1 cup powdered sugar and butter or margarine. Beat in milk, water, salt and vanilla. Add one more cup powdered sugar; beat until smooth. Spread on cooled cake. For frosting, boil sugar, margarine and milk for 1 minute only. Add chocolate chips; stir until chips melt. Spread over bars while still warm.

Serves 12 to 15

Serve an after-dinner liqueur and dessert in one sweet package with Mary Ellen Godfrey's innovative recipe. "The texture is meant to be moist and fudge-like. Also, the amount of kahlua poured over after baking can be adjusted to suit personal tastes," comments Mary Ellen. She prefers serving squares warm with a spoonful of whipped topping.

Kahlua Fudge Brownies

3 large eggs
2 cups sugar
1¼ cups kahlua, divided
⅔ cup butter
3 squares unsweetened
  baking chocolate

1½ cups sifted flour
½ teaspoon baking powder
½ teaspoon salt
¾ cup pecans, chopped

Preheat oven to 350°. In large mixer bowl, beat eggs well. Add sugar and beat until light. Melt baking chocolate and butter in double boiler. Add ¼ cup of the kahlua and chocolate mixture to eggs and sugar. Sift together flour, baking powder and salt. Add to above mixture. Fold in chopped nuts. Pour into well-greased foil-lined 8 x 8-inch pan. Bake 30 to 40 minutes or until top springs back. Cool 5 minutes. Brush top with ⅓ to ½ cup kahlua and let seep in. Cool another 8 to 10 minutes and repeat with another ½ cup kahlua. Place in refrigerator. Cut when cold. These freeze well.

Yield: 9 squares

No need to be a championship golfer to enjoy playing the game. And, no need to be a gourmet cook to whip up these nut-lover's brownies. Thanks to Lynne Kilmer, mother of P.G.A. Golf Professional Marty Lass, for sharing this speedy and sensational sweet.

Fast and Fab Fudge Nut Brownies

4 squares unsweetened
  chocolate
1 cup margarine
2 cups sugar
4 eggs

1 cup flour
1 teaspoon vanilla
2 cups chopped walnuts
  or pecans

Preheat oven to 350°. In large saucepan over low heat, melt chocolate and margarine. Remove from heat and stir in sugar. Add eggs, one at a time, beating well after each addition. Add flour, vanilla and nuts; mix well. Pour into greased 9 x 13-inch pan. Bake 35 minutes.

Yield: About 2 dozen

Brownie points for Marde Olson, who provides yet another enticing variation of this popular bar dessert. It's sure to please cheesecake fans as well as brownie lovers and is streamlined with the help of a cake mix. Definitely make-ahead because it must be chilled for eight hours before serving.

Brownie-Cheesecake Bars

1 German chocolate cake mix
½ cup coconut
⅓ cup margarine, softened
3 eggs, divided
16 ounces cream cheese, softened

2 teaspoons vanilla
¾ cup plus 3 tablespoons sugar, divided
1 cup sour cream

Preheat oven to 350°. Blend cake mix, coconut, margarine and 1 egg until crumbly. Press lightly into ungreased 9 x 13-inch pan. Beat cream cheese, ¾ cup sugar, 2 eggs and vanilla until fluffy. Spread filling over cake mixture; bake for 20 to 25 minutes until center is firm. Beat sour cream and 3 tablespoons sugar. Spread evenly over hot cake. Cool, then refrigerate at least 8 hours before serving.

Makes 2½ dozen 2 x 1½-inch bars

Tester Jacqui Jarnes had no reservations about taking Pat Clemmer's favorite brownie recipe to a Christmas party to try it out. "It was a huge hit!" says Jacqui. "The flavor reminds me of milk chocolate and preparation is super easy."

Buttermilk Brownies

¼ pound margarine or butter (½ cup)
1 cup water
2 teaspoons cocoa
2 cups sugar
2 cups flour
½ teaspoon salt
2 eggs, well beaten

1 teaspoon baking soda
1 teaspoon vanilla
½ cup buttermilk
FROSTING
¼ pound butter or margarine
3 tablespoons cocoa
4 tablespoons milk
1 pound powdered sugar

Preheat oven to 350°. Combine butter or margarine, water and cocoa in saucepan; bring to boil. Remove from heat. Sift together sugar, flour and salt. Pour cocoa mixture over dry ingredients. In separate bowl, combine eggs, soda, vanilla and buttermilk. Then, combine with other ingredients. Spread batter in greased 10 x 15-inch jelly roll pan. Bake for 15 to 20 minutes. Frost while still warm. For frosting, combine butter or margarine, cocoa and milk in small saucepan. Cook, stirring over low heat until smooth. Mix in powdered sugar. Frost brownies while still warm. **Yield: Approximately 40**

If you share Marde Olson's notion that "we all need something decadent once in a while," you will want to whip up a batch of these "fabulous" layered bars. Allow plenty of time for final refrigeration step and take care not to over-bake. Baking these and other brownies in the center of the oven is essential for even heat circulation.

French Silk Brownies

BASE:
1 cup sugar
½ cup margarine, softened
4 eggs
1 teaspoon vanilla
16-ounce can chocolate syrup
1 cup plus 1 tablespoon flour
½ teaspoon baking powder
⅛ teaspoon salt
½ cup chopped pecans

TOPPING:
1¼ cups sugar
¾ cup margarine, softened
3 eggs
3 ounces unsweetened chocolate, melted and cooled
1½ teaspoons vanilla

GLAZE:
1 ounce semi-sweet chocolate
1 tablespoon butter

Preheat oven to 350°. To make base, beat sugar and margarine. Add eggs and beat well. Beat in vanilla, chocolate syrup, flour, baking powder and salt. Stir in nuts. Pour into greased 9 x 13-inch pan. Bake 25 to 30 minutes (do not over-bake). Cool.

For topping, cream sugar and margarine with electric mixer. Add eggs one at a time, beating 2 minutes after each. Blend in chocolate and vanilla; spread evenly over cooled base.

For glaze, melt chocolate and butter over low heat in double boiler. Drizzle evenly over top of brownies. Refrigerate at least 2 hours before serving. Cut into bars.

Yield: 36 bars

These rich, buttery bars with their chewy consistency are an appealing alternative to chocolate brownies. "I've enjoyed the recipe since childhood," says Diane Aves of Bloomington. A busy mother of three young children and the owner of a health care marketing firm, she clears the calendar whenever possible for a round of golf.

Best Butterscotch Bars

1 pound brown sugar, firmly packed (2¼ to 2⅓ cups)	2 eggs
	2 cups flour
1 cup butter or margarine, softened	1 teaspoon baking powder
	½ teaspoon salt

Preheat oven to 350°. Heat sugar and butter in medium saucepan over low heat stirring until sugar dissolves, stirring constantly. Cool until lukewarm. Add eggs, one at a time, beating thoroughly after each addition. Sift together flour, baking powder and salt. Add to butter-sugar mixture. Spread evenly in ungreased 15½ x 10½-inch jelly roll pan. Bake on center rack of oven 25 minutes or until bars are a delicate brown. (A slight dent is left when you lightly touch the top.) Remove pan from oven and set on wire rack. Cut while hot.

Yield: 40 bars

Shirley Bentdahl's candy-like bars begin with a simple soda cracker base and end with mouth-watering toffee flavor. Tester Diane Aves suggests cooling completely for easier cutting and storing in a cool spot to keep chocolate from getting "gooey."

Tastes-Like-Toffee Bars

40 salted soda cracker squares	1 cup slivered almonds
1 cup butter	1 cup sliced pecans
1 cup brown sugar, firmly pressed	2 cups chocolate chips

Line a 10 x 15-inch jelly roll pan with aluminum foil rubbed with butter. Line pan with rows of soda crackers, salt-side-down. Preheat oven to 350°. In medium saucepan, melt butter. Add brown sugar, almonds and pecans. Bring mixture to boil over medium heat. Boil for 2 minutes, stirring frequently. Pour evenly over crackers and bake for 10 minutes. Remove from oven and immediately sprinkle with chocolate chips. Smooth to cover evenly. Cool and cut into squares. Store, covered, in a cool place.

Serves 40

"This sweet, buttery bar just melts in your mouth," says Edina-based home economist Pat Sinclair. "I always prepare it during the holidays." Pat specializes in recipe development and testing plus answering consumer questions for major food companies in the Twin Cities.

Dutch Treat Squares

2 cups all-purpose flour
1 cup sugar
1 cup butter, softened
1 egg, separated

1 teaspoon ground cinnamon
½ teaspoon salt
1 cup sliced almonds

Preheat oven to 350°. In large mixer bowl, combine flour, sugar, butter, egg yolk, cinnamon and salt. Beat at low speed, scraping bowl often, until well mixed, 2 to 3 minutes. Divide dough into halves. Press each half onto an ungreased cookie sheet to 1/16- inch thickness. In small bowl, beat egg white with fork until foamy. Brush over dough; sprinkle with nuts. Bake for 12 to 15 minutes, or until very lightly browned. Immediately cut into 2-inch squares and remove from pan. Cool completely.

Yield: 3 to 4 dozen squares

Judy Tucker contributes a decorative variation on the traditional Scottish shortbread theme. The jewel-like ribbons of raspberry preserves offer special-occasion status. Be sure to add glaze before pastry cools completely.

Raspberry Shortbread

1 cup softened butter
½ cup + 2 tablespoons sugar
2½ cups flour
1 cup raspberry jam

1 cup powdered sugar
2 teaspoons almond extract
2 to 3 teaspoons water

Preheat oven to 350°. Cream butter and sugar with electric mixer. Add flour and mix well. Divide dough into five equal portions. Place three parts on one cookie sheet, two parts on another sheet. Roll or pat each portion into strips which are about 2 inches wide and as long as the baking sheets. Strips should be 1 inch apart. With your finger, form an indentation down the center of each strip. Spread jam in each indentation. Bake 10 minutes or until edges are lightly browned. Combine powdered sugar, extract and water for a glaze consistency. Drizzle over pastry while still warm. Cool completely. Cut each strip diagonally into 12 pieces.

Yield: About 60 cookies

A festive looking, sugar-dusted Bundt or tube cake from Cynthia Quinn. "My family loves this moist, yummy cake and it keeps well," she says. Chop apples finely so cake will slice attractively when serving.

Apple-Cinnamon Cake

2 cups sugar
1 cup cooking oil
2 eggs, well beaten
4 cups peeled, chopped cooking apples
2½ cups flour
1 teaspoon salt
1 teaspoon baking soda
1 teaspoon cinnamon
1 teaspoon vanilla
½ cup chopped walnuts
Powdered sugar

Preheat oven to 350°. Grease a Bundt or tube pan. Combine sugar, oil, eggs and apples; let stand 20 minutes. Add remaining ingredients and mix well. Pour into prepared pan. Bake for 60 to 70 minutes (or until a toothpick inserted in the center comes out clean). Cool slightly. Carefully remove from pan. Sprinkle with powdered sugar when completely cooled. Cover and store only when completely cool.

Serves 12 to 16

What a sweet way to consume nutritious carrots! Maxine Thorkelson's recipe is made especially moist with the addition of crushed pineapple and the coconut and nuts add to the appealing texture. A traditional cream cheese frosting is the final tasty touch.

Fresh Carrot Cake

3 eggs
1½ cups cooking oil
2 cups sugar
2 teaspoons vanilla
2 cups plus 1 tablespoon flour
1 teaspoon baking soda
1 teaspoon salt
7-ounce package flaked coconut
2 cups shredded carrots
8-ounce can sweetened crushed pineapple with juice
2 teaspoons cinnamon
1 cup chopped pecans

Preheat oven to 350°. Beat eggs in large mixer bowl. Blend in oil, sugar and vanilla. In another bowl, blend flour, baking soda and salt. Add flour mixture to mixer bowl. Combine well. Stir in coconut, carrots, pineapple, cinnamon and pecans. Spread mixture in greased 9 x 13-inch baking pan. Bake for about 50 minutes or until cake tests done. Cool cake and frost with Cream Cheese Frosting.

Serves 12

Cream Cheese Frosting

8-ounce package cream cheese, softened
½ cup butter or margarine, softened
3½ cups sifted powdered sugar
1 teaspoon vanilla

Combine softened cheese and butter or margarine. Gradually add powdered sugar, mixing well. Add vanilla. Spread over cooled carrot cake.

Sugar and spice make Jean Giroulx's apple cake especially nice. And, the caramel glaze makes it even better! "Kids just love this," reports tester Jaye Vaaler. We would have to add that adults do, too!

Caramel-Glazed Apple Cake

1 cup cooking oil
2 cups sugar
3 eggs
1 tablespoon vanilla
3 cups all-purpose flour
1 teaspoon baking soda
1 teaspoon nutmeg
1 teaspoon cloves
1 tablespoon cinnamon
½ teaspoon salt
3 cups apples, peeled, quartered and thinly-sliced
Vanilla ice cream or whipped cream, optional

CARAMEL GLAZE
½ cup butter
½ cup brown sugar, firmly packed
2 tablespoons milk
1 teaspoon vanilla

Preheat oven to 350°. In large mixer bowl, combine oil and sugar. Beat in eggs; stir in vanilla. In small bowl, combine flour, soda, nutmeg, cloves, cinnamon and salt. Stir into egg mixture. Stir in apples. Pour mixture into well-greased 12-cup Bundt pan. Bake for 50 minutes, or until toothpick inserted in center comes out clean.

Before end of baking time, prepare caramel glaze. Combine all ingredients in small saucepan. Bring to a boil and cook 1 minute. Remove cake from oven and leave it in the pan. Gently pull cake away from sides of pan with a fork; pour glaze onto the cake immediately. Leave cake in pan to cool slightly, then invert onto a serving plate. Serve warm or chilled with vanilla ice cream or whipped cream.

Serves 12 to 16

A simple angel food cake is elevated to celebratory status when transformed with a tangy lemon filling. Elizabeth Kane coaxed a college classmate to give her the recipe and the Kanes have enjoyed it ever since. "A little effort brings impressive results," she says. "Make ahead so filling has time to set and flavors blend."

Mimi's Christening Cake

1 round angel food cake (from bakery or homemade)
14-ounce can sweetened condensed milk
8-ounce carton whipped topping
2 lemons (grated rind from one; juice from both)

Slice cake across into three equal layers. Gently combine sweetened condensed milk with whipped topping (do not use mixer). Fold in grated rind from one lemon and the juice from both. Spread mixture between cake layers and over sides and top. Store in refrigerator.

Serves 10 to 12

When Debbie Dimmock's sons were away at college in Arizona, this was their most requested "care package" from Mom. "It's a casual cake. We like to have it on hand so snackers can just cut a slice when hunger strikes." Formerly in the travel business, Debbie is back in school, this time to study gemology in preparation for a new career as an appraiser.

Special Request Lemon Cake

1 package lemon cake mix (2 layer size without pudding addition)
1 package instant lemon pudding (4-serving size)
4 eggs, beaten
¾ cup vegetable oil
1 cup water
2 cups powdered sugar
⅓ cup lemon juice
3 teaspoons oil

Preheat oven to 350°. Combine first five ingredients until well blended. Pour into a greased Bundt or tube pan; bake 40 to 50 minutes. Remove from oven and prick, all over, with a large fork. Combine powdered sugar, lemon juice and oil; pour over hot cake. Let cool, and remove from pan.

Serves 12 to 16

Doreen O'Toole (Marty Lass' mother-in-law) shares a "long-time family favorite. This is a big hit at showers and other gatherings," she says. The splendid sauce will become a sweet staple in your collection once you've tasted it. Try over ice cream, angel or pound cake and frozen yogurt as well as the torte.

Butterscotch Torte

6 eggs, separated
1½ cups sugar
1 teaspoon baking powder
2 teaspoons vanilla
1 teaspoon almond extract
2 cups graham cracker crumbs
1 cup chopped nuts

SAUCE
1 cup brown sugar
1 tablespoon flour
¼ cup butter
¼ cup orange juice
¼ cup water
1 teaspoon vanilla
8-ounce carton whipped topping
Chopped nuts, if desired

Preheat oven to 325°. Beat egg whites until stiff but not dry; set aside. In large separate bowl, beat egg yolks, sugar and baking powder until fluffy. Add vanilla and almond extracts. Fold in egg whites, crumbs and nuts. Spread batter in greased 9 x 13-inch pan. Bake 35 minutes. Cool before next step.

For sauce, combine all ingredients except whipped topping in saucepan. Simmer, stirring constantly until thickened. Cool. When cake is cool, cover with whipped topping. Then drizzle the sauce over top. If desired, sprinkle a few chopped nuts over each serving. Store in refrigerator.

Serves 16

A perfect blending of "the smooth taste of chocolate and the tart snap of raspberries," says ECC Pastry Chef Joe Frieler. The unadorned cake can be frozen for up to six weeks. On the day of serving, complete assembly with the chocolate coating, sauce and fresh berries for garnish. "Elegant" comments tester Romona Tokheim.

Chocolate Decadence

FOR CAKE:
6 ounces semi-sweet or
  bitterweet chocolate,
  chopped
6 ounces butter
1 single serving packet
  instant coffee
2 tablespoons vanilla
6 egg yolks (reserve whites)
1 cup brown sugar
½ cup all-purpose flour
6 egg whites
½ cup granulated sugar

FOR GANACHE COATING:
½ cup heavy whipping cream
1 cup chopped bittersweet
  or semi-sweet chocolate

FOR RASPBERRY SAUCE
¼ cup Burgundy wine
1 quarter of an orange
½ cup granulated sugar
2 tablespoons cornstarch
2 tablespoons water
2 cups fresh or frozen
  raspberries
2 to 3 fresh raspberries
  for garnish per serving

For cake, preheat oven to 400°. Melt together chocolate, butter, instant coffee and vanilla in microwave or double boiler. Whip together egg yolks and sugar on high speed. When thick and lemon colored, add flour; whip for 1 minute. Add cooled chocolate mixture to yolk mixture; mix until blended. Whip egg whites to soft peaks. Slowly add sugar, whipping to medium peak. Stir small amount of egg white mixture into chocolate mixture; then add remaining mixture. Bake in greased 8 or 9-inch greased springform pan 35 to 45 minutes or until toothpick comes out clean. Center of cake will fall slightly when cooled.

For coating, heat cream in saucepan just until it starts to simmer. Remove from heat and add chocolate. Cover, let stand 5 minutes. Stir until well blended. Pour evenly over cake to cover.

For raspberry sauce, combine first four ingredients in a saucepan; heat to a simmer. Dissolve cornstarch in water. Add slowly to raspberries while stirring until slightly thickened. Strain through fine sieve. The day cake is served, spread raspberry sauce over top of coated cake. Garnish with fresh 2 to 3 fresh raspberries.

Serves 12

"This cake is a favorite because it isn't terribly rich," says contributor Mary Ellen Godfrey. "It's barely out of the oven and a third of it has already been eaten!" adds enthusiastic tester Marie Lacy. Before baking, Mary Ellen gently presses chocolate chips and nuts into batter with a spatula so they "sink in just a bit."

Oatmeal-Chocolate Chip Cake

1¾ cups boiling water
1 cup quick rolled oats
½ cup butter, softened
1 cup granulated sugar
1 cup brown sugar
2 eggs, slightly beaten
1¾ cups flour
1 tablespoon cocoa
1 teaspoon soda
½ teaspoon salt
2 cups chocolate chips, divided
¾ cup pecans, chopped

Pour boiling water over oatmeal. Let stand ten minutes. Preheat oven to 325°. Add butter and sugars to oatmeal mixture; beat well. Stir in the eggs. Combine flour, cocoa, soda and salt; mix well. Stir in 1 cup chocolate chips. Pour into greased and floured 13 x 9-inch pan. Top with remaining cup chocolate chips and the chopped pecans. Bake about 35 minutes or until done.

Serves 12

Beverly Soshea, a Senior Engineer in Skin Health Products at 3M, shares a rich, rum-flavored delight. "This cake was developed by an Atlanta friend who was a dietitian and food editor. Glazing it is like 'gilding the lily,' but I include the glacé recipe for those who want a sweeter taste." Begin preparation the day before serving.

Sweet Georgia Brown Cake

1 package devils food cake mix (two-layer size)
4-ounce package instant chocolate pudding mix
1 cup sour cream
½ cup cooking oil
½ cup coffee
½ cup dark rum
4 large eggs
2 cups semi-sweet chocolate chips

GLACÉ
2 cups sifted powdered sugar
1 tablespoon butter, softened
1 to 2 teaspoons vanilla, rum, brandy or orange extract
2 to 3 tablespoons buttermilk

Preheat oven to 350°. Combine all ingredients, except chocolate chips, in bowl of electric mixer. Mix on low speed briefly, just to blend ingredients. Then, beat at medium speed 1 minute. Stop, scrape bowl and beat 1 more minute. Fold in chocolate chips. Pour batter into greased, floured Bundt or tube pan. Bake 40 minutes to 1 hour until cake springs back when pressed lightly with finger near center. Cool in pan on rack for 15 minutes. Turn out gently onto rack. Let stand overnight to allow chips to firm up.

For glacé, cream sugar and butter in mixer bowl. Add flavoring and buttermilk; mix until smooth. Drizzle over cake. (Adjust sugar and/or buttermilk if necessary for correct consistency.)

Serves 10 to 12

Rest assured, this doesn't taste one bit like mud! An "old standby" from Jan Collins, it's topped with a marshmallow creme layer while cake is warm from the oven, and topped again with frosting after cooling step. Jan notes that it totes well to potlucks right in the baking pan.

Mississippi Mud Cake

½ pound margarine (2 sticks)
3½ tablespoons cocoa
2 cups sugar
1 teaspoon vanilla
4 eggs
1½ cups flour
1½ cups coconut
1½ cups nuts
8-ounce jar marshmallow creme

FROSTING
¼ pound butter or margarine
3½ tablespoons cocoa
½ cup milk
1 pound powdered sugar
1 teaspoon vanilla

Preheat oven to 350°. Melt margarine. In large mixing bowl combine margarine with cocoa and sugar. Then add eggs, vanilla and flour, mixing well after each addition. Fold in coconut and nuts. Bake in a 9 x 13-inch pan for 30 to 35 minutes. While still hot, spread cake with marshmallow creme. Cool cake and top with frosting.

For frosting, melt butter in saucepan. Add cocoa and milk; boil for 1 minute. Add vanilla and powdered sugar. Beat until smooth. Frost cooled cake. Refrigerate leftovers.

Serves 8 to 12

This crowd-pleaser from Virginia Krusell of St. Paul is "moist like a brownie, but a little more cake-like in texture." Tester Judy Tucker found it "great for a group." Unlike most recipes, this one requires frosting the cake when it is hot from the oven.

Chocolate Sheet Cake

2 cups flour
2 cups sugar
1 teaspoon baking soda
1 teaspoon salt
1 cup margarine
4 tablespoons cocoa
1 cup water
1 cup sour cream
2 eggs, slightly beaten
1 teaspoon vanilla

FROSTING
½ cup butter or margarine
5 tablespoons milk
4 tablespoons cocoa
16-ounce box powdered sugar
1 teaspoon vanilla

Preheat oven to 400°. Grease and flour 15½ x 10½ x 1-inch jelly roll pan. Sift dry ingredients. Bring margarine, cocoa and water to a boil in medium saucepan. Pour over dry ingredients and blend. Add sour cream, slightly beaten eggs and vanilla; blend well. Pour into jelly roll pan. Bake 15 to 20 minutes until cake springs back when touched.

Begin making frosting 5 minutes before cake is done. Combine butter, milk and cocoa in small saucepan; bring to a boil. Remove from heat. Add powdered sugar and vanilla and blend well. Frost cake while cake is HOT!

Serves 18 to 24

When Gloria C. Kittleson of St. Paul was on the Walker Art Center staff, this was the birthday cake of choice. "We vowed to keep the recipe a secret. But, it's just tooooo good not to share," she confides. Splurge on a high-quality cocoa to make your time and effort especially rewarding.

Dutch Chocolate Birthday Cake

CAKE

1 cup sifted unsweetened cocoa
2 cups boiling water
3 cups sifted all-purpose flour
2 teaspoons baking soda
¾ teaspoon baking powder
1 cup butter or margarine,
    softened
2½ cups granulated sugar
4 eggs
1½ teaspoons vanilla extract

CHOCOLATE FILLING

1 cup sweet butter or margarine,
    softened
1 cup sifted powdered sugar
½ cup sifted unsweetened cocoa
2 eggs

FROSTING

2 cups heavy cream
¾ cup sifted powdered sugar
½ cup sifted unsweetened cocoa
1 teaspoon vanilla extract

In medium bowl, combine cocoa with boiling water, mixing well. Let cool completely. Preheat oven to 350°. Lightly grease and then flour three 9 x 1½-inch layer cake pans. Sift flour with baking soda, salt and baking powder; set aside. In large bowl of electric mixer, at high speed, beat butter with granulated sugar, eggs and vanilla until light and fluffy — about 5 minutes — occasionally scraping side of bowl and guiding mixture into beaters with rubber scraper. At lowest speed, beat in flour mixture (in fourths) alternately with cocoa mixture (in thirds), beginning and ending with flour mixture. Do not over beat. Pour batter into prepared pans. Bake 30 minutes or until surface springs back when gently pressed with fingertip. Cool in pans 10 minutes. Remove from pans; cool thoroughly on wire racks.

For filling, cream butter in small bowl of electric mixer until smooth. Add the powdered sugar, cocoa and eggs; beat until filling is fluffy and smooth.

For frosting, combine cream, powdered sugar and vanilla in medium bowl; beat with electric mixer until stiff and of spreading consistency. Refrigerate until needed.

To assemble cake, place one layer, top side up on cake platter. Spread with half of filling. Then second layer, bottom side up, spread with remaining filling. Place third layer, top side up, over filling. Frost the top and side of cake with whipped cream frosting. Refrigerate about 1 hour (or overnight) before serving.

Serves 16 to 20

In just minutes you can whip up a citrus creation fit for any menu's grand finale. Thanks to Nancy Richards and her mother, Helen Walkup, both of Edina, for sharing one of their favorite recipes. Nancy, who recently retired from Sun Country Airlines, is the wife of Fred Richards, who has served as Mayor of Edina.

Lemon-Lime Pie

14-ounce can sweetened condensed milk
6 tablespoons fresh lemon juice
2 tablespoons fresh lime juice
½ pint whipping cream
9-inch graham cracker crust

With a wire whisk, combine sweetened condensed milk and juices. Let stand briefly to thicken. Whip cream until stiff; fold into milk-juice mixture. Pour into prepared crust. Refrigerate several hours or overnight to set. If desired, garnish wish a dollop of whipped cream or topping and a slice of lemon or lime.

Serves 6 to 8

If it's been a while since you've treated your family to this old-fashioned treasure, try Adelaide Callan's favorite version. "If you prefer, omit the meringue and top the cooled pie with sweetened whipped cream," she suggests. Note that bananas should be ripe for best flavor, but still firm for first rate appearance and consistency.

Banana Cream Pie

⅓ cup flour or 3 tablespoons cornstarch
⅔ cupsugar
¼ teaspoon salt
2 cups milk, scalded
3 slightly beaten egg yolks
2 tablespoons butter
½ teaspoon vanilla
2 or 3 firm bananas
9-inch pastry shell, baked
¼ teaspoon salt

MERINGUE
¼ teaspoon salt
3 egg whites
6 tablespoons sugar

Preheat oven to 400°. Mix flour, sugar and salt; gradually add scalded milk. Cook in double boiler until thick, stirring constantly. Add small amount of hot mixture to egg yolks. Stir into remaining hot mixture. Cook 2 minutes. Remove from heat and cool. Add butter and vanilla. Slice bananas into shell. Top with cooled filling. Spread meringue over filling. Bake 8 to 10 minutes.

For meringue, beat salt and egg whites until frothy. Add sugar, a tablespoon at a time, and continue beating until mixture forms moist, lustrous peaks. Spread over cooled filling, sealing to edge of pastry.

Serves 8

Take it from tester Romona Tokheim — "This just melts in your mouth. I will definitely make it again, especially when we have dinner guests." Contributor Marie Lacy points out that the bread crumbs serve a dual purpose. "They keep pastry shell from becoming soggy and they enhance filling consistency."

Luscious Lemon Pie

6 ounces butter
1 cup sugar
Juice and grated rind of 2 lemons
3 eggs, separated
1 whole egg
1 or 2 slices white bread
6 tablespoons sugar
8-inch pastry shell, baked

Preheat oven to 350°. Melt butter over low heat; stir in sugar and lemon rind and juice. Beat egg yolks and whole egg together and add to mixture when sugar is dissolved. When thickened, remove from heat. DO NOT ALLOW TO BOIL! Remove the crusts from bread and cut or tear gently into small pieces. Scatter over bottom of pie shell. Make stiff meringue of the egg whites sweetened with the 6 tablespoons of sugar. While lemon mixture is still hot, spoon it over bread crumbs and cover with meringue. Seal meringue to edges of pie shell. Bake in oven just until meringue is delicately brown. Cool and serve at room temperature.

Serves 6

One reason ECC members are so fond of desserts is this creation from Club Pastry Chef Joe Frieler. For variety, tester Peggy Dodge suggests serving it with colorful fresh berries and substituting a cookie or graham cracker crust. "I found it can be prepared in advance quite nicely and the flavor is wonderful," she adds.

Make-Ahead Lemon Chiffon Pie

9-inch pie shell, baked and cooled
¼ ounce envelope unflavored gelatin
2 tablespoons water
1 teaspoon salt
4 pasteurized eggs, separated
¼ cup water
1 tablespoon lemon zest
1 cup heavy cream, whipped

Sprinkle gelatin over 2 tablespoons water; let sit for 5 minutes. Heat gelatin, salt, ½ cup sugar, lemon juice, the egg yolks and ¼ cup water in saucepan over medium heat until slightly thickened, stirring constantly. Add lemon zest. Let cool until it is the consistency of syrup. Whip the egg whites until soft peaks form. Slowly add ½ cup sugar and whip until stiff peaks form. Fold into yolk mixture. In the same bowl, whip cream until thick and fold into mixture. Put in pre-baked and cooled 9-inch pie shell. Cool overnight or for several hours. Before serving, top with whipped cream

Serves 6 to 8

Begin June Randall's divine dessert the day before serving to allow ample chilling time. The meringue-type crust is a perfect complement for the delicately-flavored layers of fresh peaches and whipped cream.

Peaches and Cream Pie

CRUST

3 egg whites, beaten until foamy
1 cup sugar
1 cup saltine cracker crumbs
1 teaspoon baking powder
Dash salt
½ teaspoon vanilla
1 cup whipping cream, whipped

FILLING

2 cups chopped fresh peaches
3 tablespoons lemon juice
½ teaspoon salt
1 cup sugar
1½ tablespoons unflavored gelatin
1 cup whipping cream, whipped
1 teaspoon vanilla
½ teaspoon almond extract

Preheat oven to 300°. Beat egg whites until foamy. Gradually beat in sugar. Fold in cracker crumbs, baking powder, salt and vanilla. Pour into 10-inch pie plate which has been buttered, then floured. Bake 40 to 45 minutes. Cool. Spread 1 cup whipping cream over macaroon shell. Spread with peach filling. Top with sweetened whipped cream, if desired.

For filling, combine fresh peaches, lemon juice, salt and sugar. Let stand one hour. Soften gelatin in ½ cup peach syrup (drained from peaches) and dissolve over low heat. Combine with peach mixture. Chill until thick and syrupy. Fold in whipped cream, vanilla and almond extract. Chill about 12 hours before serving.

Serves 8

Here's a peachy dessert presented by ECC chefs. You can make it year around using fresh or frozen peaches, but it's particularly delightful when fresh are available. Preparation is uncomplicated, but requires several steps. Allow plenty of time for final chilling.

Cajun Peach Pie

PASTRY

1¼ cups flour

⅓ teaspoon salt

¼ cup powdered sugar, heaping

1 teaspoon baking powder

¼ teaspoon cinnamon

⅛ teaspoon nutmeg

⅓ cup butter

1 egg

¼ teaspoon vanilla

FILLING

12 ounces cream cheese

1½ cups sugar

½ teaspoon almond extract

1 teaspoon vanilla

3 eggs

2 to 3 peaches, sliced, or 16 ounces frozen sliced peaches

About ½ cup apricot or peach preserves

Whipped cream for garnish, optional

For pastry, combine dry ingredients. Cut in butter. Mix in 1 egg and vanilla. Roll into ball. Wrap dough in plastic film; chill 10 minutes. Roll out on a floured surface. Place in a 9-inch pie pan which has been coated with vegetable spray. Set aside.

Preheat oven to 350°. For filling, cream first four ingredients until smooth. Scrape bowl and add eggs. Beat another minute and pour into crust. Bake 30 minutes or until center is set. Remove from oven and cool. When pie is cool, top with sliced peaches. In a saucepan, heat apricot or peach preserves just enough to glaze fruit. Stir preserves constantly. Brush evenly over peaches. Chill to set topping. Garnish with sweetened whipped cream.

Serves 6

Mary Schrock's party-perfect pie was eagerly tested by Jo Ellen Saylor and her daughter Meredith. They found that the rewarding results made up for the time involved and the waiting periods between steps. Since it must be partially completed the day before serving, there is minimal effort involved in the finishing touches.

Coffee-Toffee Pie

PASTRY

½ package pie crust mix (not sticks)

¼ cup light brown sugar, firmly packed

¾ cup finely-chopped walnuts

1 square unsweetened chocolate, grated

1 tablespoon water

1 teaspoon vanilla extract

FILLING

½ cup butter, softened

¾ cup granulated sugar

2 teaspoons instant coffee

2 pasteurized eggs

1 square unsweetened chocolate,
   melted and cooled to room temperature

TOPPING

2 cups heavy cream

2 tablespoons instant coffee

½ cup powdered sugar

Chocolate curls

Preheat oven to 375°. In a medium bowl, combine pie crust mix, brown sugar, walnuts and grated chocolate. Add water and vanilla. Mix until well blended with fork. Press into a well-greased 9-inch pie plate. Bake 15 minutes.

For filling, beat butter until creamy. Gradually add sugar, beating until light. Add instant coffee. Add eggs one at a time; beat 5 minutes after each egg. Add chocolate. Spoon filling into pie shell. Cover and refrigerate overnight.

For topping, combine cream, coffee and sugar. Cover and refrigerate unmixed for one hour. Put beaters in freezer. Beat topping ingredients until stiff. Spoon or pipe over filling with pastry tube. Garnish with chocolate curls.

Serves 8

After a "run for the roses" or any other time a rich reward is appropriate, try this prize winner from Sally Froslid of St. Paul. "An old friend blessed me with this southern recipe we all love," says Sally. It will remind you of conventional pecan pie in appearance, but has unique additions which add more flavor and texture.

Kentucky High Pie

½ cup (1 stick) butter or margarine
3 eggs
1 cup sugar
¼ cup cornstarch
¾ to 1 cup chocolate chips
1 cup pecans
¾ cup coconut
1 tablespoon vanilla
9-inch unbaked pie shell
Whipped cream or topping, as desired

Preheat oven to 325°. Melt butter; set aside to cool. Whisk together eggs, sugar and cornstarch until well blended. Mix in chocolate chips, nuts, coconut and vanilla. Add cooled butter and stir until mixture is thoroughly mixed. Pour into pastry shell. Bake 45 minutes to an hour or until set in center. Serve with a dollop of whipped cream or topping, if desired.

Serves 8

Another dessert contest winner with a southern accent. "My brother brought this recipe home from New Orleans many years ago," says contributor Rosemary Geist of St. Paul. "We adapted it slightly to suit our own tastes and we've been enjoying it ever since.

Bourbon-Walnut Pie

9-inch unbaked pie shell
4 eggs
¼ teaspoon salt
¼ cup melted butter
1¼ cups light corn syrup
1¼ cups packed brown sugar
1 teaspoon vanilla
1 jigger bourbon whiskey
1 cup walnuts
Whipped cream

Preheat oven to 350°. Beat eggs with whisk. Add salt, butter, syrup, sugar, vanilla and bourbon to eggs. Sprinkle walnuts over bottom of pastry shell. Pour egg mixture over nuts. Bake 45 to 50 minutes or until set. Serve with whipped cream.

Serves 6 to 8

ECC Pastry Chef Joe Frieler has this glorious recipe at the ready when the fresh fruits of summer come to market. He suggests orange marmalade as a substitute for the difficult-to-find apricot jelly. Tester Gene Gaasedelen found apple jelly works well, too. "It's a pleasure to be able to serve this favorite Club dessert at home," she remarks.

Raspberry-Macaroon Pie

BASE:

5 egg whites

2 cups sugar

½ teaspoon baking powder

⅓ teaspoon salt

1 cup chopped nuts, such as pecans

1½ cups quick oats (or instant)

½ teaspoon vanilla

FILLING:

1 cup apricot jelly

1 cup fresh raspberries
   (can use strawberries, peaches or other fruit)

Sweetened whipped cream for garnish.

Preheat oven to 375°. Butter a 9 or 10-inch pie pan. Whip egg whites, sugar, baking powder and salt until stiff. Fold in nuts, oats and vanilla. Bake 30 to 35 minutes until lightly browned.* Cool. (Base will rise and crack and may collapse slightly in the center.) For filling, heat apricot jelly in microwave or double boiler. Fold in fresh fruit. Spoon mixture over base. At serving time, garnish with whipped cream.

Serves 6 to 8

*If using an electric oven, place oven rack in highest possible position and place a cookie sheet under pie pan during baking. This will shield delicate base from intense "bottom heat" which may cause it to scorch.

Pat Clemmer's tantalizing little tarts feature an uncommon filling of currants, which are small dried seedless grapes grown in California and the Mediterranean countries. Add these dainty delights to a holiday cookie tray or serve any time with a scoop of lemon sorbet or French vanilla ice cream.

Currant Tarts

Uncooked pastry dough   1 cup currants
  for 2 crusts   1 tablespoon butter
1 egg   3 tablespoons milk or cream
1 cup brown sugar   ½ teaspoon cinnamon

Preheat oven to 450°. Combine all ingredients and beat until well mixed. Cut pastry into circles and fit into 48 mini muffin tins. Fill each cup with currant mixture. Bake until crust is slightly brown, about 10 minutes.

Yield: 48 tarts

"Absolutely addictive" is how testers described Kay Bach's favorite sweet snack for munching and gifting. Well known as an enthusiastic Edina volunteer, Kay co-chaired the city's centennial observation in 1988 and is a past President of the city's League of Women Voters. In addition, she served two terms on the Hazeltine National Golf Club Board of Directors.

Candied Pecans

1 tablespoon water   ½ cup sugar
1 egg white   ½ teaspoon cinnamon
1 pound pecan halves   ¼ teaspoon salt

Preheat oven to 225°. In small bowl, beat water and egg white until frothy. Coat pecans with mixture. Mix sugar, cinnamon and salt in separate small dish. Sprinkle pecans with mixture until evenly coated. Bake on well-buttered jelly roll pan or cookie sheet for 1 hour. Serve like candy.

Yield: 1 pound candied nuts

June Randall's mother-in-law, Jenella Randall, delighted her friends with gifts of this sweet treat at holiday time. Without too much effort and a candy thermometer to guide you, you can turn your own kitchen into an old-fashioned sweet shoppe. Let the children wrap cooled pieces in waxed paper.

Grammy's Caramels

2 cups white sugar
1⅓ cups light corn syrup
2 cups half-and-half, divided
1 cup butter
1 cup chopped walnuts, optional
1 teaspoon vanilla.

Cook sugar, syrup, 1 cup of the cream and butter to soft ball stage (use candy thermometer). Add remainder of cream and cook to 245° on candy thermometer, stirring constantly. Add vanilla and pour at once onto buttered pan. Do NOT pour onto waxed paper. Do not stir or beat after removing from stove. Do not overcook! Cut into pieces and wrap each in waxed paper. Store in cool place.

Yield: About 5 dozen

Shirley Bard describes her dessert dip as "instant gratification." Tester Mary L. Miller follows up with her own adjective — "scrumptious!" This retains its dipping consistency even after refrigeration, which makes it handy to have on hand for impromptu serving.

Caramel Dip for Fresh Fruits

8-ounce package cream cheese, softened
⅔ cup brown sugar
¼ cup granulated sugar
1 teaspoon vanilla
Granny Smith apples, sliced
Strawberries
Fresh pineapple chunks

Combine softened cream cheese with sugars and vanilla until well blended. Cover and refrigerate. Serve at room temperature with firm, ripe fruits.

Serves 6

Thank You

Recipe Contributors and Testers . . .

The Edina Country Club salutes members, friends, and our own culinary staff for their enthusiastic participation in the production of this unique collection. We are most appreciative of the talents shared and the time volunteered. We thank them for "serving" to us special dishes they bring to their own tables around the clock, throughout the year and for all ages of satisfied diners.

Testing results, recipe similarities, and spatial restrictions were chief factors guiding the selection process. Regrettably, not every recipe submitted could be published. (In cases of duplication, the recipe with the earliest postmark was included.) Also, we certainly do not claim that every selection is an "original." However, comments accompanying the recipes along with conversations with contributors convince us that each is a personal favorite. We feel certain that many recipes and serving suggestions will become favorites at your home as well.

Norine Ahmann
Anita Anderson
Pauline Anderson
Diane Aves
Kay Bach
Betty Bajwa
Shirley Bard
Mary Alice Bell
Shirley Bentdahl
Sylvia Berg
Peggy Bishop
Virginia Bodine
Mickie Borg
Pat Borth
Nancy Bros
Jan Brower
Jack Bucklin
Ann Burckhardt
Adelaide Callan
Laura Carlson
Chef Jerry Cegla, CFBE
Tim Cegla
Marian Clay
Pat Clemmer
Jan Collins
Marjorie Connelly
Mary Cooper
Helen Couper
Carol Cronk
Chef Jerry Cross

Bonnie Damkroger
Kathleen Danford
Deborah Dimmock
Peggy Dodge
Norma Dolliff
Elizabeth Eisenbrey
Shirley Erickson
De Evenson
Susan Fee
Susan Flynn
Angela Fox
Joyce Franzen
Joe Frieler
Sally Froslid
Gene Gaasedelen
Allison Gaasedelen
Ken Galloway, CEC
Rosemary Geist
Jean Giroulx
Mary Ellen Godfrey
Britton A. Goetze, Jr.
Terri Gulliford
Marian Hamilton
Glenna Hammond
Kathy Hanson
Diane Lacy Harr
Jenifer Harris
Chef Hallie Harron
Ruth Hauskins
Donna Healy

Diana Hedges
Betty Hemstad
Mary Jo Hendricks
Maryanne Herman
Karen Gaasedelen Herman
Mitzi Hlavac
Joan Hoch
Storey Holland
Richard Hoyt
Sharon Hundt
Leslie Walter Jacobson
Jacqueline Jarnes
Marianne Jasper
Patricia Jesperson
Sarah Jean Jesperson
Linda Johnson
Elizabeth Kane
Vicki Kattke
Jim Keeler
Peggy Kelly
Jan Winters Keprios
Hille Kersten
Rick Kettelhohn
Lynne Kilmer
Heather Randall King
Richard King
Gloria Kittleson
Liz Krezowski

Virginia Krusell
Marjorie Kugler
Marie Lacy
Gwen Ladner
Michelle & Marty Lass
Mary Laukka
Jean Lein
Sheila Lind
Nancy Lindahl
Donna Lundstrom
LeAnn Lyon
Janet Markee
Karen McKay
Sheran McNulty
Kathleen McReavy
Verna Melius
Patricia Meyers
Mary L. Miller
Dale C. Miller, CCM Minneapolis Club
Gerry Johnson Mooers
Mary Morton
Mary Mulheran
Annette Nelson
Janet M. Nelson
Eleanor Nelson
Jean Nickolatos
Doreen O'Toole

Lynda Oliver
John Olson
Marde Olson
Mary Olson
Eleanor Ostman
Sabra Otteson
Betsy Palecek
Susan Passolt
Marion Payne
Elisa Peltola
Nathalie Person
Liana Peterson
Julian G. Plante,
 Ph.D.
Kathy Powers
Gretchen Pracht
Ellena Prickett

Sharon Quenemoen
Beth Quinn
Cynthia Quinn
June Randall
Robert & Karen
 Remund
Nancy Richards
Mary Richardson
Mary Rischmiller
Scott Rochat
Dorothea Roskam
Louise Saunders
JoEllen & Meredith
 Saylor
Margy Schaller
Kathryn Schmid
Helen Schnobrich

Bob Schranck
Mary Schrock
Patty Simmons
Pat Sinclair
June Smith
Beverly Soshea
Pat Spring
Pat Stark
Jeff Stone
Don Stork
David Striefel
Terry Swanson
Evelyn Teegen
Maxine Thorkelson
Judy Tillson
Romona Tokheim
Judy Tucker

Charlotte Tudor
Trish Ura
Jaye Vaaler
Pat & James Van
 Valkenburg
Marlys Wahlberg
Theresa Waldman
Helen Waldron
Helen Walkup
Rebecca Walser
Julie Waychoff
Betty Weingartner
Helen Winder

The name of this cookbook, "Savor the Flavor,"
was submitted by Theresa Waldman

300

INDEX